ADVANCE PRAISE FOR *THE STATE OF AFFAIRS*

"In this generous, soulful book, Esther Perel guides us through the devastation of affairs, helping us come out the other side with wisdom and compassion. If an affair is a torrent of misery and judgment, Perel is a beacon of solace and compassion."
—Eli J. Finkel, professor of psychology, Northwestern University, and author of *The All-Or-Nothing Marriage*

"Perel goes where few others dare. Always honest and always fair, in *The State of Affairs* she guides us through a complicated journey, fraught with moral and emotional bumps, to a place where we can better understand ourselves and our relationships."
—Simon Sinek, *New York Times* bestselling author of *Start With Why* and *Leaders Eat Last*

"Esther Perel is known for challenging old, fusty ideas about relationships. If you think affairs are taboo, or beyond forgiveness, or the worst form of betrayal, think again. The state of affairs, as described by Esther Perel, is nothing short of what you and those you love decide to make of it." —Stan Tatkin, PsyD, MFT, author of *Wired for Dating*

"Read this book! It challenges us to move beyond psychological correctness and to look both deep into the human heart and at the culture we live in. It is a serious, powerful, and courageous contribution, which redefines the field of couples' therapy." —Diana Fosha, PhD

"Esther Perel has an uncanny way of mining the greatest challenges of long-term relationships and therein finding humanity, meaning, opportunity, and hope. In *The State of Affairs*, she tackles the ultimate transgression of infidelity without judgment or an ideological agenda. In its unflinching honesty and intelligence, this ambitious and courageous book is invaluable to anyone in (or helping someone through) the throes of an affair, recovering from one, or saying goodbye as a result of one."
—Marta Meana, PhD, professor of psychology, University of Nevada, and former president of the Society for Sex Therapy and Research

"If you are a human being and you interact with other human beings, you should read this inclusive book. Perel explores every dynamic of modern day relationships. *The State of Affairs* gives you the tools you need to understand and forgive yourself and others for being human."
—Cara Delevingne, actor and model

ALSO BY ESTHER PEREL

Mating in Captivity

THE
STATE OF
AFFAIRS

Rethinking Infidelity

ESTHER PEREL

HARPER

An Imprint of HarperCollins*Publishers*

For Jack,
whom I have loved for three decades,
and
for anyone who has ever loved.

CONTENTS

CONTENTS

ACKNOWLEDGMENTS

What possessed me to write a book about one of the most controversial facets of our nature? Few events so encompass the breadth of human drama, and it has been an endless source of fascination for me since writing my first book, *Mating in Captivity*. That was back in the halcyon days of writerly innocence, before the Internet radicalized communication. Roughly a decade has elapsed, and today production occurs in full view. I have been in dialogue with my readers throughout the book's creation. Thank you all for the illuminating input.

A few of you, however, have held my hand offline. Simply put, I couldn't have done it without you. That's because I think while I write. And I talk while I think. For that, I have been blessed with dear friends, esteemed colleagues, and welcomed strangers. My debt of gratitude transcends these modest acknowledgments.

Master editor and collaborator Ellen Daly, if ever I've seen genius at work, you are it. Your clarity in navigating where I was coming from and where I needed to go kept me on course. I will always hear your voice, my personal GPS, recalculating the way. Laura Blum, my coeditor and poetic muse, you are a living thesaurus. There is no one with whom I love to play with words and refine ideas more than you. Gail Winston, my fearless editor at HarperCollins, thank you for believing in me again. Sarah Manges, you and I began this adventure with a daring proposal. Your editorial contribution was invaluable. Tracy Brown, my literary agent, I trust you wholeheartedly, a scarce commodity, as these pages will demonstrate. Yuli Masinovsky, you always remind me of the importance of telling a story, on the page or on the screen.

The best ideas rarely arise in one isolated mind, but rather develop in networks of curious and creative thinkers. Throughout these pages, I have quoted many of those whose pioneering insights—both in conversation and in writing—have helped me shape the ideas in this book. I am particularly grateful to Michelle Scheinkman, Ulrich Clement, Janis Abrahms Spring, Janet Reibstein, Tammy Nelson, Ellyn Bader, Meg John Barker, Helen Fisher, Marta Meana, Eric Klinenberg, Eric Berkowitz, and Pepper Schwartz.

The cross-fertilization that comes from being in an interdisciplinary study group has been critical to honing both my questions and my conclusions. Diana Fosha, Doug Braun-Harvey, George Faller, Natasha Prenn, and Megan Fleming, thank you for holding me accountable during the early stages of this project. Joshua Wolf Schenk, you made being stuck less frightening.

I would not have dared to let this book see the light of day without my discerning team of readers. Your comments showed me the cracks and shone light through them. Katherine Frank, every therapist who takes up the quill should be so lucky as to have a cultural anthropologist with your creativity and depth of insight by her side. Peter Fraenkel and Harriet Lerner, you are cherished colleagues and uniquely astute and direct critics. Steve Andreas, Guy Winch, Aviva Gitlin, Dan McKinnon, Ian Kerner, Margie Nichols, Carol Gilligan, and Virginia Goldner, I needed the authoritative feedback of leading clinicians, teachers, and thinkers. Jesse Kornbluth, Hanna Rosin, David Bornstein, and Patricia Cohen, you are wizards of the pen, and your comments helped me to speak a language understood by all. Dan Savage and Terry Real, you are my kindred spirits. David Lewis, Daniel Mandil, Irina Baranov, Blair Miller, and Daniel Okulitch, nothing gets past your penetrating faculties. Diana Adams and Ed Vessel, I am especially thankful for your guidance as I wrote about nonmonogamy. Olivia Natt and Jesse Baker, you added a valuable younger perspective with your feedback. Alissa Quart, brainstorming titles with you is a lot of fun.

My team. Malika Bhowmik, my research intern, hats off on a job exquisitely done. You brought order to my chaos. And speaking of order, Lindsay Ratowsky and Amanda Dieker, you made it possible for me to dedicate my time and attention to my book. Early on, I was also helped by a quartet of talented students: Brittany Mercante, Annabelle Moore, Nicole Arnot, and Alexandra Castillo. I look forward to seeing you blossom in your careers. Thank you to all the colleagues who attend my monthly training and supervision groups—there is no better way to clarify one's thinking than by teaching. Jonas Bamert, your research was much appreciated. Bruce Milner, you opened your bucolic home in Woodstock and offered me calm and beauty so I could write.

And now, family. To my parents, who taught me to speak up, and whose harrowing experience of betrayal showed me that there is always hope for healing—even if it's only partial. Jack Saul, my husband, we have shared the adventure of love and life. You are my intellectual interlocutor. Writing a book takes up a lot of space, and you respond with such generosity. Adam and Noam, I hope these pages offer you wisdom you can use in your relationships. Talking with you about the trials and tribulations of millennial love kept me current and gave me such joy.

There's no exaggerating the role of my patients and all of you who allowed me into your private lives. Your trust was essential. It is through stories like yours that we connect and make meaning. Throughout my travels, my work, and my personal exchanges, I have had the richest conversations. For these I can offer thanks, even if I can't name you all. It was so good not to feel alone throughout this arduous creation, and now that it's done, I can't wait to engage with you further.

INTRODUCTION

There is one simple act of transgression that can rob a couple of their relationship, their happiness, their very identity: an affair. Yet this extremely common act is poorly understood.

I have been probing the intricacies of love and desire in modern couples for almost three decades as a therapist, writer, trainer, and lecturer. My first book, *Mating in Captivity*, explored the nature of erotic desire in long-term relationships and included a single chapter on infidelity. To my surprise, every time I gave a talk or an interview about my book, no matter where in the world, the topic of infidelity took precedence over all others. It would come to consume my waking hours. Whereas *Mating in Captivity* probed the dilemmas of desire within committed relationships, *The State of Affairs* tracks the trajectory of desire when it goes looking elsewhere.

That being said, this is not just a book about infidelity. Affairs have a lot to teach us about relationships—what we expect, what we think we want, and what we feel entitled to. They offer a unique window into our personal and cultural attitudes about love, lust, and commitment. Through examining illicit love from multiple angles, I hope to engage you, the reader, in an honest, enlightened, and provocative exploration of modern relationships in their many variations. I would like to stimulate a conversation between you and your loved ones about issues such as fidelity and loyalty, desire and longing, jealousy and possessiveness, truth-telling and forgiveness. I encourage you to question yourself, to speak the unspoken, and to be unafraid to challenge sexual and emotional correctness.

My role as a therapist is to create a safe space where the diversity of experiences can be explored with compassion. As an author, I hope to do the same. In that sense, this is not a prescriptive book for overcoming the crisis of an affair, though I hope it will be helpful to those of you who are currently in the midst of one, whatever part you are playing. Instead, my goal is to introduce a more productive conversation about the topic, one that will ultimately strengthen all relationships by making them more honest and more resilient.

The conversation about affairs today tends to be divisive, judgmental, and shortsighted. As a culture, we are ever more open about sex, but infidelity remains shrouded in a cloud of shame and secrecy. I hope this book will help to lift that silence and launch a new way of thinking and talking about one of our most ancient ways of being. Much has been written about prevention and recovery; much less about the meanings and motives of affairs. Even less has been said about what we can learn from them and how it might inform and transform our relationships.

Some people will dismiss these as irrelevancies. Only the facts matter, they tell me. The plane is down; grab the survivors and run. But more and more people come to me because they want to know what happened, why it crashed, and whether it could have been prevented. They want to understand it, learn from it, and fly again. For all of these people, I would like to start the conversation where it usually stops and tackle some of the more unsettling questions that infidelity raises.

In the pages ahead I will explore the many faces of affairs—addressing the pain and destruction of betrayal as well as the thrill and self-discovery inherent in transgression. I want to parse the tension between the expansive opportunities of an affair and the imminent danger that is immediately attached to it. What are we to make of the duality between the liberating and empowering dimensions of adulterous love and the damage that it can inflict?

I also want to include the broader circles of family, community, and culture. I hope to root this discussion of our most personal relationships in a broader historical and social context.

In broaching a different kind of discussion on this most inflammatory subject, I am well aware of the risks I take. Beliefs about infidelity run deep in our cultural psyche, and questioning them will no doubt be perceived by some as dangerous irreverence or as a compromised moral compass on my part. While I prefer to sidestep flat-out condemnation to allow for a thoughtful inquiry, I do not approve of deception or take betrayal lightly. I sit with the devastation in my office every day. Understanding infidelity does not mean justifying it. Yet in all but the most extreme cases, residing in the flats of judgment is simply not helpful.

Let me tell you a bit how I have gathered the information for this book. Mine is not an evidenced-based scientific survey, nor is it a sociological study based on data collected by the various websites for people seeking affairs. Rather, my approach is akin to that of an anthropologist and an explorer. I talk to people, and I listen. The raw material for this book has come from my therapy sessions, trainings, lectures around the world, informal conversations, and from the hundreds of people who have sent me letters and left comments on my website, my blog, my TED Talks, and my Facebook page.

In my psychotherapy practice, I have focused for the past six years primarily on couples dealing with infidelity. With these people, I have plumbed the depths of the subject. Because I meet with partners alone as well as together, I have been afforded an unusual window into the experience of the unfaithful partner, not only the pain of the betrayed. I am fortunate to work with people from around the globe, which has helped me to provide different cultural perspectives, but I am aware that my patients—being self-selected—do not necessarily represent a diversity of economic and social groups.

Affairs and secrets go hand in hand, and this book contains many secrets. Often it is impossible to tell one person's secret without betraying another's. Some of the details that give a story its signature poignancy are exactly the ones I had to conceal for confidentiality's sake. Every person in this book has been carefully disguised to protect his or her anonymity, but I have striven to preserve their particular words and the emotional accuracy of each scenario.

Finally, a note of gratitude. In researching and writing this book, I have been inspired and educated by numerous other thinkers, writers, and experts. But one book that stands out above all others is the one to which I am indebted for my title. The original *The State of Affairs: Explorations in Infidelity and Commitment* is a compendium of sociological perspectives on infidelity that establishes the subject as worthy of serious academic inquiry. Reading essay after thoughtful essay, I felt emboldened to delve into the theme of adultery and to probe its psychological dimensions with an inclusive and layered approach.

Whether we like it or not, philandering is here to stay. And all the ink spilled advising us on how to "affair-proof" our relationships has not managed to curb the number of men and women who wander. Infidelity happens in good marriages, in bad marriages, and even when adultery is punishable by death. It happens in open relationships where extramarital sex is carefully negotiated beforehand. And the freedom to leave or divorce has not made cheating obsolete. After immersing myself in the topic, I have come to see that there is no singular truth, no comprehensive typology to describe this crucible of passion and betrayal. The only thing I can say for certain is that nothing I'm about to tell you is made up.

Esther Perel, New York City, January 2017

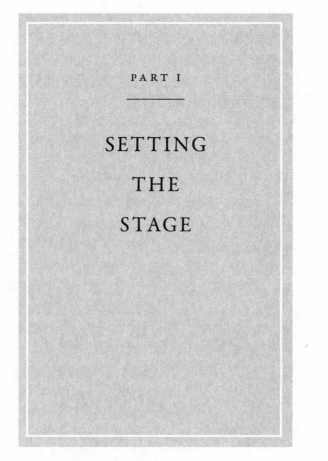

PART I

SETTING

THE

STAGE

CHAPTER 1

A NEW CONVERSATION ABOUT MARRIAGE AND INFIDELITY

It would take too long to explain the intimate alliance
of contradictions in human nature which makes love itself wear
at times the desperate shape of betrayal.
And perhaps there is no possible explanation.
—Joseph Conrad, *Some Reminiscences*

At this very moment, in all corners of the world, someone is either cheating or being cheated on, thinking about having an affair, offering advice to someone who is in the throes of one, or completing the triangle as a secret lover. No aspect of a couple's life elicits more fear, gossip, or fascination than an affair. Adultery has existed since marriage was invented, and so too has the taboo against it. It has been legislated, debated, politicized, and demonized throughout history. Yet despite its widespread denunciation, infidelity has a tenacity that marriage can only envy. So much so that it is the only sin that gets two commandments in the Bible, one for doing it and one just for thinking about it.

In every society, on every continent, and in every era, regardless of the penalties and the deterrents, men and women have slipped the confines of matrimony. Almost everywhere people marry, monogamy is the official norm and infidelity the clandestine one. So what are we to make of this time-honored taboo—universally forbidden yet universally practiced?

For the past six years I have been having this conversation—not just within the cloistered walls of my therapy practice, but on airplanes, at dinner parties, at conferences, at the nail salon, with colleagues, with the cable guys, and of course, on social media. From Pittsburgh to Buenos Aires, Delhi to Paris, I have been conducting my own open-ended survey about affairs today.

Around the globe, the responses I get when I mention "infidelity" range from bitter condemnation to resigned acceptance to cautious compassion to outright enthusiasm. In Bulgaria, a group of women seem to view their husbands' philandering as unfortunate but inevitable. In Paris, the topic brings an immediate frisson to a dinner conversation, and I note how many people have been on both sides of the story. In Mexico, women proudly see the rise of female affairs as a form of social rebellion against a chauvinistic culture that has forever made room for men to have "two homes," *la casa grande y la casa chica*—one for the family and one for the mistress. Infidelity may be ubiquitous, but the way we make meaning of it—how we define it, suffer from it, and talk about it—is ultimately linked to the particular time and place where the drama unfolds.

Let me ask you: When you think of infidelity, what are the first words, associations, and images that come to mind? Do they change if I use the words "love affair" or "romance"? What about "tryst" or "fling" or "hookup" or "fuck buddy"? Do you find your reactions skewed toward disapproval or toward understanding? Where do your sympathies fall—with the jilted, with the unfaithful, with the lover, with the children? And have your responses changed because of events in your own life?

Convictions about extramarital affairs run deep in our cultural psyche. In the United States, where I live and work, the conversation tends to be visceral, loaded, and polarized.

"Infidelity? It's a dealbreaker," says one. "Once a cheater, always a cheater."

"Come on," counters another, "monogamy just isn't natural."

"That's total bullshit!" retorts a third. "We're not cats in heat, we're humans. Grow up already."

In the American marketplace, adultery is sold with a mixture of denunciation and titillation. Magazine covers peddle smut while preaching sanctimony. As a culture we've become sexually open to the point of overflowing, but when it comes to sexual fidelity, even the most liberal minds can remain intransigent. Curiously, our insistent disapproval keeps infidelity's vigor in check without revealing how rife it really is. We can't stop the fact that it happens, but we can all agree that it shouldn't. Constituents clamor for public apologies as they pore over the tawdry details. From the upper echelons of the political and military elite to Angie down the block, infidelity bespeaks narcissism, duplicity, immorality, and perfidy. In this view, it can never be a simple transgression, a meaningless fling, or a genuine love.

Contemporary discourse about the topic can be summed up as follows: Infidelity must be a symptom of a relationship gone awry. If you have everything you need at home, there should be no reason to go elsewhere. Men cheat out of boredom and fear of intimacy; women cheat out of loneliness and hunger for intimacy. The faithful partner is the mature, committed, realistic one; the one who strays is selfish, immature, and lacks control. Affairs are always harmful and can never help a marriage or be accommodated. The only way to restore trust and intimacy is through truth-telling, repentance, and absolution. Last but not least, divorce affords more self-respect than forgiveness.

The moralizing tone of the current conversation tends to pin the "problem" on deficient couples or individuals, sidestepping the bigger questions that the scope of the phenomenon might invite. Infidelity says a lot about marriage—not just your marriage, but marriage as an institution. It also plunges us into today's culture of entitlement, where we take our privileges for granted. Do we really think we can distill the proliferation of cheating to a few bad apples? Surely millions of renegade lovers can't all be pathological.

For or Against?

There are few neutral terms to describe adultery. Moral opprobrium has long been the prime tool for containing our unruly impulses, so much so that we have no words to speak of them without it. The language that is available to us clasps to its bosom the taboo and the stigma that infidelity represents. While the poets speak of lovers and adventurers, most people's preferred vocabulary includes cheaters, liars, traitors, sex addicts, philanderers, nymphos, womanizers, and sluts. The entire lexicon is organized around an axis of wrongdoing that not only reflects our judgment but fosters it. The term "adultery" itself is derived from the Latin word meaning corruption. Even as I strive to bring a more balanced perspective to this topic, I am aware of the compromised language I will often be using.

Among therapists, too, balanced, unbiased dialogue is rare. Affairs are overwhelmingly described in terms of the damage caused, with a focus on either prevention or recovery. Borrowing from the language of criminalization, clinicians often label the faithful spouse as the "injured party" and the unfaithful one as the "perpetrator." Generally, there is much concern for the betrayed, and detailed repair advice for the unfaithful to help his or her partner overcome the trauma.

The revelation of an affair can be so wrecking; it's no surprise that most people want to take sides. Whenever I tell someone I'm writing a book about infidelity, the immediate reaction is usually "Are you for or against?" as if there were only two options. My answer is "Yes." Behind this cryptic response lies my sincere desire to initiate a more nuanced and less judgmental conversation about infidelity and its concomitant dilemmas. The intricacies of love and desire don't yield to simple categorizations of good and bad, victim and culprit. To be clear, not condemning does not mean condoning, and there is a world of difference between understanding and justifying. But when we reduce the conversation to simply passing judgment, we are left with no conversation at all.

We are also left with no room for people like Benjamin, a mild-mannered gentleman in his early seventies, who approached me after a talk in Los Angeles to ask, "Is it still called cheating when your wife no longer knows your name?" "My wife has Alzheimer's," he explained. "She has been in a nursing home for the past three years, and I visit her twice a week. For the past fourteen months, I have been seeing another woman. Her husband is on the same floor. We have found great comfort in each other." Benjamin may be one of the nicest "cheaters" I've ever met, but he is by no means alone. Plenty of people care deeply for the well-being of their partners even while lying to them, just as plenty of those who have been betrayed continue to love the ones who lied to them and want to find a way to stay together.

For all of these people, I am committed to finding a more compassionate and effective approach to infidelity. People often see an affair as a trauma from which there is no return, and indeed, some affairs will deliver the fatal blow to a relationship. But others may inspire change that was sorely needed. Betrayal cuts to the bone, but the wound can be healed. Affairs can even become generative for a couple.

Because I believe that some good may come out of the crisis of infidelity, I have often been asked, "So, would you recommend an affair to a struggling couple?" My response? A lot of people have positive, life-changing experiences that come along with terminal illness. But I would no more recommend having an affair than I would recommend getting cancer.

Have You Been Affected by Infidelity?

When I first became interested in the topic of infidelity, I used to ask audiences if anyone had ever experienced an affair. Not surprisingly, no hands went up. There are not many people who will publicly admit to fooling around or being fooled.

Bearing this in mind, I changed my question to "How many of you have been affected by infidelity in your lives?" Overwhelmingly, hands went up, and have done so in every audience to whom I have addressed this query. A woman saw a friend's husband kissing a beautiful stranger on the train. Now the question of whether or not she should tell hangs heavy over her friendship. A teenage girl discovered that her father's double life was as old as she was. A mother cannot fathom why her son has stayed with "that hussy," as she refers to her daughter-in-law, no longer welcome at Sunday dinner. The echoes of secrets and lies resound across generations, leaving unrequited loves and shattered hearts in their wake. Infidelity is not merely a story of two or three; it binds entire networks.

The wanderers themselves may not readily raise their hands in public, but they tell me their tales in private. People take me aside at parties or visit my office to deposit their secrets and suspicions, transgressive desires and forbidden loves.

The majority of these stories are much more banal than those that make the headlines: no babies, no STDs, no stalking ex-lover extorting money. (I suppose those couples go to lawyers, not therapists.) Of course, I've come across my share of narcissists, sexual omnivores, and careless, selfish, or vengeful people. I have seen extreme acts of deceit, where unsuspecting partners have been blindsided by the discovery of second families, covert bank accounts, reckless promiscuity, and elaborate schemes of duplicity. I've sat across from men and women who brazenly lie to me for the entire duration of the therapy. But more often, what I see are scores of committed men and women with shared histories and values—values that often include monogamy—whose stories unfold along a more humble human trajectory. Loneliness, years of sexual deadness, resentment, regret, marital neglect, lost youth, craving attention, canceled flights, too much to drink—these are the nuts and bolts of everyday infidelity. Many of these people are deeply conflicted about their behavior, and they come to me seeking help.

The motives for straying vary widely, as do the reactions and possible outcomes. Some affairs are acts of resistance. Others happen when we offer no resistance at all. One person may cross the border for a simple fling, while another is looking to emigrate. Some infidelities are petty rebellions, sparked by a sense of ennui, a desire for novelty, or the need to know one still has pulling power. Others reveal a feeling never known before—an overwhelming sense of love that cannot be denied. Paradoxically, many people go outside their marriages in order to preserve them. When relationships become abusive, transgression can be a generative force. Straying can sound an alarm that signals an urgent need to pay attention, or it can be the death knell that follows a relationship's last gasp. Affairs are an act of betrayal and they are also an expression of longing and loss.

Hence, I approach infidelity from multiple perspectives. I try to appreciate and empathize with the point of view of both parties—what it did to one *and* what it meant to the other. I also consider, and sometimes work with, other relational stakeholders—the lover, the children, the friends. An affair is one story that is experienced by two (or more) people in completely different ways. Hence, it becomes many stories, and we need a frame that can contain these highly differentiated and clashing accounts. Either-or discourses don't invite understanding or reconciliation. To look at straying simply in terms of its ravages is not only reductionistic but also unhelpful. On the other hand, to dismiss the harm done and only glorify our human propensity for exploration is no less reductionistic and no more helpful. A both/and approach may be much more appropriate for the majority of cases. We need a bridging narrative to help real people navigate the multifaceted experience of infidelity—the motives, the meanings, and the consequences. There will always be some who insist that even trying to understand it is giving cheating more dignity than it deserves. But such is the work of this therapist.

On a typical day, my first patient is Rupert, a thirty-six-year-old man who followed his wife to New York from the UK. He knows she has been having an affair, but he has decided not to confront her. "I have a marriage to rebuild, and a family to save," he says. "My focus is on us. I get that she fell for someone else, but what I keep wondering is, can she fall back in love with me?"

Next are Delia and Russell—college sweethearts who reconnected through LinkedIn long after they'd gone on to build their own respective families. As Delia says, "We couldn't spend our entire lives wondering what could have been." Now they've found the answer, but it comes with a moral dilemma. "We have both done enough therapy to figure that affairs are rarely sustainable," Russell tells me. "But I think Delia and I are different. This isn't a flash in the pan. This is a lifelong love story that was interrupted. Should I throw away the opportunity to be with the woman of my life, deny all my feelings, for the sake of preserving a marriage that was never that great?"

Farrah and Jude, a lesbian couple in their mid-thirties, have been together six years. Jude is trying to understand why Farrah had a secret affair *after* they'd agreed to open up their relationship. "We had an arrangement where it was okay to sleep with other women, so long as we told each other," Jude recounts. "I thought being open would protect us—but she lied anyway. What more can I do?" Even an open relationship is no guarantee against deception.

During my lunch break, I read emails. One comes from Barbara, a sixty-eight-year-old woman from Minnesota, recently widowed. "In the midst of my grieving process, I discovered evidence of my husband's long-standing affair. Now I'm dealing with questions I never expected—like, should I tell my daughter? And to make matters worse, my husband was highly respected in our community and I continue to be invited to tributes to him, which all my friends attend. I feel in such a bind—part of me wants to leave his legacy untarnished, and part of me aches to tell the truth." In our exchanges, we discuss the power of one discovery to change the view of an entire life. How does one come to rebuild both a life and an identity after the dual loss of betrayal and widowhood?

Susie's message is full of righteous anger, on her mother's behalf. "She was a saint who stayed with my father until death despite his long-standing affair." I wonder if she has ever considered telling the story another way. What if her father sincerely loved another woman but stayed and sacrificed himself for his family?

Adam, a young therapist, has sent me a message on Facebook

after attending one of my training sessions. "I always thought that cheaters were lowlifes," he writes. "They should at least have the decency to respect the people they married enough not to sneak behind their backs. And yet, sitting in that discussion, suddenly I had a rude awakening. The room we were in was safe and comfortable, yet I kept shifting in my chair as though hot coals were in the cushions waking me up to a truth. I had always overlooked the fact that my parents were both married when they met; in fact, my father was counseling my mother as she tried to leave an abusive husband. Their affair was how I came to be on this earth. Thirty-four years ago, adultery was the act that allowed my parents to find the person they wanted to spend the rest of their lives with." Adam's black-and-white thinking was rattled, both personally and professionally.

My last session of the day is with Lily, a thirty-seven-year-old ad rep who has been pushing back her ultimatums for almost a decade, waiting for her lover to divorce his wife. He has had two more children since their affair began, and Lily feels her fertility diminishing day by day. "I froze my eggs last month," she confides in me, "but I don't want to tell him that—I need all the leverage I can get." She unpacks her ambivalence in session after session—one week convinced that he's just stringing her along; and the next, grasping at every straw of hope that indeed she is the love of his life.

In the middle of a dinner, I receive an "emergency" text. Jackson is having a meltdown and needs to speak immediately. His wife just discovered that too many pills were missing from the Viagra bottle and kicked him out. "To be honest," he says, "I felt terrible about lying to her, but I couldn't bear seeing disgust on her face every time I tried to share my sexual needs with her." Jackson's fantasy life was colorful, but his wife found it a total turnoff, and told him so, repeatedly. After years of rejection, he took his fantasy palette elsewhere. "I should have been honest," he says, "but too much was at stake. My sexual needs were important, but not important enough not to see my kids every day at breakfast."

As I listen to all these people's stories, I find myself shocked, judgmental, caring, protective, curious, turned on and turned off, and sometimes all in one hour. I have cried with them, felt hopeful and hopeless, and identified with everyone involved. Because I see, on a daily basis, the devastation this act can cause, I also see how inadequate much of the current conversation about the topic is.

A Window into the Human Heart

Affairs have a lot to teach us about relationships. They open the door to a deeper examination of values, human nature, and the power of eros. They force us to grapple with some of the most unsettling questions: What draws people outside the lines they worked so hard to establish? Why does sexual betrayal hurt *so much*? Is an affair always selfish and weak, or can it in some cases be understandable, acceptable, even an act of boldness and courage? And whether we have known this drama or not, what can we draw from the excitement of infidelity to enliven our relationships?

Must a secret love always be revealed? Does passion have a finite shelf life? And are there fulfillments that a marriage, even a good one, can never provide? How do we negotiate the elusive balance between our emotional needs and our erotic desires? Has monogamy outlived its usefulness? What is fidelity? Can we love more than one person at once?

For me, these conversations are part and parcel of any adult, intimate relationship. For most couples, unfortunately, the crisis of an affair is the first time they talk about any of this. Catastrophe has a way of propelling us into the essence of things. I encourage you not to wait for a storm, but to address these ideas in a quieter climate. Talking about what draws us outside our fences, and about the fear of loss that accompanies it, in an atmosphere of trust can actually promote intimacy and commitment. Our desires, even our most illicit ones, are a feature of our humanity.

As tempting as it is to reduce affairs to sex and lies, I prefer to use infidelity as a portal into the complex landscape of relationships and the boundaries we draw to bind them. Infidelity brings us face-to-face with the volatile and opposing forces of passion: the lure, the lust, the urgency, the love and its impossibility, the relief, the entrapment, the guilt, the heartbreak, the sinfulness, the surveillance, the madness of suspicion, the murderous urge to get even, the tragic denouement. Be forewarned: Addressing these issues requires a willingness to descend into a labyrinth of irrational forces. Love is messy; infidelity more so. But it is also a window, like none other, into the crevices of the human heart.

The New Shame

Divorce. In all the heated debates about infidelity, online and off, that one word crops up over and over again. If you're thinking of having an affair, get a divorce. If you're unhappy enough to cheat, you're unhappy enough to leave. And if your partner has an affair, call the lawyer immediately.

Jessica, a Brooklynite in her early thirties with a two-year-old son, contacted me a week after she learned that her husband of four years, Julian, had been having an affair with a coworker. "I found a secret Facebook account with messages to this woman." A child of the digital age, she took her problem online. "Everything I read made me feel awful," she explains. "It was like bad advice from a women's magazine. *Move on and don't look back! He did it once, he'll do it again! Kick him to the curb!*

"None of the websites I looked at addressed the fact that I still had very strong feelings about this man," she says. "We had a whole life planned together and he's the father of my son. I'm attached to his family, and they've been a tremendous support for me in the past week. All of these articles and writers, not to mention my own parents, are telling me he is garbage and that my feelings for him are misguided. My dad even went so far as to suggest that I have Stockholm syndrome! I feel judged, like I'm one of 'those women' who just let their husbands get away with cheating."

Jessica is a financially independent woman with options, unlike the many women who have no recourse in the face of their husbands' patriarchal privileges. And precisely because she lives with a different bill of rights, our culture demands that she exercise them. As I listen to her, my mind flashes back to a workshop I had recently led with a group of women from a village in Morocco. When I explained to them that today in America, women like Jessica are encouraged to take a stand and leave, one young woman laughed. "*Mais*, madame, if we were to leave all the husbands who chase skirts, all of Morocco would be divorced!"

Once divorce carried all the stigma. Now, choosing to stay when you can leave is the new shame. Exhibit A is Hillary Clinton. Many women who otherwise admire her have never reconciled themselves with her decision to stay with her husband when she had the power to leave. "Where is her self-respect?"

Certainly there are times when divorce is unavoidable, wise, or simply the best outcome for all involved. But is it the only righteous choice? The risk is that in the throes of pain and humiliation, we too hastily conflate our reactions to the affair with our feelings about the whole relationship. History is rewritten, bridges are burned along with the wedding photos, and children divide their lives between two homes.

Jessica isn't ready to kick her husband to the curb. "People make mistakes. I'm no saint myself; though I haven't slept around, I don't have the best coping skills either—I shut down and drink too much when things get bad or I'm stressed. If we didn't allow for our partners to stumble, we would all be miserable and alone." She's ready to give Julian a second chance.

The rush to divorce makes no allowance for error, for human fragility. It also makes no allowance for repair, resilience, and recovery. And it makes no allowance for people like Jessica and Julian, who want to learn and grow from what happened. They tell me, "We both want to make things work. We've had some of the most incredible conversations since this started. Really soul-baring and also constructive, like we haven't talked in years." But then they ask, "Did we really have to go through an affair just to be able to be truly honest with each other?" I hear this often and share their regret. But here's one of the unspoken truths about relationships: for many couples, nothing less extreme is powerful enough to get the partners' attention and to shake up a stale system.

Ultimately, the problem with the judgmental, highly charged, and repressive conversation about infidelity is that it precludes any possibility for deeper understanding, and therefore for hope and healing—together or apart. Victimization makes marriages more fragile. Of course, when Julian cheats on Jessica while she is home changing her toddler's diapers, it is helpful for her to get in touch with her anger, an appropriate response to this disfigurement of their relationship. But the more I speak to those affected by infidelity—the actor and the acted upon, the lovers, the children—the more strongly I feel the need for a view of life and love that steers away from blame. We have nothing to gain from breeding bitter, vengeful, and divisive sentiments. Exhibit A is the woman I met whose indignation was so intense that she told her five-year-old about her husband's years of sexual misconduct "because my son should know why Mommy's crying."

Although infidelity has become one of the prime motives for divorce, a large number of couples will stay together despite an affair. But for how long and under what conditions? Will they have the opportunity to emerge stronger as a result? Or will they bury the affair under a mountain of shame and mistrust? How they metabolize the affair will shape the future of their relationship and their lives.

Today in the West most of us are going to have two or three significant long-term relationships or marriages. And some of us are going to do it with the same person. When a couple comes to me in the aftermath of an affair, I often tell them this: Your first marriage is over. Would you like to create a second one together?

CHAPTER 2

DEFINING INFIDELITY

Is Chatting Cheating?

I did not have sexual relations with that woman.
—President Bill Clinton

Everyone wants to know, "What percentage of people cheat?" But that's a tough question to answer, because first you have to answer, "What is cheating?" The definition of infidelity is anything but fixed, and the digital age offers an ever-expanding range of potentially illicit encounters. Is chatting cheating? What about sexting, watching porn, joining a fetish community, remaining secretly active on dating apps, paying for sex, lap dances, massages with happy endings, girl-on-girl hookups, staying in touch with one's ex?

Because there is no universally agreed-upon definition of what constitutes infidelity, estimates of its prevalence among American couples vary widely, ranging from 26 to 70 percent for women and from 33 to 75 percent for men. Whatever the exact numbers may be, everyone agrees that they are rising. And many fingers point to women as being responsible for the increase, as they rapidly close the "infidelity gap" (research indicates a 40 percent jump since

1990, while men's rates have held steady.) In fact, when the definition of infidelity includes not only "sexual intercourse" but also romantic involvement, kissing, and other sexual contact, female college students significantly outcheat their male counterparts.

Data gathering is hampered by one simple fact: When it comes to sex, people lie—especially about sex they are not supposed to be having. Even under the cloak of anonymity, gender stereotypes persist. Men are socialized to boast, exaggerate, and overrepresent their sexual exploits, while women minimize, deny, and underrepresent theirs (which isn't surprising, considering that there are still nine countries where women can be put to death for straying). Sexual honesty is inseparable from sexual politics.

Furthermore, we are walking contradictions. While most people say that it would be terribly wrong for their partner to lie about an affair, those same people say that is exactly what they would do if they were having one. And in response to the golden question "Would you have an affair if you knew you'd never get caught?" the numbers skyrocket. Ultimately, no amount of statistics, however accurate, can give us real insight into the complex reality of infidelity today. Therefore, my focus is stories, not numbers. For it is the stories that lead us into the deeper human concerns of longing and disenchantment, commitment and erotic freedom. Their common theme is that one partner feels betrayed by the other. But it's everything else that makes these dramas compelling. Seduced by the need for labels, we tend to cluster far too many experiences under the single signifier "infidelity."

If Only It Were So Simple . . .

"Have you had intercourse with anyone other than your spouse in the past twelve months?" If defining infidelity were as simple as a yes or no answer to that question, my job would be a lot easier. The painful arguments I am privy to remind me every day that while some forms of trespassing are indeed straightforward, the world of transgression is as murky as the world of sexuality itself.

Elias has suggested to his wife, Linda, that they consult an expert. They are in deep disagreement about the interpretation of cheating. A regular at strip clubs, he mounts the defense: "I watch, I talk, I pay, but I don't touch. Where's the cheating?" In his mind, he's perfectly faithful. Linda thinks otherwise and is making him sleep on the couch.

Ashlee just found out that her girlfriend Lisa occasionally has been hooking up with her old boyfriend Tom. "She says it doesn't count as cheating because he's a guy! But as far as I'm concerned, that makes it worse. Not only is she going behind my back, but she's getting something I can't give her. Am I just her lesbian phase?"

Shannon feels betrayed when she discovers that her boyfriend, Corbin, just bought a box of condoms—something they don't need, since they're trying to get pregnant. Corbin protests, "I didn't do anything! It was just an idea! Do you want to snoop in my mind now as well as in my phone?" "The buying of condoms is not an idea to me!" she retorts. No, but is it an infidelity?

And what about porn? While most people would agree that an old copy of *Playboy* under the mattress doesn't amount to betrayal, the boundaries can get blurry when we shift from print to screen. Many men see watching porn as falling into the same category as masturbation—some even proudly claim it prevents them from cheating. Women are less likely to see it that way. Violet, however, always thought she was quite open-minded about porn. When she walked into Jared's study and caught him watching a panting blonde on his screen, she just rolled her eyes and joked that he needed a new hobby. But when the woman said, "Where'd you go, Jared? Did you finish?" she realized that he was on Skype. "The worst part of it is that he's trying to convince me it isn't cheating," she tells me. "He calls it *customized pornography*."

The possibilities for dalliance are endless in our connected era. Today, 68 percent of Americans own a smartphone, which means, as comedian Aziz Ansari quips, "you're carrying a 24-7 singles bar in your pocket." And it's not just singles. The marrieds have their own sites, like the infamous AshleyMadison.com. The Internet is a great democratizer, offering equal access to our forbidden desires.

You no longer even need to leave your home to stray. You can actually have an affair while lying next to your partner in bed. My patient Joachim was spooning his husband, Dean, when he noticed him messaging another guy on Manhunt. Kit was sitting right beside his girlfriend, Jodi, on the couch watching TV when he recognized that familiar swiping motion on her iPhone. "She says she was just curious, that it's like a game and she never acts on it," he tells me. "But we both agreed to delete Tinder as part of our commitment ceremony!"

The Internet has made sex "accessible, affordable, and anonymous," as the late researcher Al Cooper pointed out. All of these apply equally to infidelity, and I'd add another a-word: ambiguous. When it's no longer an exchange of kisses but an exchange of dick pics; when the hour in a motel room has become a late-night Snapchat; when the secretive lunch has been replaced with a secret Facebook account, how are we supposed to know what constitutes an affair? As a result of this burgeoning field of furtive activities, we need to carefully rethink how we conceptualize infidelity in the digital age.

Who Gets to Draw the Lines?

Defining adultery is at once quite simple and quite complicated. Today, in the West, relationship ethics are no longer dictated by religious authority. The definition of infidelity no longer resides with the Pope, but with the people. This means more freedom, as well as more uncertainty. Couples must draw up their own terms.

When someone comes forward and admits, "I had an affair," nobody argues over the hermeneutics. When you catch your partner in bed with another, or find the email trail of a multiyear parallel life, again, it's pretty obvious. But when one partner decides that the other person's behavior is a betrayal, and the reaction is "It's not what you think," "It didn't mean anything," or "That's not cheating," we enter more nebulous territory. Typically, the task of marking the fault lines and interpreting their significance falls to the one who feels betrayed. Does feeling hurt entitle one to claim ownership over the definition?

What is clear is that all characterizations of modern infidelity involve the notion of a breach of contract between two individuals. It is no longer a sin against God, a breaking of a family alliance, a muddying of the bloodline, or a dispersion of resources and inheritances. At the core of betrayal today is a violation of trust: We expect our partner to act according to our shared set of assumptions, and we base our own behavior on that. It's not necessarily a particular sexual or emotional behavior that comprises the betrayal; rather, it is the fact that the behavior is not within the couple's agreement. Sounds fair enough. But the problem is that for most of us, these agreements are not something we spend much time explicitly negotiating. In fact, to call them "agreements" at all is perhaps a stretch.

Some couples work out their commitments head-on, but most go by trial and error. Relationships are a patchwork of unspoken rules and roles that we begin stitching on the first date. We set out to draft boundaries—what is in and what is out. The me, the you, and the us. Do we get to go out alone or do we do everything together? Do we combine our finances? Are we expected to attend every family reunion?

We review our friendships and decide how important they should be, now that we have each other. We sort out ex-lovers—do we know about them, talk about them, keep pictures of them on our phones, stay friends with them on Facebook? Particularly when it comes to these outside attachments, we see how much we can get away with before stepping on each other's toes. "You never told me you were still in touch with that girl from college!" "We've slept together ten times, but I see that you still have your profile on Hinge." "I get that he's your best friend and you've known him since kindergarten, but do you have to tell him *everything* about us?"

Thus we stake out the turf of separateness and togetherness, outlining the implicit contract of the relationship. More often than not, the version that one person files away in the inner cabinet is different from that of his or her partner.

Gay couples are sometimes an exception to this rule. Having lived for so long outside the standard social norms and fought valiantly for sexual self-determination, they are highly aware of the price of sexual confinement and not so eager to shackle themselves. They are more likely to openly negotiate monogamy than tacitly assume it. Likewise, a growing minority of straight couples are experimenting with forms of consensual nonmonogamy, where the borders are more permeable and also more explicit. This does not mean they are immune to the agony of betrayal, but they are more likely to be on the same page about what constitutes it.

For modern love's idealists, however, the very act of explicitly addressing monogamy seems to call into question the assumption of specialness that is at the heart of the romantic dream. Once we have found "the one," we believe there should be no need for, no desire for, and no attraction to any other. Hence, our rental agreements are much more elaborate than our relational agreements. For many couples, the extent of the discussion is about five words: "I catch you, you're dead."

A New Definition

For me, infidelity includes one or more of these three constitutive elements: secrecy, sexual alchemy, and emotional involvement. Before I go any further, I want to make clear that these are not three rigid criteria; rather, a three-sided prism through which to view your experience and assumptions. To broaden the definition, however, does not mean descending into moral relativism. Not all infidelities are created equal. In the end, these issues are personal and value-laden. My purpose is to give you a framework to make sense of your own circumstances and to communicate more deeply with those you love.

Secrecy is the number one organizing principle of an infidelity. An affair always lives in the shadow of the primary relationship, hoping never to be discovered. The secrecy is precisely what intensifies the erotic charge. "Sex and subterfuge make a delicious cocktail," writes journalist Julia Keller. We all know from childhood the glee of hiding and keeping secrets. They make us feel powerful, less vulnerable, and more free. But this dark pleasure is frowned on in adulthood. "I've always been a what-you-see-is-what-you-get kind of person," says Angela, a punctilious Irish American paralegal who realized, through her affair with a client, that she enjoys sneaking around. "Discovering that I could act in total breach of my own long-held values was both bewildering and exciting at the same time. Once I was speaking with my sister, who was rattling away about the wrongdoing of cheaters, all the while smiling inwardly at my own secret. Little did she know that she was looking into the face of the 'villain.'"

Describing this volatile mix of guilt and delight, Max admits, "One moment I felt like I was scum, but the next, I knew I was touching the essence of something I desperately needed to feel again." A forty-seven-year-old devoted father of three, one of whom has cerebral palsy, he's adamant about his silence: "I'll never tell my wife I had found a lifeline with another woman, but I'll never regret that I did. It had to exist in silence. There was no other way to do it! The affair is over, the secret is alive and well."

One of the powerful attributes of secrecy is its function as a portal for autonomy and control. It's a theme that I hear repeatedly, most often from women, but also from men who feel disempowered in one way or another. "As a black man in the white world of academia, you play tightly by the rules. There's not much leeway for someone like me," Tyrell explains. I'm not surprised when he tells me that his affairs were the space where *he* could define the rules. "You don't get to control me everywhere" was the mantra that accompanied his dalliances.

Affairs are a pathway to risk, danger, and the defiant energy of transgression. Unsure of the next date, we are ensured the excitement of anticipation. Adulterous love resides in a self-contained universe, secluded from the rest of the world. Affairs blossom in the margins of our lives, and as long as they are not exposed to broad daylight, their spell is preserved.

Secrets aren't all fun and games, however, even for the one who carries them. As the crux of adultery, they fuel the lying, the denying, the deception, and the elaborate strategies. Being wrapped in duplicities can be isolating, and with the accumulation of time, can lead to corrosive shame and self-loathing. When I ask Melanie why she decided to end her six-year affair now, she responds, "As long as

I felt guilty, I still saw myself as a good person doing bad things. But the day I stopped feeling guilty, I lost respect for myself. I'm just a bad person."

For the deceived partner, the uncovered secrets are devastating. For many, particularly in the United States, it is the endless cover-ups that leave the deepest scars. I hear this over and over: "It's not that he cheated; it's that he lied about it." And yet the concealment that is frowned upon in one corner of our planet is reframed as "discretion" in others. In the stories I hear there, it's a given that affairs come with lying and hiding. It's the fact that the person didn't hide it well enough that is humiliating and hurtful.

Any discussion about infidelity requires that we reckon with secrets. But it may also require that we ask ourselves, What about privacy? And where does privacy end and secrecy begin? Is snooping a legitimate preemptive tactic? Does intimacy require absolute transparency?

Sexual alchemy is a term I choose to use rather than "sex" because I prefer a definition of sexuality that goes beyond Bill Clinton's—one that does not stop at a narrow repertoire of sexual acts but includes a broader understanding of the erotic mind, body, and energy. By talking about sexual alchemy, I want to clarify that affairs sometimes involve sex and sometimes not, but they are always erotic. As Marcel Proust understood, it's our imagination that is responsible for love, not the other person. Eroticism is such that the kiss we only imagine giving can be as powerful and exciting as hours of actual lovemaking. I am thinking of Charmaine, a fifty-one-year-old Jamaican woman with a contagious smile who has been sharing lingering lunches with her younger colleague Roy. She insists that their connection does not tear at her marriage vows. "We didn't technically have sex. We never even touched; we only talked. Where's the cheating in that?" But we all know that renunciation can be as erotic as consummation. Desire is rooted in absence and longing. When I press her, she concedes, "I've never been so aroused. It was like he was touching me without touching me." What is she describing if not sexual alchemy? An innocent lunch can indeed be steamy, even if Charmaine is only, as Cheryl Strayed puts it, "dry dating."

"Nothing happened!" is the common refrain of the sexual literalists. After a few too many drinks at his coworker Abby's birthday party, Dustin accepted her invitation to stay over. When quizzed about it the next day by his girlfriend, Leah, he repeated those two words insistently. "All right, since you must know, we slept together in the same bed. But I'm telling you, nothing happened." At what point does "something happen"? I wonder. Leah, meanwhile, is plagued by her own questions. Did they get naked? Did she sleep in his arms? Did he brush his nose against her sleeping face? Did he get hard? Is that really nothing?

These stories make a critical point—many affairs are less about sex than about desire: the desire to feel desired, to feel special, to be seen and connected, to compel attention. All these carry an erotic frisson that makes us feel alive, renewed, recharged. It is more energy than act, more enchantment than intercourse.

Even when it comes to the act of intercourse, the adulterous defense system is impressively agile at finding loopholes. People go to great lengths to take the sex out of sex. My colleague Francesca Gentille compiled a list of some of the more imaginative completions to the sentence beginning "It wasn't sex because . . ."

". . . I didn't know her name."

". . . no one came."

". . . I was drunk/high."

". . . I didn't enjoy it."

"... I'm not sure I remember the details."

"... it was with a gender I don't usually have sex with."

"... no one else saw it."

"... we still had our clothes on."

"... we still had some of our clothes on."

"... one foot was on the floor."

These contortions all relate to the physical world. Cyberspace adds further twists. Is virtual sex real? When you watch a naked ass on your screen, are you just freely roaming in the sanctuary of your imagination, or have you stepped into the dangerous zone of betrayal? For many people, the Rubicon is crossed when there is an interaction involved—when the porn star becomes the live woman on a webcam, or the nude pics are not on an anonymous Tumblr account but arriving on her cellphone from an actual guy. But what about virtual reality? Is it real or imagined? These are significant questions that we as a culture are pondering, without definitive answers. As philosopher Aaron Ben-Ze'ev pertinently states, "The move from passive imaginary reality to the interactive virtual reality in cyberspace is much more radical than the move from photographs to movies." We may debate what is real and what is imagined, but the alchemy of the erotic is unmistakable.

Even if we agree to widen the lens to include a variety of sexual expressions, we may still disagree about what they mean and where they belong. All these discussions inevitably raise the thorny question of the nature of our erotic freedom. Do we expect our partners' erotic selves to belong entirely to us? I'm talking about thoughts, fantasies, dreams, and memories, and also turn-ons, attractions, and self-pleasure. These aspects of sexuality can be personal, and part of our sovereign selfhood—existing in our own secret garden. But some people view everything sexual as a domain that must be shared. Discovering that their partner masturbates or still has feelings for an ex is tantamount to betrayal. In this view, any independent expression of sexuality—real or imagined—is a breach. From another perspective, however, making space for some degree of erotic individuality can convey a respect for privacy and autonomy, and is a token of intimacy. In my decades of working with couples, I've observed that those who are most successful in keeping the erotic spark alive are those who are comfortable with the mystery in their midst. Even if they are monogamous in their actions, they recognize that they do not own each other's sexuality. It is precisely the elusiveness of the other that keeps them coming back to discover more.

Every couple has to negotiate each other's erotic independence as part of the larger conversation about our individuality and our connection. In our efforts to protect ourselves from intimate betrayal, we demand access, control, transparency. And we run the risk of unknowingly eradicating the very space between us that keeps desire alive. Fire needs air.

Emotional involvement is the third element that may play a role in infidelity. Most affairs register an emotional component, to one degree or another. At the deep end of the spectrum we have the love affair, where the accompanying bouquet of passionate feelings is integral. "I thought I knew what love was, but I have never felt like this before" is a common refrain. People in this state talk to me about love, transcendence, awakening, destiny, divine intervention—something so pure that they could not pass it by, because "to deny those feelings would have been an act of self-betrayal." For those involved in such an unparalleled love story, the term "affair" is inadequate, for it doesn't begin to capture the emotional depth of the experience. "When you call it cheating, you reduce it to something vulgar," Ludo says. "Because she had gone through something similar, Mandy was the first person with whom I've ever been able to open up about my father's abuse. Yes, we had sex, but it was so much more than that."

As we move further along the continuum, there is a whole range of encounters that include varying degrees of emotional intimacy. At the shallow end, we have flings that are recreational, anonymous, virtual, or paid. In many of these cases, people insist that there's no emotional involvement in their transgressions. Some even go so far as to argue that therefore these don't constitute a betrayal. "I pay the girl so she will leave!" says Guy. "The whole point of the hooker is not to fall in love, so therefore it doesn't threaten my marriage." Here the common refrain is "It meant nothing!" But is sex ever really just sex? There may be no feelings attached to a random fuck, but there is plenty of meaning to the fact that it happened.

It is ironic that some people, like Guy, will minimize the emotional involvement to lessen the offense ("It meant nothing!"), while others, like Charmaine, will highlight the emotional nature of the bond for exactly the same purpose ("Nothing happened!").

A lot of ink has been spilled trying to determine which is the greater evil—stolen love or forbidden sex. Our individual sensitivities are idiosyncratic. Some people aren't bothered by emotional attachments to others, so long as they keep their hands to themselves. Others don't see sex as a big deal and give each other freedom to play—so long as there are no feelings involved. They call it "emotional monogamy." For most of us, sex and emotions are difficult to untangle. You can have a lot of each, more of one, or more of the other, but they are usually both at play in the adulterous sandbox.

What About Emotional Affairs?

In recent years, a new category has emerged: the "emotional affair." It's the "it" term in today's infidelity lexicon. Generally, it's used to indicate that the betrayal does not involve actual sex, but rather, an inappropriate emotional closeness that should be reserved for one's partner and that is depleting the primary relationship.

This is a concept that requires some careful unpacking. So many "emotional affairs" are pulsing with sexual tension, regardless of whether genitals have made contact, and giving them a new label seems to me to promote erotic reductionism. Clearly, affairs can be sexual without involving a penis entering a vagina, and in such cases, it is more helpful to call a spade a spade.

Sometimes, however, the term "emotional affair" is applied to relationships that are genuinely platonic but are perceived to be "too close." This is a notion that is deeply entwined in our ideals of modern coupledom. Because for many today, marriage is wedded to the concept of emotional intimacy and naked honesty, when we open our inner life to someone else, it can feel like a betrayal. Our model of romantic love is one in which we expect our partner to be our principal emotional companion—the only one with whom we share our deepest dreams, regrets, and anxieties.

We're on uncharted ground here. Emphasizing the "emotional" as infidelity never even occurred to earlier generations, whose concept of marriage was not organized around emotional exclusiveness. It is still foreign in many parts of the world. Is it a helpful concept for couples today? Marriages have always been strengthened when partners can vent to others or find multiple outlets for emotional connection. When we channel all our intimate needs into one person, we actually stand to make the relationship more vulnerable.

Clearly, the waters get muddy very fast when we try to parse out the subtleties of emotional betrayal. On the one hand, claiming a connection of the heart is often used as a cover-up for an erotic tryst. When a woman complains that her partner is completely absorbed with his new "friend"—Snapchatting at all hours, texting, making her playlists—I sympathize with her frustration but also clarify that what's bothering her is not just emotional, it's sexual. On the other hand, deep emotional relationships with others are legitimate outlets for feelings and needs that can't all be met in the marriage. I walk that fine line in session after session. Given the treacherousness of the territory, it's no wonder that many people cling to the narrowest take on infidelity—that is, forbidden sex.

With all of that being said, I encourage you to consider what infidelity means to you, and how you feel about it—and to inquire openly about what it means to your partner.

Changing Roles, Changing Stories

At times, we define infidelity; other times, it defines us. We may be tempted to see the roles in the adulterous triangle as quite set—the betrayed spouse, the cheater, the lover. But in reality, many of us may find ourselves in several positions, and our perspective on the meaning of it all will shift as we do, depending on the situation.

Heather, a single professional New Yorker at the cusp of her fertility peak, is still hoping for happily ever after. A couple of years ago, she broke up with her fiancé, Fred. She had discovered a folder on his computer filled with messages to escorts with all sorts of kinky requests and scheduled rendezvous. She felt betrayed by this sexual sidebar, but she was even more upset that he had checked out on *her*. She craved a dynamic hot monogamy, but he took his testosterone elsewhere and brought home a phlegmatic passion-less version of himself. Their therapist told her that Fred needed to grow up, and he was going to be a great partner in four to five years. "The cost-benefit analysis wasn't worth it," she says. "When I thought about what I wanted to do from thirty-seven to forty, it wasn't to mother Fred into adulthood."

Last summer she met a new guy, Ryan, on the train from Boston to New York. Their eyes locked, and they knew what it meant. He was straightforward about his situation: "I'm in a thirteen-year marriage, with two kids, and I'm on my way out." Ryan and his wife, Blair, had agreed it was over, but they were taking it slow, carefully figuring out whether to break the news to the kids during family weekend at summer camp or in the fall when they returned to school.

It strikes me that, not long ago, Heather herself had felt cheated on. Does she realize that she is now the one having an affair with a married man? "It's the last thing I wanted," she says. "But this *isn't* really an affair. Ryan's marriage may not be legally over, but in every other way, it is."

I poke her a little. "But his wife doesn't know? It's not like you said to him, go home and take care of your unfinished business, then come back to me."

She's quickly defensive: "Well, when's a marriage really over? Is it when you're sleeping in separate bedrooms? Is it when you've made the public announcement to family and friends? Is it when you file for divorce? It's such a long process, and I couldn't figure out what would be a satisfying landmark in time for me." I'm glad to see Heather glowing. I am also aware that her notion of infidelity has become conveniently elastic now that she is on the other side.

A few weeks later, the glow has gone. She tells me that after discreetly dating for two months, she and Ryan finally spent an entire weekend together and it was one of the happiest times of her life. But she was jolted out of Eden when Ryan called days later to tell her that Blair knew everything, even Heather's name, thanks to his iPad, which he had left on the nightstand.

Blair is no longer interested in the slow road to divorce. She has taken the kids away for the week, leaving Ryan to explain the situation to his parents and their friends. In one gesture, what was merely a budding romance between two people turned into a systemic unraveling. Everyone is involved, and everyone's fate has taken a new turn.

For Blair the timing is irrelevant. "We've grown apart" has become "He cheated on me." For Ryan, "I'm trying to do the right thing and not hurt anyone" has become "How do I explain this to my kids and my parents?" And Heather has become the agent of their fatal blow. Betrayed by Fred, the last thing she ever imagined was that she would become the other woman. She has always had strong opinions about committed partners who cheat, and even stronger ones about their lovers. She is no man snatcher. She felt like a proud member of the sisterhood of women who had one another's backs. Now she is in the very position of those that she used to dis. The image of Blair reading their idyllic exchanges, message by message, makes her blood freeze.

It's not the first time I've heard such a tale of role reversal and judgment turned into justification. When it comes to infidelity, like most things in life, human beings commit what social psychologists call the actor-observer bias. If you cheat, it's because you are a selfish, weak, untrustworthy person. But if I do it, it's because of the situation I found myself in. For ourselves, we focus on the mitigating circumstances; for others, we blame character.

Our definitions of infidelity are inseparable from the stories we tell ourselves, and they evolve over time. Nascent love listens with an eager ear that has a way of edging the boundaries and circumventing the obstacles. When Ryan told Heather that he no longer slept in the same bed as his wife, she easily saw him as more divorced than married, and herself as innocent. Scorned love listens with an unforgiving ear, and attributes ill intent to every move. Blair is now convinced that Ryan never had the intention to spare her feelings and was probably cheating all along.

Heather's starry-eyed love has taken a battering. One moment she was imagining herself pregnant with Ryan's child, holding the hands of her adoring new stepkids, all of them on the way to visit his parents. Now she'll have to meet them all in the humiliating role of the mistress. To the children, she will forever be the woman with whom their father cheated on their mother. Despite her sincere intentions, Heather is tainted.

"This may be a long road, but I'm up for the challenge," she tells me. And in time her persistence pays off. Today she and Ryan are married, and she has a nice connection with his parents and his kids. Next summer they are expecting their first child. I wonder, how would she define infidelity now?

CHAPTER 3

AFFAIRS ARE NOT WHAT THEY USED TO BE

Love is an ideal thing, marriage a real thing;
a confusion of the real with the ideal never goes unpunished.
—Johann Wolfgang von Goethe

When Maria discovered a love note in the pocket of her husband Kenneth's dress blues, she threw it away and never mentioned it. It was 1964. "What would I do? Where would I go? Who would take a woman with four kids?" When she confided in her mother, her reasoning was confirmed. "Your kids are young. Marriage is long. Don't let your pride take everything away from you." Besides, they both figured, this was just what men did.

Fast-forward to 1984. Now it was the turn of Maria's eldest daughter, Silvia, to confront marital duplicity. Her detection came in the form of several charges from Interflora on her husband Clark's American Express bill—flowers that clearly had not been delivered to her desk. When she told her mother, Maria was sympathetic, but also glad that her daughter was not condemned to the same fate she had endured: "Men don't change.

You don't have kids *and* you have a job. Pack your bags and get out."

Two years later, Silvia fell in love again, remarried, and eventually—when the time was right—gave birth to twins, Michelle and Zac. The freedoms that she experienced—to have a blue-chip career, to choose if and when to have children, to divorce without stigma, and to remarry—would have been inconceivable for her mother's generation, and still are for many women all over the world. But in much of the Western hemisphere, in the past half-century, marriage has undergone an extreme makeover. And it continues to transform before our eyes. When Silvia's son, Zac, came of age, he could choose to legally marry his boyfriend. And when he too uncovered an unwelcome truth about his beloved, it manifested as a secret profile on Grindr.

People often ask, Why is infidelity such a big deal today? Why does it hurt so much? How has it become one of the leading causes of divorce? Only by taking a brief trip back in time to look at the changes in love, sex, and marriage over the last few centuries can we have an informed conversation about modern infidelity. History and culture have always set the stage for our domestic dramas. In particular, the rise of individualism, the emergence of consumer culture, and the mandate for happiness have transformed matrimony and its adulterous shadow. Affairs are not what they used to be because marriage is not what it used to be.

The Way We Were

For millennia, matrimony was less a union of two individuals than a strategic partnership between two families that ensured their economic survival and promoted social cohesion. It was a pragmatic arrangement in which children were not sentimentalized and husbands and wives dreamed of productive compatibility. We fulfilled our conjugal responsibilities in return for a much-needed sense of security and belonging. Love might arise, but it certainly was not essential. In any event, it was too flimsy an emotion to support such a weighty institution. Passion has always burned in the human heart, but it arose independent of the bonds of wedlock. In fact, historian Stephanie Coontz makes the intriguing point that when marriage was primarily an economic alliance, adultery was sometimes the space for love. "Most societies have had romantic love, this combination of sexual passion, infatuation, and the romanticization of the partner," she writes. "But very often, those things were seen as inappropriate when attached to marriage. Because marriage was a political, economic, and mercenary event, many people believed that true, uncontaminated love could only exist without it."

Traditional wedlock had a clear mandate based on well-defined gender roles and division of labor. As long as each person did what she or he was supposed to do, it was a good match. "He works hard. He doesn't drink. He provides for us." "She's a good cook. She's given me many children. She keeps a tidy household." It was a system in which gender inequality was etched in the law and encoded in the cultural DNA. When women married, they relinquished their individual rights and property, and indeed, they became property themselves.

It's worth remembering that until recently, marital fidelity and monogamy had nothing to do with love. It was a mainstay of patriarchy, imposed on women, to ensure patrimony and lineage— whose children are mine and who gets the cows (or the goats or the camels) when I die. Pregnancy confirms maternity, but without paternity tests, a father could be tormented for life when his only son and heir was blond and his entire family had not one light hair among them. A bride's virginity and a wife's monogamy were critical for protecting his pride and his bloodline.

For women, venturing outside the marital bed was highly risky. They could end up pregnant, publicly humiliated, or dead. Meanwhile, it is old news that in most cultures, men had the tacitly sanctioned freedom to roam with little consequence, supported by a host of theories about masculinity that justified their predilections for tasting widely. The double standard is as old as adultery itself.

"I love you. Let's get married." For most of history, those two sentences were never joined. Romanticism changed all that. In the late eighteenth and early nineteenth centuries, amidst the societal sea change of the Industrial Revolution, marriage was redefined. Gradually it evolved from an economic enterprise to a companionate one—a free-choice engagement between two individuals, based not on duty and obligation but on love and affection. In the move from the village to the city, we became more free but also more alone. Individualism began its remorseless conquest of Western civilization. Mate selection became infused with romantic aspirations meant to counter the increasing isolation of modern life.

Yet despite these changes, a few social realities remained intact well into the mid-twentieth century. Marriage was still intended to last for life; women were economically and legally dependent on their husbands; religion defined morality and dictated the code of conduct; divorce was rare and a cause of great shame and ostracism. And above all, fidelity remained a sine qua non, at least for the female of the species.

As a woman of the fifties, Maria was well aware of her limited options. She had grown up in a world where she had four breakfast cereals to choose from, three TV channels, and two men she knew personally who might be eligible. The fact that she had a say at all in her choice of partner was quite a new development—even today, more than 50 percent of marriages globally are arranged.

While she loved her husband, Kenneth, sex was primarily about procreation. "After bearing four children in six years, frankly, I was done," she says. Pleasure just didn't factor in when she occasionally fulfilled her wifely duty. And Kenneth, whom she described as "a decent and generous man," had never been initiated into the mysteries of the female anatomy, nor did anyone tell him he should have been. But neither their lackluster sexual relations nor his subsequent compensatory conquests were grounds for divorce.

While the men of Kenneth's generation had tacit permission to sweeten their marital dissatisfaction with extramarital delicacies, women like Maria were expected to find sweetness in marriage itself. For Maria and Kenneth, as for their contemporaries, matrimony was a lifetime pact, with few ways to exit. They entered their nuptials for better or for worse, till death do us part. Fortunately for those who were miserable, death came sooner than it does today.

One Person at a Time

Silvia didn't wait for death to part her from her husband. These days, marriage ends when love dies. As a baby boomer growing up in San Francisco, she had come of age during a cultural turning point that altered coupledom almost beyond recognition. Feminism, contraception, and abortion rights all empowered women to take control of their own loves and lives. Thanks to no-fault divorce laws, passed in California in 1969 and in many more states soon thereafter, leaving an unhappy union was now part of a woman's menu of choices. And if women *could* leave, they needed a better reason to stay. Henceforward, the bar of marital quality had been raised significantly.

After her divorce, Silvia put her career first, fighting her way up the corporate ladder in the still-male-dominated world of banking. She dated a few guys—"boring bankers and account executives, like my first husband"—but it wasn't until she met Jason, a violin maker and music teacher, that she felt ready to give Cupid another chance.

In one of our conversations, I asked Silvia if she was monogamous. She looked at me, surprised. "Yes, of course. I've been monogamous with all my boyfriends and both my husbands." Did she realize the cultural shift implicit in the words she had so casually uttered?

Monogamy used to mean one person for life. Now monogamy means one person at a time.

With her second husband, Silvia demanded equality in her kitchen and her bedroom. Jason swept her off her feet by how well he swept the floor and how well he anticipated her needs. Instead of being defined by unique, gender-based roles, their attachment was conceived in terms of flexible divisions of labor, personal fulfillment, mutual sexual attraction, and intimacy.

First we brought love to marriage. Then we brought sex to love. And then we linked marital happiness with sexual satisfaction. Sex for procreation gave way to sex for recreation. While premarital sex became the norm, marital sex underwent its own little revolution, shifting from a woman's matrimonial duty to a joint pathway for pleasure and connection.

Modern Love

Today we are engaged in a grand experiment. For the first time ever, we want sex with our spouses not just because we want six children to work on the farm (for which we need to have eight, since at least two might not make it), nor because it is an assigned chore. No, we want sex just because we *want* it. Ours is sex that is rooted in desire, a sovereign expression of our free choice, and indeed, of our very selves. Today we have sex because we're *in the mood*, we *feel like* it—hopefully, with each other; preferably, at the same time; and ideally, with unflagging passion for decades on end.

In *The Transformation of Intimacy*, Anthony Giddens explains that when sex was decoupled from reproduction, it became no longer just a feature of our biology but a marker of our identity. Our sexuality has been socialized away from the natural world and has become a "property of the self" that we define and redefine throughout our lives. It is an expression of who we *are*, no longer merely something we *do*. In our corner of the world, sex is a human right linked to our individuality, our personal freedom, and our self-actualization. Sexual bliss, we believe, is our due—and it has become a pillar of our new conception of intimacy.

The centrality of intimacy in modern marriage is unquestioned. Emotional closeness has shifted from being the by-product of a long-term relationship to being a mandate for one. In the traditional world, intimacy had referred to the companionship and camaraderie born out of sharing the vicissitudes of everyday life—working the land; raising children; weathering loss, sickness, and hardship. Both men and women were more likely to seek friendship and a shoulder to lean on in same-sex relationships. Men bonded over work and beer, women connected through motherhood and borrowing flour.

The modern world is in constant motion, spinning faster and faster. Families are often dispersed, siblings are scattered across continents, and we uproot ourselves for new jobs more easily than a plant is repotted. We have hundreds of virtual "friends" but no one we can ask to feed the cat. We are a lot more free than our grandparents were, but also more disconnected. In our desperate search for a safe harbor, where are we to dock? Marital intimacy has become the sovereign antidote for lives of growing atomization.

Intimacy is "into-me-see." I am going to talk to you, my beloved, and I am going to share with you my most prized possessions, which are no longer my dowry and the fruit of my womb but my hopes, my aspirations, my fears, my longings, my *feelings*—in other words, my inner life. And you, my beloved, will give me eye contact. No scrolling while I bare my soul. I need to feel your empathy and validation. My significance depends on it.

One Ring to Rule Them All

Never before have our expectations of marriage taken on such epic proportions. We still want everything the traditional family was meant to provide—security, children, property, and respectability—but now we also want our partner to love us, to desire us, to be *interested* in us. We should be best friends, trusted confidants, and passionate lovers to boot. The human imagination has conjured up a new Olympus: that love will remain unconditional, intimacy enthralling, and sex oh-so-exciting, for the long haul, with one person. And the long haul keeps getting longer.

Contained within the small circle of the wedding band are vastly contradictory ideals. We want our chosen one to offer stability, safety, predictability, and dependability—all the anchoring experiences. And we want that very same person to supply awe, mystery, adventure, and risk. Give me comfort and give me edge. Give me familiarity and give me novelty. Give me continuity and give me surprise. Lovers today seek to bring under one roof desires that have forever had separate dwellings.

In our secularized society, romantic love has become, as Jungian analyst Robert Johnson writes, "the single greatest energy system in the Western psyche. In our culture, it has supplanted religion as the arena in which men and women seek meaning, transcendence, wholeness, and ecstasy." In our quest for the "soul mate," we have conflated the spiritual and the relational, as if they are one and the same. The perfection we long to experience in earthly love used to be sought only in the sanctuary of the divine. When we imbue our partner with godly attributes and we expect him or her to uplift us from the mundane to the sublime, we create, as Johnson puts it, an "unholy muddle of two holy loves" that cannot help but disappoint.

Not only do we have endless demands, but on top of it all we want to be happy. That was once reserved for the afterlife. We've brought heaven down to earth, within reach of all, and now happiness is no longer just a pursuit, but a mandate. We expect one person to give us what once an entire village used to provide, and we live twice as long. It's a tall order for a party of two.

At so many weddings, starry-eyed dreamers recite a list of vows, swearing to be everything to each other, from soul mate to lover to teacher to therapist. "I promise to be your greatest fan and your toughest adversary, your partner in crime, and your consolation in disappointment," says the groom, with a tremble in his voice.

Through her tears, the bride replies, "I promise faithfulness, respect, and self-improvement. I will not only celebrate your triumphs, I will love you all the more for your failures." Smiling, she adds, "And I promise never to wear heels so you won't feel short." Their declarations are heartfelt mantras of committed love. But what a setup. The more they pile up the promises, the more I wonder if they'll make it through the honeymoon with that list intact. (Of course, in their less dreamy moments, today's newlyweds are well warned of the fragility of matrimony, hence the prosaic prenups that precede the poetic vows.)

We have brought into our conception of marriage everything we once used to look for outside—the adoring gaze of romantic love, the mutual abandon of unbridled sex, the perfect balance of freedom and commitment. In such a blissful partnership, why would we ever stray? The evolution of committed relationships has brought us to a place where we believe infidelity shouldn't happen, since all the reasons have been removed.

And yet, it does. As much as we hopeless romantics hate to admit it, marriages based on attraction and love are often more fragile than marriages based on material motives. (Although that's not to say the old, steady marriages were happier.) They leave us *more* vulnerable to the vagaries of the human heart and the shadow of betrayal.

The men and women I work with invest more in love and happiness than ever before, but in a cruel twist of fate, the resulting sense of entitlement is precisely what's behind today's exponential rise of infidelity and divorce. Once we strayed because marriage was not supposed to deliver love and passion. Today we stray because marriage fails to deliver the love, passion, and undivided attention it promised.

Every day in my office I meet consumers of the modern ideology of marriage. They bought the product, got it home, and found that it was missing a few pieces. So they come to the repair shop to fix it so that it looks like what's on the box. They take their relational aspirations as a given—both what they want and what they deserve to have—and are upset when the romantic ideal doesn't jibe with the unromantic reality. It's no surprise that this utopian vision is gathering a growing army of the disenchanted in its wake.

Romantic Consumerism

"My needs aren't being met," "This marriage is not working for me anymore," "It's not the deal I signed up for"—these are laments

I hear regularly in my sessions. As psychologist and author Bill Doherty observes, these kinds of statements apply the values of consumerism—"personal gain, low cost, entitlement, and hedging one's bets"—to our romantic connections. "We still believe in commitment," he writes, "but powerful voices coming from inside and outside tell us that we are suckers if we settle for less than we think we need and deserve in our marriage."

In our consumer society, novelty is key. The obsoleteness of objects is programmed in advance so that it ensures our desire to replace them. And the couple is indeed no exception to these trends. We live in a culture that continually lures us with the promise of something better, younger, perkier. Hence we no longer divorce because we're unhappy; we divorce because we could be happier.

We've come to see immediate gratification and endless variety as our prerogative. Previous generations were taught that life entails sacrifice. "You can't always get what you want" made sense a half century ago, but who under thirty-five vibes with this message? We doggedly reject frustration. No wonder the constraints of monogamy can induce panic. In a world of endless options, we struggle with what my millennial friends call FOMO—the fear of missing out. FOMO drives what is known as the "hedonic treadmill"— the endless search for something better. The minute we get what we want, our expectations and desires tend to rise, and we end up not feeling any happier. The swiping culture lures us with infinite possibilities, but it also exerts a subtle tyranny. The constant awareness of ready alternatives invites unfavorable comparisons, weakens commitment, and prevents us from enjoying the present moment.

Mirroring a shift in Western society at large, relationships have left the production economy for the experience economy. Marriage, as philosopher Alain de Botton writes, went "from being an institution to being the consecration of a feeling, from being an externally sanctioned rite of passage to being an internally motivated response to an emotional state." For many, love is no longer a verb, but a noun describing a constant state of enthusiasm, infatuation, and desire. The quality of the relationship is now synonymous with the quality of the experience. What good is a stable household, a good income, and well-behaved children if we are bored? We want our relationships to inspire us, to transform us. Their value, and therefore their longevity, is commensurate with how well they continue to satisfy our experiential thirst.

It is all these new prerogatives that drive the story of contemporary infidelity. It's not our desires that are different today, but the fact that we feel we deserve—indeed, we are obligated—to pursue them. Our primary duty is now to ourselves—even if it comes at the expense of those we love. As Pamela Druckerman points out, "Our high expectations for personal happiness might even make us more likely to cheat. After all, aren't we entitled to an affair, if that's what it takes to be fulfilled?" When the self and its feelings are central, a new narrative of justification is added to the age-old story of straying desires.

The Next Generation

All of this brings us to Silvia's twins, Zac and Michelle. Now in their late twenties, they are quintessential millennials. The cultural landscape they inhabit is shaped by the values laid out by their parents—individualism, self-fulfillment, egalitarianism—to which they have added a fresh focus on authenticity and transparency. Technology is at the center of their every activity, including the sexual variety. Their libidinal pursuits play out on apps like Tinder, Grindr, Hinge, Snapchat, and Instagram.

Neither Zac nor Michelle is married—like all their friends, they've spent their twenties completing their education, traveling, working, and playing. They've grown up in a wide-open sexual terrain that no previous generation has encountered—one with more opportunity, but also more ambiguity; fewer limits but few guidelines. As a young queer man, Zac has never known what it was like to sneak into an underground gay club where all the men are married to women. He didn't have to "come out," because in some sense he was never in. He knows about the AIDS crisis from movies, but he has a prophylactic pill in his pocket that will keep him safe. When marriage equality became the latest chapter in the evolution of the institution, he got down on one knee and proposed to his boyfriend, Theo, in front of the entire law office where they work. Someday they hope to have a family of their own.

Michelle, an entrepreneur who runs a small virtual reality company, is not sitting at home waiting for the phone to ring. If she wants to be with someone, she's one swipe away. She dreams of one day getting married, but she's in no hurry. In fact, she has her eggs on ice so she doesn't have to fret about her biological clock, and enough money saved that she'll never be dependent. "Even if I met the right guy tomorrow, I wouldn't want to have kids for at least five years," she explains. "I'd want to live with someone and enjoy being a couple before we became parents." Some refer to this cohabitation period as "beta testing" a relationship. "Besides," Michelle adds, "if I don't meet someone, I don't need a guy to become a mother." Sex, marriage, and parenthood used to be a package deal. No longer. The boomers separated sex from marriage and reproduction; their children are separating reproduction from sex.

Michelle's attitudes are common among her generation. "Culturally, young adults have increasingly come to see marriage as a 'capstone' rather than a 'cornerstone,'" say the researchers at the project Knot Yet, "that is, something they do after they have all their other ducks in a row, rather than a foundation for launching into adulthood and parenthood."

Walking down the aisle is something Michelle will only do once she feels emotionally mature, professionally settled, financially secure, and ready to move on from the fun of singledom. At that time, she will be looking for a partner who will complement her and who will bestow upon her the deep experience of recognizing her carefully crafted identity. In contrast, for her grandmother Maria, marriage was a formative experience, the cornerstone upon which she and her husband were building their identities together as they moved into adulthood.

Will Michelle's calculated delay protect her from the adulterous betrayal that Maria suffered? Or will it leave her more vulnerable? Hugo Schwyzer comments in *The Atlantic* that the "cornerstone" paradigm has an expectation of difficulty built into it, while the "capstone" does not. Couples who marry young are expected to struggle and to come out stronger for it. Hence, the cornerstone model "doesn't condone infidelity so much as it concedes its near-inevitability." In contrast, he observes, "The capstone model is much less forgiving of sexual betrayal because it presumes that those who finally get around to marrying should be mature enough to be both self-regulating and scrupulously honest. . . . The evidence suggests, however, that the capstoners are more than a little naïve if they imagine that a rich set of premarital life experiences will serve as an inoculation against infidelity."

Shattering the Grand Ambition of Love

Maria, now almost eighty and widowed, will attend her grandson's wedding next month, and perhaps her mind will drift back to her own nuptials. The institution into which Zac and Theo are entering bears little resemblance to that into which she and Kenneth solemnly stepped, more than half a century before.

In order to keep up with modern life, marriage has turned itself inside out, offering ever-greater equality, freedom, and flexibility. And yet there is one matter about which it remains, for the most part, unflinching: infidelity.

The more sexually active our society has become, the more intractable its attitude toward cheating. In fact, it is precisely because we can have plenty of sex before marriage that exclusiveness within marriage has assumed entirely new connotations. These days, most of us arrive at the altar after years of sexual nomadism. By the time we tie the knot, we've hooked up, dated, cohabited, and broken up. We used to get married and have sex for the first time. Now we get married and we stop having sex with others.

The conscious choice we make to rein in our sexual freedom is a testament to the seriousness of our commitment. (Of course, in the continuing evolution of this most elastic institution, there are now some who bring multiple partners inside marriage as well.) Faithfulness is now an elective, an expression of primacy and loyalty. By turning our backs on other loves, we confirm the uniqueness of our "significant other." "I have found The One. I can stop looking." Miraculously, our desire for others is supposed to evaporate, vanquished by the power of this singular attraction. In a world where it is so easy to feel insignificant—to be laid off, disposable, deleted with a click, unfriended—being *chosen* has taken on an importance it never had before. Monogamy is the sacred cow of the romantic ideal, for it confirms our specialness. Infidelity says, *You're not so special after all*. It shatters the grand ambition of love.

In her seminal book *After the Affair*, Janis Abrahms Spring eloquently gives voice to this existential torment: "Swept away . . .

is your own conviction that you and your partner were meant for each other, that no one could make your partner happier, that together you formed a primal and irreducible union that could not be shared or severed. The affair marks the passing of two innocent illusions—that your marriage is exceptional, and that you are unique or prized."

When marriage was an economic arrangement, infidelity threatened our economic security; today marriage is a romantic arrangement and infidelity threatens our emotional security.

Our individualistic society produces an uncanny paradox: As the need for faithfulness intensifies, so too does the pull toward unfaithfulness. In a time when we depend on our partners emotionally for so much, never have affairs carried such a devastating charge. But in a culture that mandates individual fulfillment and lures us with the promise of being happier, never have we been more tempted to stray. Perhaps this is why we condemn infidelity more than ever even as we practice it more than ever.

PART II

———

THE

FALLOUT

CHAPTER 4

WHY BETRAYAL HURTS SO MUCH

Death by a Thousand Cuts

I used to think I knew who I was, who he was, and suddenly I don't
recognize us, neither him nor me . . . My entire life, as I've led it up
to this moment, has crumbled, like in those earthquakes where the
very ground devours itself and vanishes beneath your feet while
you're making your escape. There is no turning back.
—Simone de Beauvoir, *The Woman Destroyed*

"It was like my whole life had been erased. Just like that. I was so devastated that I called in sick and took the rest of the week off. I could barely stay upright. I forgot to eat, which for me is a very big deal." Gillian tells me that in all of her fifty-plus years, she has never experienced this kind of pain before. "How can this hurt so badly when no one has died?"

The revelation of an affair is eviscerating. If you really want to gut a relationship, to tear out the very heart of it, infidelity is a sure bet. It is betrayal on so many levels: deceit, abandonment, rejection, humiliation—all the things love promised to protect us from. When the one you relied upon is the one who has lied to your face, treated you as unworthy of basic respect, the world you thought you lived in is turned upside down. The story of your life is so fractured you can't piece it together. "Tell me again," you demand. "How long has this been going on?"

Eight years. In Gillian's case, the number works like dynamite. "That's a third of our marriage!" she says, astounded. She and Costa have been together for twenty-five years and have two grown sons. She works as the in-house legal counsel for a major music publisher and is at the top of her career. Costa, born and raised on the Greek island of Paros, owns an Internet security company that has had to ride out the storm of the economic downturn. Gillian has just confirmed Costa's long-standing affair with Amanda, his marketing manager.

"I'd had my suspicions" she admits, "and I had asked him more than once, but he absolutely and persuasively denied it. And I believed him."

Then she discovered the emails and the texts, the Skype account, the selfies, the credit card receipts that went back years and years.

"I felt full of shame and very, very stupid. I was so gullible, so easy to lie to, that at one point he actually concluded that I probably knew because, hey, who could be so dumb? I have so much shock, rage, and jealousy inside. When the anger subsides, it's all pure hurt. Disbelief followed by crushing belief. I really have no compass for this."

Adultery has always hurt. But for modern love's acolytes, it seems to hurt more than ever. In fact, the maelstrom of emotions that are unleashed in the wake of an affair is so overwhelming that many contemporary psychologists borrow from the field of trauma to explain the symptoms: obsessive rumination, hypervigilance, numbness and dissociation, inexplicable rages and uncontrollable panic. Treating infidelity has become a specialty among mental health professionals—myself included—in part because the experience is so cataclysmic that couples can't manage the emotional fallout alone and need intervention if they hope to make it through.

In the immediate aftermath, feelings do not lay themselves out neatly along a flowchart of appropriateness. Instead, many of my patients describe swinging back and forth in a rapid succession of contradictory emotions. "I love you! I hate you! Hold me! Don't touch me! Take your shit and get out! Don't leave me! You scumbag! Do you still love me? Fuck you! Fuck me!" Such a blitz of reactions is to be expected and is likely to go on for some time.

Couples will often reach out to me in the midst of this onslaught. "We are facing a massive marital crisis," Gillian wrote in her first email. "My husband is in terrible pain, too. He feels eaten up by guilt even as he tries to comfort me. We want to try to stay together if we can." Her blow-by-blow account closed with a plea: "I fervently hope you can help us use this awful experience to get to a better place." I intend to do everything I can to help them move forward. But first, I need to help them be where they are.

Emergency Response

The disclosure is a pivotal moment in the story of an affair and of a marriage. The shock of discovery galvanizes the reptilian brain, triggering a primal response: fight, flight, or freeze. Some just stand there, dumbfounded; others can't get away fast enough—hoping to escape the upheaval and regain some sense of control over their lives. When the limbic system has been activated, short-term survival trumps well-thought-out decisions. As hard as it is to do in these moments, I often caution couples to separate their feelings about the affair from their decisions about the relationship. Too often their impulsive responses, while meant to be protective, can destroy years of positive marital capital in an instant. As a therapist, I too must be mindful of my reactions. The drama of infidelity elicits a cornucopia of feelings—sympathy, envy, curiosity, and compassion but also judgment, anger, and disgust. Being emotionally affected is natural, but projections are unhelpful.

I divide post-affair recovery into three phases: crisis, meaning making, and visioning. Gillian and Costa are in the crisis phase, and what they *don't* do at this stage is just as critical as what they do. It's a delicate moment, requiring a safe, nonjudgmental container for the intensity of emotions that are running wild inside and between them. At this point, they need calmness, clarity, and structure, as well as reassurance and hope. Later, in the meaning making phase, there will be time to delve into why the affair happened and what role each of them played in the story. And finally, in the visioning phase, we will ask what lies ahead for them, separately or together. For now, however, we are in the emergency room performing triage. What needs most urgent attention? Is anyone at risk? Reputations, mental health, safety, children, livelihood, and so on, must all be taken into consideration.

As a first responder, I stand right by the couple, sometimes on a daily basis. It speaks to both the isolation of modern coupledom and the stigma of infidelity that the therapist is often the only person to know what is going on at this early stage—the stable base to support their collapse.

So many flying pieces—two people grappling with the fact that they have been living in different realities and only one of them knew it. Few other events in the life of a couple, except perhaps death and illness, carry such ruinous force. Couples therapist Michele Scheinkman emphasizes how important it is to hold a dual perspective that encompasses the differentiated experiences of the couple, something they are unable to do for themselves at this time.

I do this in my sessions, as well as in our correspondence. I encourage writing—in a diary, to me, or to each other—as a release valve. Journal writing provides a safe place to purge, unrestricted. Letter writing is a more deliberate, carefully edited process. Couples often need separate coaching to find the right words. Sometimes the letters are read aloud in our sessions. Other times they are sent, with me copied. There is something deeply intimate in being the witness to the epistolary exchanges between these wounded souls. It offers a whole other window into the relationship that one cannot see only on the couch.

In a way that I have come to anticipate, Gillian and Costa tell me that they have had some of the deepest, most honest conversations with each other since all of this came out—into the middle of the night. Their history is laid bare—unfulfilled expectations, anger, love, and everything in between. They listen to each other. At this critical juncture, they have cried, they have argued, and they have made love—a lot. (It is uncanny how the fear of loss can rekindle desire.) They are once again, as my colleague Terry Real likes to say, face-to-face—the way we are when we first fall in love, before we settle into the side-by-side alignment of everyday coupledom.

Every Betrayal Was Once a Love Story

The discovery of an affair can be all-consuming. So much so that we forget that it is only one chapter in the larger story of a couple. The acute trauma will give way to a process of recovery, however long it may take, either together or apart. Shock has a constricting effect, like a punch in the stomach. My task is to help couples catch their breath and relocate themselves in the bigger picture of their relationship, beyond the immediate ordeal. To begin, sometimes even in the first session, I will ask them to share with me how they met—their origin story.

Gillian and Costa fell in love during her last year of law school. He pulled up on his motorcycle outside the library and invited her to go for a ride. She was charmed by his boldness, his gallantry, and his warmth, all delivered in an exotic accent. Surprising herself, she hopped on board.

She affectionately describes him as "volcanic"—unafraid of conflict and confrontation, and with an unabashed zest for life. She characterizes herself as more of a peacemaker, erring on the side of pragmatism. "Costa was good for me," she says, "he encouraged me to shake off my New England properness and be more spontaneous."

Before Costa, she had been engaged to Craig, a Wharton-groomed MBA who was poised to take over his family business. But she had been ambivalent for quite a while: "Craig loved being loved by me more than he loved me." In the end, she broke off the engagement because she "wanted to be adored."

Her Mediterranean man adored her and knew how to show it. He was totally smitten with this powerful, elegant, and independent woman. "I had just moved to the States, and she was so American," he explained. She was a stark contrast to the women of his childhood, whose strength was often measured by how stoically they endured lifelong mistreatment by their philandering husbands.

Gillian remarks that she had always suspected that her ex-fiancé, Craig, in his unconditional self-love, would one day cheat on her. It wasn't like him to put anyone else's needs ahead of his own. At the core of her choosing Costa lay her certainty that he, on the other hand, would never be so selfish. She just *knew* it. She banked on his devotion. How could she have been so mistaken?

They got married at his family home in Paros—white walls, blue awnings, red-tiled roofs set off with pink bougainvillea blossoms. As she watched her impeccably coiffed mother stumbling happily through the *syrtaki* dance, our bride felt deeply affirmed in her decision to give up the man with the right degree and the right pedigree for the man who would forever cherish her. Reflecting the emancipatory values of her time and ignoring her parents' misgivings, Gillian traded in their model of marriage for her own ideal.

When Costa's secret came to light, her disillusion was all the more searing. It wasn't just an attack on her, it was an attack on her entire belief system—a breach of some of the most dearly held assumptions about coupledom today. Marriage has become a mythical castle, designed to be everything we could want. Affairs bring it tumbling down, leaving us feeling like there is nothing to hold on to. Perhaps this goes some way toward explaining why modern infidelity is more than painful. It is traumatic.

Discovery in the Digital Age

Whether we were totally blindsided or had been tracking the spores of evidence all along, nothing prepares us for the actual unveiling. After years of hovering around the truth, Gillian noticed one day that Costa had left his computer at home. "I finally had to look," she says. "And then I couldn't stop looking."

On what she calls "D-Day," she sat for hours digging through the digital evidence. She was flattened by the images. Hundreds of photos, emails exchanged, desires expressed; the vivid details of Costa's eight-year affair unfolded before her eyes. Just a few decades ago, she might have found a phone number in a suit pocket, lipstick on a collar, or a dusty box of letters. A nosy neighbor might have blabbered. Caught, Costa would have told her the story as he saw fit, omitting choice facts to protect her or himself. Today, courtesy of technological memory, Gillian is more likely to burrow into the excruciating details of her husband's duplicity. She can study her own humiliation, memorizing pages of painful electronic evidence.

Betrayal in the digital age is death by a thousand cuts. She sees them swilling oysters, laughing in Taos; she sees Amanda posing seductively. Here, a shot of them riding his Yamaha, Amanda wearing Gillian's helmet; there, an email with a romantic itinerary in Greece. And everywhere, endless texts chronicling the minute details of Amanda's life.

For everything Gillian sees, there is more she imagines. Him kissing her. The wedding ring on his finger, his hand on her breast. She remembers the way Amanda looked at him at the Christmas party last year—and herself dismissing that look, "like an idiot." She recalls how Amanda complimented her on her chocolate mousse the night Costa invited her to dinner at their home—and herself playing the good hostess, "what a fool." Now she's wondering, "Was his hand on *her* knee under *our* dining room table? Were they laughing about it at work the next day?" The images play over and over, unrelenting, and as soon as she gets one out of her mind, another takes over.

I think it's safe to say that the majority of affairs today are revealed through technology. Current discoveries have taken a graphic turn, occasionally even happening in real time. While Gillian's excavations into Costa's computer were deliberate, for others, technology breaks the news, unsolicited. The iPad left at home makes an unsuspecting husband witness to the text conversation his wife is having with the lover she is on her way to meet. The baby monitor is inexplicably transmitting a moaning sound, even though the woman has her baby in her arms when she arrives home early from a weekend away. The kitty cam, meant to provide reassurance that his beloved pets were okay, instead gives a man a window into a drunken encounter between his girlfriend and a stranger.

In the early hours of New Year's Day, Cooper was on the dance floor in a Berlin nightclub when his phone screen lit up. It was a picture of his girlfriend, back in New York on another dance floor, grinding with some guy. The accompanying text from his buddy said, "Yo man, FYI, just saw Aimee making out with some random dude."

Anyone can be a hacker these days. For all the years that Ang was watching porn, Sydney thought, *That's his business.* But when he lost all interest in sex with her, she decided that now it *was* her business. A girlfriend told her about some spyware she could use to track his online activities. "I would sit there at my desk, watching these videos, knowing that he was watching them at the same time, jerking off, for hours on end. It messed with my head. At first I started dressing and acting more like those porn girls, thinking I could win him back. In the end, I felt betrayed, not only by him but more by myself."

You no longer need to hire a private detective—you have one in your pocket. The accidental slip of the send button. "Why is Dad sending me a naked picture?!" The butt call. "What's that heavy breathing in the background?" The "unusual activity alert" from the fraud department at Visa. "I've never even been to Montreal!"

And in this parade of technological whistleblowers, let's not forget the marvels of GPS. It's been a while since César began to suspect that Andy's extended hours at the gym might not have been confined to the weight room. "For all the time he's supposedly lifting, I'd expect to see a bit more muscle! And I know he sits in the sauna, but how long can you stay in there before you melt?" Since he couldn't very well follow Andy without being seen, he followed his phone instead. The blue dot on the map left the gym after only thirty minutes and headed downtown.

I've Looked at Love from Both Sides Now

Not only do our gadgets enable disclosure, but they preserve a digital record. "It's become an obsession, almost pathological," Gillian tells me. "I keep reading the emails, trying to fit it all together. Hundreds of texts between them in a single day—from seven A.M. till midnight. The affair was present all the time, in the midst of our life. What was I doing when he wrote that? At nine-twelve P.M. on August 5, 2009, we were celebrating my fifty-first birthday. Did he run to the bathroom to text her just before he sang 'Happy Birthday,' or was it after?"

Infidelity is a direct attack on one of our most important psychic structures: our memory of the past. It not only hijacks a couple's hopes and plans but also draws a question mark over their history. If we can't look back with any certainty and we can't know what will happen tomorrow, where does that leave us? Psychologist Peter Fraenkel emphasizes how the betrayed partner is "rigidly stuck in the present, overwhelmed by the relentless progression of disturbing facts about the affair."

We are willing to concede that the future is unpredictable, but we expect the past to be dependable. Betrayed by our beloved, we suffer the loss of a coherent narrative—the "internal structure that helps us predict and regulate future actions and feelings [creating] a stable sense of self," as psychiatrist Anna Fels defines it. In an article describing the corrosive effects of all kinds of relational betrayals, she reflects, "perhaps robbing someone of his or her story is the greatest betrayal of all."

In the obsessive drive to root out every facet of an affair lies the existential need to reweave the very tapestry of one's life. We are meaning-making creatures and we rely on coherence. The interrogations, the flashbacks, the circular ruminations, and the hypervigilance are all manifestations of a scattered life narrative trying to piece itself back together.

"I feel so broken," Gillian says. "My mind goes back and forth, sweeping through the timeline, adjusting the memories and wedging all the new stuff into place so that it starts to align with reality."

Anna Fels uses the image of a dual screen, where people are constantly reviewing the life they remember on one side and the newly revealed version on the other. A sense of alienation creeps up inside. It isn't just their lying partner they feel estranged from, but also themselves.

This crisis of truth is captured poignantly in the movie *Love Actually*. Karen, played by Emma Thompson, retreats to her bedroom to digest the realization that the gold necklace she saw her husband buy was not in the Christmas package she just opened. Her gift was a Joni Mitchell CD, which we hear playing as the scene cuts to his young secretary, in sexy lingerie, putting on the necklace, and then back to a tearful Karen retro-gazing at her life as depicted in the family photographs on her dresser. Joni sings, "It's love's illusions I recall/I really don't know love at all."

Gillian's dual screens are often X-rated. "Our sex versus their sex. My body; her body. Those hands I love caressing another, those lips kissing hers. Him inside of her, whispering with that irresistible voice, telling her how hot she is. Did they have favorite positions? Was it better than our sex? Did he alternate days between her and me?"

Her marriage and her memories have been infiltrated. Once a source of comfort and security, they now fill her with nagging uncertainty. Even the happy times can no longer be remembered fondly—they have all become tainted. Costa insists that when he was with Gillian and the boys, he was fully there—physically, emotionally, all of it. Their life together wasn't false, he asserts. But to her, it feels "like a distortion mirror."

Costa is patient in answering her questions, and their conversations help her to reconstruct their full chronology. He has tried to console her. He has expressed his regret multiple times. Is he going to live in purgatory forever? Will he be guilty till he dies? From his perspective, things are clear. "I want to rebuild with you, not rehash the same things over and over." I have explained to him that repetition helps restore coherence and is intrinsic to healing; nevertheless, when days turn into weeks, he becomes increasingly frustrated. And so does Gillian.

"He begs me to leave the past in the past and move on," she tells me, "but that just makes me feel that he is minimizing my pain. I keep feeling as though I'm on one of those waterwheels. I come up for air and glimpse the future, and then I get pulled back into the water and I think I'm going to die if I don't come back up."

Unfortunately for repentant adulterers, the broken heart takes a long time to mend. "You think that because you've taken responsibility, apologized, and said ten Hail Marys that you've done your part!" she says. "I see how that works for you, but it doesn't for me. I need to hear it again." This is a situation that many couples find themselves in, and I explain to Costa that in the crisis phase, it is to be expected. Gillian is not doing this simply to annoy him. "You've known this history for eight years, she just caught on. And she's got a lot of catching up to do." If she is still incessantly interrogating him three years from now, then it will be a problem.

Infidelity: The Identity Thief

For Gillian, as for many, many others, infidelity is not just a loss of love; it is a loss of self. "I am now a member of the cuckolded wives club," she tells Costa. "This is inalterable and will be true for the rest of my life, no matter what the outcome. *You* made me this person. I don't know who I am anymore."

When love goes plural, the spell of oneness is broken. For some, this dissolution is more than their marriage can bear. Costa and Gillian want to find a way to stay together, but each in their own way fears that even if their love is to survive, it will remain contaminated forever.

"I love you; it has always been you," Costa assures her. "Amanda is something that happened. I would have ended it after a year, but then her daughter got sick and I felt guilty. I know you may not believe me, but you are the love of my life and that hasn't changed." Indeed, why should she believe him when she now knows that for eight years he has slept beside her every night and then woken up to text Amanda "Good morning, my love"? And yet, she wants to.

The sense of obliteration that Gillian describes is a story I hear all the time from modern Western couples, but it is not the same everywhere. We would love to think that pain is pain, democratic and universal. In fact, an entire cultural framework shapes the way we give meaning to our heartbreak. In my conversations with a group of Senegalese women, several of whom had been cheated on by their husbands, none talked about having lost their entire identity. They described sleepless nights, jealousy, endless crying, outbursts of anger. But in their view, husbands cheat because "that's what men do," not because their wives are mysteriously inadequate. Ironically, their belief about men underscores their ongoing oppression but protects their sense of identity. Gillian may be socially more emancipated, but her identity and self-worth have been mortgaged to romantic love. And when love calls in its debts, it can be a ruthless creditor.

My Senegalese friends draw much of their identity and sense of belonging from their community. Historically, most people anchored their sense of self-worth in complying with the values and expectations of religion and family hierarchy. But in the absence of the old institutions, we are now each in charge of the making and maintaining of our own identity, and the burdens of selfhood have never been heavier. Hence, we are constantly negotiating our sense of self-worth. Sociologist Eva Illouz astutely points out that "the only place where you hope to stop that evaluation is in love. In love you become the winner of the contest, the first and only." No wonder infidelity throws us into a pit of self-doubt and existential confusion.

Men and women alike affirm this tale. Of course, there are nuances in what they highlight; the conversation on affairs carries an implicit gender bias. Perhaps because men have always been given more permission to pursue and to boast about their conquests, their tears have been suppressed. Men whose wives turned elsewhere were more likely to express rage or embarrassment than sadness. They were allowed to grieve the loss of face, not of self. We know much more about hurt women and straying men than we know about hurt men or straying women. But as women are leveling the playing field of infidelity and it is becoming more culturally acceptable for men to show emotion, I hear more and more men who have been blindsided by betrayal giving voice to their own loss of identity.

"The world as I knew it was over," Vijay wrote to me. A forty-seven-year-old Anglo-Indian deli manager, with two kids, he'd just discovered an email that his wife, Patti, had sent to her best friend, containing a series of texts between her and her lover. "I felt like I was falling through dark, gravity-less space. I desperately tried to find something to cling to. But almost immediately she was changed. Me too. She seemed cold, retreated. She cried, but it didn't seem like she was crying for us."

Milan's voice cracks as he tells me, "I fell in love hard. I really believed in a future with Stefano, and I gave it everything. Then he totally shut down on me sexually. He got hooked on meth, and then he fell in love with some kid. I came home and he was screwing him in our bed. And he just ignored me, pretending I was his roommate. This went on for months. I was so humiliated, but I couldn't leave. And as a gay man, I was not supposed to be jealous: it was only fucking, after all. I needed him. I have so much contempt for myself, for allowing him to treat me this way. I barely recognize myself anymore."

"I Am Not That Guy!"

The crisis of identity is not only reserved for the partner who was betrayed. When the veil on a secret is lifted, the shock is not only for the one who discovers the affair but also for the one who was engaged in it. Looking at his or her behavior through the newly opened eyes of the aggrieved, the protagonist of the affair confronts a self-image that is barely recognizable.

Costa is having his own breakdown. Confronted by Gillian's excruciating pain, he is awakened to the reality of what he has done and what it has done to her. The partition between his public life and his secret life has come crumbling down.

In our private conversations, he struggles to come to terms with his own disparate pieces. He has never been to therapy, is rather suspicious of so-called experts, and doesn't expect much sympathy to come his way. I make a point of letting him know that I'm not the moral police. "Even though you had an affair, and a rather long one at that, I don't pretend to know you. I'm here to help, not to judge."

Costa has to reckon with the discrepancy between his self-image and his actions. From childhood on, he had promised himself that he would *never* act like his philandering and domineering father, who had treated his mother with contempt. Costa has always seen himself as a principled man—morally upright and deeply attuned to the pain of a woman whose love has been desecrated.

"I am not that guy" was the pillar around which he organized his entire sense of self (and won Gillian's heart). It also was the phrase used to dissuade Gillian of her suspicions over the years. Determined to shore up this better-than-my-father identity, Costa became a man who was rigid and quick to judge. Unconsciously, he believed that his absolutism would help to hold his paternal heritage at bay, but in a twist of fate, it drove him to act in the very way he always hoped to avoid. "I felt like my life had flatlined. I was becoming an automaton. I was bound up, tied tight, stiff and formal like I had a stick up my ass." He describes how he had begun to feel irrelevant, his own business struggling and the salary gap between them steadily growing. Gillian was busy with everybody else. "And then she started talking about retirement plans and long-term care, and I felt like she was burying me alive!" Enter Amanda, who offered him a way "to loosen up and reconnect with passion."

Costa assures me that he never stopped loving his wife and had no intention of leaving her. He wanted to end it with Amanda many times, but felt obligated to her too, especially when she seemed to be facing one crisis after another. The sensitive boy who had witnessed his mother's humiliations became the man who could not leave a damsel in distress—a weakness his mistress had detected early and played on skillfully. Furthermore, he is convinced that because he had changed so much—become less depressed and stopped moping around the house—so had their marriage, for the better. (Gillian, I know, concurs with this assessment but rejects his justifications.)

He seems to think that because, unlike his old man, he didn't publicly strut down the street with his mistress, his principles remain intact. His identity politics have created a blind spot. Only now, in the harsh light of the voluminous evidence, does he see the stretch of his rationalizations. Is Gillian's pain and shame really so different from his mother's? I ask him.

Aware of his need to recalibrate his personality with the unwelcome additions, I begin to help him parse out what the affair meant to him and what it represents in the fuller context of his life. As the process unfolds, our repentant Romeo is eager to share his new insights with his wife. I caution him that this conversation is premature. Her angst takes precedence over the analysis. We are still in the crisis phase, and at this stage the compassion goes toward her. Only when the betrayed partner feels emotionally met will he or she be able to listen to explanations without hearing them as justifications. It is too soon to expect Gillian to see Costa's point of view, let alone consider what part she might have played.

For now, he needs to listen. This is going to take some work, because he is so invested in preserving an image of himself as not being a "sleazebag" (as he puts it) that he feels compelled to justify himself and his actions. He sees how bad she feels, but it makes him feel bad about himself (shame), which prevents him from feeling bad for her (guilt).

The shift from shame to guilt is crucial. Shame is a state of self-absorption, while guilt is an empathic, relational response, inspired by the hurt you have caused another. We know from trauma that healing begins when perpetrators acknowledge their wrongdoing. Often, when one partner insists that they don't yet feel acknowledged, even as the one who hurt them insists they feel terrible, it is because the response is still more shame than guilt, and therefore self-focused. In the aftermath of betrayal, authentic guilt, leading to remorse, is an essential repair tool. A sincere apology signals a care for and commitment to the relationship, a sharing of the burden of suffering, and a restoration of the balance of power.

I know it won't be easy for Costa. If you've cheated on someone, it's hard to watch the suffering that you've caused and to give your partner the time and space to really grieve, knowing you're the cause of it. But that's exactly what she needs. "If you want to help Gillian feel better," I tell Costa, "first you need to let her feel like shit." Holding space for her pain is important, and physically holding her is equally so. Costa is doing a lot of this. Obviously, it is easier for him to respond empathically when his wife is sad than when she goes on the attack. That said, the lashing out is unavoidable, at least for a while. The time will come for telling her to ease off. Meanwhile, it is his consistent empathic stance that will help her anger subside gradually.

Costa makes a great effort to be available for her anguish. He tells her over and over that he loves her. Gillian calms down for a while—an hour; sometimes two or more; on occasion, a whole day. She believes him, of course she does—he's her husband. But then, BOOM, she remembers. "I used to believe him before, and look where that got me."

Her suspicions mount again. This time, she's not going to shut her eyes and pretend nothing is happening. So she starts to scavenge for more information. He has forfeited his right to privacy. Who is this woman whose picture he liked on Instagram? What was the dentist doing for three hours? Did he even have an appointment? She will call and find out for herself. Fear and rage merge and she explodes. Sparing nothing, she goes after his family, his culture, his genes, and of course, Amanda. It's open season.

"Cheater! Liar!" Now she's pushed Costa over the edge. He is willing to take responsibility, but in no way will he let this be the final verdict on his identity. "I have cheated *once* and I have lied many times about that *one* thing," he insists, "But I am not a cheater or a liar." Her pain mirrors back an image of himself that he can't tolerate, so he gets mad. When she continues to feel bad, it confirms that he *is* bad. The tension mounts again. "I am not that guy! I will not allow her, this affair, or anything else to define me."

I decide to take him on. "I hear your conflict and I see your conscience. But when you consider the duplicity, year in, year out, you are closer to being 'that guy' than you would like to admit."

Acts of Repair

The early stages of post-affair therapy are highly volatile, to say the least. Weeks of careful reconstruction can crumble with one remark. Both are on edge, eyeing each other, fearful of the next emotional blow. As Maria Popova writes, "The dance of anger and forgiveness, performed to the uncontrollable rhythm of trust, is perhaps the most difficult in human life, as well as one of the oldest."

During the crisis phase, the responsibility for repair lies primarily with the one who had the affair. In addition to expressing contrition and being receptive to the pain of their partner, he or she can do several other important things.

Janis Abrahms Spring identifies one of these steps as the "transfer of vigilance." Essentially, this means that the one who acted outside the relationship takes on the role of remembering and holding the affair in awareness. Typically, the partner who has been betrayed feels compelled to ask questions, to obsess, to make sure that this terrible thing does not get swept under the rug. The wanderer is usually all too eager to put the unpleasant episode behind them.

By reversing these positions, we change the dynamic. Surveillance rarely breeds trust. If Costa holds the memory of the affair, then he relieves Gillian from having to be the one to ensure that it isn't forgotten. If he brings it up on his own and invites conversation about it, then he communicates that he is not trying to hide or minimize it. If he volunteers information, he frees her from the constant rehashing. One time, Amanda called him. He told Gillian right away, defusing a potential source of distrust. Another time, when they were at a restaurant, he sensed that Gillian was wondering if he had been there with Amanda. He didn't wait for her to ask—he told her, unsolicited, and made sure she was comfortable staying there. All of this, abundantly displayed, helps to restore trust, as it makes her feel that they are on the same side.

For her part, Gillian needs to begin to curb her angry outbursts—not because they are unjustified, but because they will not give her what she is really seeking. Anger may make her feel more powerful, temporarily. However, psychologist Steven Stosny observes that "if loss of power was the problem in intimate betrayal, then anger would be the solution. But the great pain in intimate betrayal has little to do with loss of power. Perceived loss of value is what causes your pain—you feel less lovable."

In the wake of betrayal, we need to find ways to restore our own sense of self-worth—to separate our feelings about ourselves from the way the other person has made us feel. When it seems like your entire being has been hijacked and your self-definition rests in the hands of the person who did this to you, it is important to remember that there are other parts to who you are.

You are not a reject, although part of you has been rejected. You are not a victim, although part of you has been abused. You are also loved, valued, honored, and cherished by others and even by your unfaithful partner, although you may not feel that in this moment. Realizing that she had totally disconnected from her friends after she merged her entire life with the boyfriend who had now left her, one woman made a list of five people she needed to bring back into her life. She took a two-week road trip, rekindling the friendships and reclaiming the parts of herself that each of them valued, and in so doing, she separated the injury from her own essence.

Holocaust survivor Viktor Frankl distills a profound truth: "Everything can be taken from a man but one thing: the last of the human freedoms—to choose one's attitude in any given set of circumstances, to choose one's own way."

Dress up, even if you don't feel like it. Let your friends cook you a beautiful dinner. Take that painting class that you've been meaning to take for so long. Do things to take care of yourself, that make you feel good, to counter the humiliation and your urge to hide. Many people feel too much shame to do these things when they've been cast aside, but that's exactly what I urge them to do.

Gillian needs to find her own ways to reclaim her value. Costa's contrition is not enough to ease that pain. Expressing guilt and empathy is crucial for the hurt but insufficient for healing damaged self-worth. Where Costa can help is in resisting self-concern and instead reaffirming her importance and centrality in his life. As he puts aside his worries about himself, he sets out to reclaim the girl who got on the back of his motorcycle all those years ago and made a bargain with the god of love. When he tells her in no uncertain terms, "It's you I want to be with. It was always you," he begins the process of reassigning her value, her cherished presence. For the first time, she starts to believe that he is not staying simply out of principle. He is choosing her.

Two minutes later, his phone buzzes. I see a flash of suspicion in her eyes and she recoils. Another trigger, another question. Here we are, in the trenches of romantic recovery. And we will be here for some time.

CHAPTER 5

LITTLE SHOP OF HORRORS

Do Some Affairs Hurt More than Others?

A strange thing, indeed, that those words, "two or three times,"
nothing more than a few words, words uttered in the air, at a
distance, could so lacerate a man's heart, as if they had actually
pierced it, could sicken a man, like a poison that he had drunk.
—Marcel Proust, *Swann's Way*

Are some affairs "worse" than others? Do some kinds of infidelity hurt less and prove easier to recover from? Much as I've tried to identify patterns in the interplay between action and reaction, I have yet to find a tidy correspondence between the severity of the offense and the intensity of the response.

It's tempting to try to organize affairs according to a hierarchy of violation, where jerking off to porn is a minor infraction, which is certainly less than getting a massage with a happy ending, which is in turn preferable to actual penetration with a Russian hooker, which is still milder than finding your girlfriend in bed with your friend or discovering that your husband has a four-year-old son living three blocks away. Certainly, not all transgressions are created equal. However, as appealing as it may be to create a gradation of betrayals, it's not especially helpful to measure the legitimacy of the reaction by the magnitude of the offense.

When we traverse the landscape of romantic suffering, countless considerations are at play that steer the story of an individual or a couple in one direction or another. Shock comes in varying degrees. Even after decades of this work, I still cannot predict what people will do when they discover a partner's affair. In fact, many have told me that their response is far from what they would have predicted themselves.

The impact of an affair is not necessarily proportional to its length or seriousness. Some relationships will collapse upon the discovery of a fleeting hookup. In a moment of unguarded intimacy, a woman slipped into reminiscence and told her husband about a brief extramarital fling that happened decades earlier. She was flabbergasted when he promptly ended their thirty-year marriage. Others will exhibit a surprisingly robust capacity to bounce back after extensive treachery. It's striking how some people barely react to life-changing revelations, while others respond with great fanfare to mere wandering eyes. I have seen people devastated from knowing that their partner even fantasized about someone else or masturbated to porn, while others philosophically accept the nameless encounters that accompany business trips to far-flung places.

In the tangled tale of infidelity, every nuance matters. As a therapist, I need emotional specifics. Researcher Brené Brown explains that in the wake of a shocking or traumatic event, "our emotions get the first crack at making sense of the pain." Some things inflame the heartbreak ("he did *what?*") and others become markers of relief ("at least she didn't do *that*"). To borrow terms from healthcare entrepreneur Alexandra Drane, some are magnifiers—particular elements that increase the suffering. Others are buffers—protective shields against the hurt.

How infidelity will land on you and how you will respond has as much to do with your own expectations, sensitivities, and history as it has to do with the egregiousness of your partner's behavior. Gender, culture, class, race, and sexual orientation all frame the experience of infidelity and give shape to the pain.

A magnifier can be a circumstance. Pregnancy, economic dependency, unemployment, health challenges, immigration status, and countless other life conditions can add to the burden of betrayal. Our family history is a prime magnifier—affairs and other breaches of trust we grew up with or suffered in past relationships can leave us more susceptible. Infidelity always takes place within a web of connections, and the story started long before the acute injury. For some, it confirms a deep-seated fear: "It's not that he doesn't love me, it's that I don't feel lovable." And for others, it shatters the image they had of their partner: "I picked you because I was so sure you were not that kind of person."

Buffers include a strong network of friends and family who are patient and provide a safe space for the complexity of the situation. A well-developed sense of self or a spiritual or religious faith can also mitigate the impact. The quality of the relationship itself, prior to the crisis, always plays a major part. And if one feels that one has options—real estate, savings, job prospects, dating prospects—it not only tempers vulnerability but gives one room to maneuver, inside and out. Parsing the pain points of betrayal helps to identify opportunities for strengthening these protective buffers.

In my early meetings with infidelity's casualties, I scan the wounds until I locate their specific emotional quality, identifying magnifiers and strategizing for buffers. Where does it hurt the most? What twisted the knife? The slight, the disloyalty, the abandonment, the breach of trust, the lies, the humiliation? Is it loss or rejection? Is it disillusion or shame? Is it relief, resignation, or indignation? What is the particular feeling or constellation of feelings around which you circle?

"Of All People, Why Him?"

Some people are able to express their feelings immediately. Their emotional literacy enables them to recognize, name, and own the particulars of their suffering. But I also encounter many who have shut down without ever identifying their emotional pain points. They live haunted by unnamed feelings, which are no less powerful for their anonymity. "You're only the second person I've ever told my story to," a young man named Kevin wrote after reaching out to me on Facebook. "It's been ten years. Perhaps finally writing this all out is my own form of therapy."

For Kevin, a twenty-six-year-old programmer who lives in Seattle, what hurt the most was not that his first love cheated on him—it was *whom* she did it with. Years of carrying the shame "of being clueless" have left Kevin with some serious trust issues. He met Taylor at sixteen—she was the gorgeous senior who took his virginity and held most of his attention during high school. Kevin introduced Taylor to his older brother, Hunter, and the three became inseparable.

Initially, when Taylor broke off the relationship, it took Kevin by surprise. He was "hurt, but not heartbroken." Strangely, Taylor and Hunter were still hanging out together. "Even my mom asked if I was okay with this. But I trusted him so unconditionally that when he told me they were studying, I believed him. I couldn't imagine that he of all people could betray me."

Looking back, he asks himself, "How could I not see?" But it is human nature to cling to our sense of reality, to resist its possible shattering even in the face of irrefutable evidence. I assure him that his "cluelessness" is not something to be ashamed of. This kind of avoidance is not an act of idiocy but an act of self-preservation. It is actually a sophisticated self-protective mechanism known as trauma denial—a type of self-delusion that we employ when too much is at stake and we have too much to lose. The mind needs coherence, so it disposes of inconsistencies that threaten the structure of our lives. This becomes more pronounced when we are betrayed by those we feel closest to and are dependent on—a testament to the lengths we will go to preserve our attachments, however fraught they may be.

Finally one day a kid at school blurted out to Kevin, "Do you realize your brother is sleeping with Taylor?" "It made no sense to me," Kevin recalls, and yet a few minutes later, he walked to a place that was quiet and called his brother asking if it was true. "He knew he had royally fucked up and apologized profusely. I remember crying for hours, with my head buried in a blue pillow. Things between my brother and me changed forever."

In his writing, I can hear the voice of his sixteen-year-old self. His story is frozen in time, with vivid details—the time of day, the name of the kid who told him the humiliating truth, the minutes he waited before his brother picked up the phone, the color of the pillow he cried into. Psychologists refer to these as screen memories—when we fixate on specific details in order to conceal the more distressing emotional aspects of the experience, making the trauma more tolerable.

In Kevin's next email, I can hear the relief as it starts to make sense to him why he can see the pillow more clearly than Taylor's face. The depth of a betrayal goes hand in hand with the depth of the attachment. For many, the betrayal of a friend goes even deeper than that of their own partner. Taylor's duplicity smarted, but

Hunter's cut deeper. When it is someone in one's own social circle, a member of one's own family (in all its intergenerational permutations), or a person in whom one placed one's trust (nanny, teacher, clergy, neighbor, doctor), the rupture is exponential. Where do we turn? I have heard more than one story where the friend and confidant turned out to be the lover. The more synapses of coherence are snapped, the crazier people feel and the longer it takes to recover.

For years, Kevin had been stuck in embarrassment and shame at his "dumbness." As a result, he couldn't trust his own perceptions. "Whenever I hooked up or dated a girl, I was constantly thinking, 'There must be someone else in the picture.'" Understanding that the issue was not his failure to see the signs, but rather his brother's profound failure to honor his trust was pivotal for Kevin. He's working on the relationship with Hunter. And he has discovered newfound compassion for his younger self, which allows him not to immediately close off when things get more serious with a girl he likes.

From Suspicion to Certainty

Certainty is searing, but gnawing suspicion is its own kind of agony. When we begin to suspect that our beloved is duplicitous, we become relentless scavengers, sniffing out desire's carelessly strewn clothes and clues. Sophisticated surveillance experts, we track the minute changes in his face, the indifference in her voice, the unfamiliar smell of his shirt, her lackluster kiss. We tally up the slightest incongruities. "I kept wondering why she had so many early meetings at the office when she is supposed to start at ten." "Her Instagram posts didn't match where she said she was. Dates don't lie!" "It was puzzling that he had to take a shower and put on deodorant before going for his run." "All of a sudden, she was so eager to invite Brad and Judy to dinner, when for so long she didn't even like them." "Does he really need his phone in the bathroom?"

At first we may keep our questions to ourselves, afraid to falsely accuse, if we're wrong, and even more afraid to face the facts, if we're right. But eventually the desire to know trumps the fear of knowing, and we begin to probe and to interrogate. We test, asking questions to which the GPS has already given irrefutable answers. We set traps. "Every dark secret I'll discover better by pretending," sings a scheming Figaro in Mozart's classic opera. We act like we know when we only fear. Anton tells Josie he has proof that she has been sleeping around—there's no point in continuing to lie about it. "You can tell me," he says. "I already know everything." But it's a bluff. Feeling caught, Josie tells him more than he had ever bargained for. Now he can't get the images out of his head. In a common twist, Josie tells me later that initially Anton's suspicions had been unfounded. However, as his snooping increased, so did her frustration and evasiveness. Eventually, resenting her life under surveillance, she says, "He was so convinced I had been cheating on him all along that I decided to do it for real."

Sometimes the corrosive torment of doubting a partner's fidelity is made worse by the cruel practice of gaslighting. For months Ruby was asking JP if something was up, and he kept telling her she was crazy, jealous, paranoid. She was almost at the point where she believed him, were it not for the day he left his phone at home. In hindsight, his vociferous denial should have been proof enough. Now she feels doubly betrayed. He made her doubt not just him but her own sanity.

When suspicion turns to certainty, for an instant, there may be relief, but then a new arrow strikes. The moment of revelation often leaves an indelible scar. How did you discover the affair? Did you find your husband's email address in the Ashley Madison data dump? Did someone else make sure to inform you? Or were you treated to a full-frontal view? Simon walked in on his wife and the contractor in his own bed. He hasn't slept in it since.

Jamiere was prepared for the discovery, but not for the way it happened. She recognized the signs, for Terrence had done this to her before: the sudden interest in grooming, the new shirts and clean nails, the high volume of emergency meetings at work. "You'd think the second time around he'd have gotten better at it, but he made all the same mistakes." Yet he steadfastly denied it. Finally she got her proof: an email from the husband of the woman. "He sent me a trail of their texts, which included some really nasty comments about me. How Terrence was repulsed when I got so big with the twins. My crooked teeth. My ghetto accent. There was so much contempt and ridicule it made me vomit."

Jamiere was distraught at the tone of Terrence's texts, but she also was upset at the fact that they had been sent to her, unsolicited and unabridged. Determined not to let any man continue to push her around, she confronted Terrence. Then she wrote a letter to the man who had unilaterally decided to dump the offensive texts in her lap, pretending that it was for her benefit, when it screamed "revenge." Our work now focuses on rebuilding her self-esteem.

Secrets, Gossip, and Bad Advice

Not only do people discover their partners' secrets; they sometimes become unwilling parties to the deception. Afraid to let on to their friends, their parents, the kids, the colleagues, the neighbors, and in some cases, the media, the betrayed become accomplices in the secret. Now they too must lie—to protect the very person who lied to them.

"I was standing there holding two identical pairs of earrings," Lynn recalls. "I started to ask him why he bought me the same gift twice, when the answer crystallized like an apparition. Six years with his secretary. That's a lot of matching earrings."

For the sake of the kids, Lynn and Mitch have decided to stay together. And for the sake of the kids, she has kept it hidden. "I don't want anyone to know," she told me. "So now I am the one lying, to my parents, to my own daughters. I make waffles in the morning and kiss him goodbye like it's just another day. What a farce! I want to protect them, but in the end I feel like I'm protecting him—how twisted is that?" The secret that was kept from her is now the secret she must keep from others. Mitch seems liberated by the disclosure; Lynn now feels imprisoned. Sometimes she has to remind herself that she is not the guilty one.

What will help both Lynn and Mitch is to carefully select one or two trusted confidants so that the wound does not fester. They may not want to notify the entire village, but lifting the shame of silence matters a great deal. Inviting one or two people into their grief lets some air into a situation that is often hermetically sealed.

When the secret is out, often the anguish is reinforced by the punishment of social disapproval and pity. Ditta hates all those mothers at school looking at her with false compassion while secretly feeling glad that it didn't happen to them. "How could she not know?" they whisper. "What did she expect, working on four continents and leaving him alone with the kids?" The collective voice of condemnation ranges from mild criticism to full blaming of the victim—for "allowing" it to happen, for not doing enough to prevent it, for not seeing it when it was happening, for letting it go on so long, and of course, for staying after everything that happened. The gossip hisses around every corner.

Not only can an affair destroy a marriage; it has the power to unravel an entire social fabric. Its emotional trajectory tends to intersect with many other relationships—friends, family, and colleagues. After nine years, Mo will no longer go on his annual kayak trip with his best buddies. He has just learned that one had been his wife's friend with benefits; the other the provider of the Airbnb; the third, a silent witness. Betrayed on all sides, he asks, "Who am I supposed to talk to now?"

For these people, the specific injuries are shame and isolation. The revelation of an affair can leave the unsuspecting partner in a difficult bind: At the moment they most need others for comfort and affirmation, they are least able to reach out. Unable to draw on the support of friends, they feel doubly alone.

Social isolation and silence are difficult, but so too is the advice of others. Friends are often all too quick to offer hasty judgments, simplistic solutions, and unsolicited rants on how "I never liked him/her anyway." In extreme cases, friends and family are so outraged and reactive themselves that they usurp the role of victim, leaving the deceived partner in the strange position of defending the very person who hurt them. "All my mother could say was 'I told you so,' followed by a long list of Sara's faults, which of course she'd seen from the beginning." Arthur laughs bitterly. "I found myself telling her to back off, reminding her what a great mom Sara was, how hard she worked. Then I said, 'Wait a minute. I'm the one who was hurt here!'"

Everyone seems to know exactly what to do. Friends offer their couch, to help pack his things, to change the locks, to take the kids for the weekend. They send numbers for therapists, for mediators, for detectives, for lawyers. Sometimes this is exactly what is needed. But other times, while these actions may be well intentioned, they fail to make space for the full implications of the dilemma.

"Why Now?"

Affairs hurt enough, but sometimes the timing is the particular nail in the coffin. "Our baby was just two months old!" is an all-too-common refrain, as is "I'd just miscarried." Lizzy was in her third trimester when she found out about Dan's affair. But she felt that she couldn't say anything because it would harm the baby in her belly and disconnect her from the growing life she was nurturing. All she wanted was for the baby not to be contaminated by the negative energy.

"My mother was dying and my wife was off banging a total loser," Tom tells me. Drake knows that the timing is the least of his worries, but that doesn't make it less hurtful: "The fact that I found out on our ten-year anniversary is mostly irrelevant, but it's an ironically torturous element that just adds to my despair."

When the particular timing is personally charged, the emphasis is on "how could he or she do this to me *then*?" The *then* almost overrides the *what*.

"Did You Not Think of Me?"

In some cases, it's the intentional duplicity that burns—the degree of planning it took to pull off such a calculated series of deceptions. The deliberateness implies that the unfaithful partner has weighed his or her desires against their consequences and decided to proceed anyway. Furthermore, the significant investment of time, energy, money, and ingenuity point to the conscious motivation to pursue the selfish motives at the expense of the partner or family.

"Walk me through this," Charlotte asked Steve after she uncovered his elaborate adventures in the world of high-end escorts.

"How did you get to the prostitute? Did you just happen to have five thousand dollars lying around? Or did you go to the ATM ten times to get it? Did you already know what it would cost? Are you such a regular?" Every step of premeditation around the escort meant an active disregard of his wife. There are so many things that Charlotte is angry about when it comes to Steve's escapades in the sex industry, but what really cuts at the heart of her being is the way he was able to erase her so completely from his awareness.

Was he not thinking of her at the bank? Over tapas? When he changed the sheets? When he emptied the trash? "The discovery was painful in and of itself," she tells me, "but when it became clear how much energy and planning it took, that really stung. No wonder he had so little time or energy for us."

Charlotte understands desire, and has had her own opportunities to stray. But she never acted on them. "I know what you did because it was what I *didn't* do," she tells Steve. "When it got right down to it, I couldn't do it because I couldn't stop thinking about you. I knew how much it would hurt you. How could you not know that, too? Or did you just not care?"

Carefully premeditated affairs sting, but the opposite scenario can hurt just as badly. In these cases, it is the carelessness of cheating that took place by happenstance. "She told me it was just a spur-of-the-moment fling, it meant nothing." Rick laughs bitterly. "And I said, 'That's supposed to make me feel better? That you would hurt me this much for something that meant nothing?'"

"Was I Just a Placeholder for His True Love?"

Most of us today take for granted that we will not be the first lover of our chosen partner, but we hope to be the last. We can accept that our beloved has had other relationships, even other marriages, but we like to think of them as transient and past. They are over, for they were not the real thing. We know we have not been the only one, but we believe we are *the* one. Because of this, one twist in the infidelity narrative that is particularly painful is the relighting of an old flame.

Helen and Miles have been together for eighteen years, and married for fourteen. For the last two years, it turns out, Miles has been having an affair with his ex-wife, Maura, who nearly destroyed him when she left with another man. "Why her?" Helen kept asking. "Why his ex? She hurt him so much. You would think he would want nothing to do with her." When I asked Miles, he confessed that he had never accepted that Maura had stopped loving him, and part of him still believes that the hand of fate is guiding their relationship. "After all these years, I ran into her while hiking on the Pacific Crest Trail. What are the chances?"

Helen has always known that Maura was Miles's first love—he married her in college and they were together twelve years. And now she finds herself wondering, "Did he ever really love me? Despite our kids and everything we built, was I ever really the one? Or was it her all along? Perhaps I was just a placeholder for his true love." Being replaced is always harsh, but when the ex returns and the new is actually old, the added twist is feeling that perhaps we are competing with destiny.

Babies and Blood Tests

There is a unique edge when the affair rubs up against life or death, birth and disease. We have long known that one moment of lust can leave a legacy for generations. For much of history, the inevitable consequences of adultery were illegitimate children. Contraception notwithstanding, there are still plenty of cases where there is living proof of the illicit liaison, bringing an additional level of shame and a long-lasting reminder. Men raise children they did not conceive. "Most days, I don't think about it. I'm just her dad. Every once in a while, though, I ache, knowing that this little girl I love more than anything in the world carries the DNA of the man I despise." Women live with the knowledge that their partners have fathered children elsewhere. "At first he didn't want kids. When we started trying, it was too late, even for IVF. It was painful to accept childlessness, but I thought we worked through it together. Then I find out that not only was he getting comfort with a younger woman, but she gave him the one thing I couldn't. She sent me the sonogram pictures out of spite when he told her he wasn't leaving me. The affair, I can handle, but not the baby."

Affairs can create new life; they can also pose a threat to life. These days, it has become standard practice to send the partner who has been unfaithful to take an STD test. But sometimes it is too late. At first Tim was pissed to learn of Mike's multiple hookups. He had told Mike clearly that he wanted a monogamous relationship. But to add insult to injury, Tim is now anxiously awaiting the results of his blood work. "We've always practiced safe sex. The most difficult thing for me to grasp is his lack of concern for my health and the risk he put both of us in. My stomach goes cold every time I think about it. And I still don't know whether he's sorry he did it or just sorry he got caught."

The Price Tag of Philandering

Economic circumstances also play an important role in how we experience and react to a betrayal. For the financially dependent partner, it may literally be a case of "I cannot afford to leave." For the financial provider, the idea that "I've been working all these years to support you and this family and now I will have to pay alimony while you go to live with this loser" can be unbearable. For either partner, what is at stake is not just the family and the life they've built together, but also the lifestyle they have become accustomed to. When Devon cheated on Annie for the second time, she told him he had twenty-four hours to "get the hell out of *my* apartment." Later, she told me, "I pay all the bills, including his car payment, so he can work on his music. I've been generous to a fault, but now I'm done." Her economic freedom is a buffer, giving her a range of options that are out of reach for many others.

Darlene can't even attend a support group because she can't afford a babysitter for her kids. She doesn't say, "I'm done." She says, "I'm trapped." She isn't ready to leave, despite the urging of a number of therapists and members of her congregation. So we work on finding her a new church with a supportive minister, as well as an online community that will respect her choice and lend her an ear. Until she can develop a space to think for herself, she can hardly contemplate her options.

Edith is well into her fifties when she discovers her husband's decades-long prostitute habit. The lurid nature of it all bothers her, but what really kicks her in the gut is the cost. "I don't want to sound mercenary," she tells me, "but twenty years of paid sex—that's the price of a mortgage!" As she sits at home in their small, rented one-bedroom poring over the credit card bills, those tens of thousands of dollars hurt much more than the sex they paid for.

Money. Babies. STDs. Premeditation. Carelessness. Shame. Self-doubt. Gossip and judgment. The particular person, gender, time, place, social context. If this brief compendium of love's horror stories shows us anything, it is that while every act of betrayal shares common features, every experience of betrayal is unique. We do no one a service when we reduce affairs to sex and lies, leaving out the many other constitutive elements that create the nuances of the torment and inform the path to healing.

CHAPTER 6

JEALOUSY

The Spark of Eros

The Green-eyed Monster causes much woe,
but the absence of this ugly serpent argues the presence of
a corpse whose name is Eros.
—Minna Antrim

Q: Are there any secrets to long-lasting relationships?
A: Infidelity. Not the act itself, but the threat of it. For Proust,
an injection of jealousy is the only thing capable of rescuing
a relationship ruined by habit.
—Alain de Botton, *How Proust Can Change Your Life*

Euripides, Ovid, Shakespeare, Tolstoy, Proust, Flaubert, Stendhal, D. H. Lawrence, Austen, the Brontës, Atwood—countless literary giants have delved into the subject of infidelity. And the stories keep on coming, continuously supplied by new pens. At the center of many of these works lies one of the most complex emotions, jealousy—"that sickening combination of possessiveness, suspicion, rage, and humiliation [that] can overtake your mind and threaten your very core as you contemplate your rival," as evolutionary anthropologist Helen Fisher describes it. Indeed, the canon of literature, along with theater, opera, music, and film, would be almost decimated were it to shed infidelity and its haunting companion, jealousy. The pages and stages of the masters are filled with characters contorted by this most excruciating and high-risk emotion.

And yet, when infidelity finds its way into the therapist's office, particularly here in the United States, suddenly jealousy is nowhere to be found. My colleagues, Brazilian couples therapists Michele Scheinkman and Denise Werneck, highlight this interesting gap: "The literature on infidelity deals with the impact of betrayals and affairs in terms of the trauma of revelation and discovery, confession, decisions about the third party, forgiveness, and repair—all matters related to a concrete situation of betrayal in the here and now. However, it does not deal with jealousy. The word is absent from the tables of contents and indices in the most widely read infidelity books."

Scheinkman and Werneck are particularly attuned to cultural differences in the interpretation of jealousy. They write, "Recognized all over the world as a motivation for crimes of passion, jealousy is construed in some cultures as a destructive force that needs to be contained, while in others it is conceived as a companion of love and gatekeeper of monogamy, essential for the protection of a couple's union."

My own experience working in the United States and around the world confirms Scheinkman and Werneck's observations. In Latin America, the term "jealousy" is bound to appear in the first breath. "In our culture, jealousy is the gut issue," a woman in Buenos Aires told me. "We want to know, does he still love me? What does she have that I don't?"

"What about the lying?" I asked. She laughed dismissively. "We've been lying since the Spanish arrived!"

Such cultures tend to emphasize the loss of love and the desertion of eros over the deception. Hence, jealousy is, in the words of Italian historian and philosopher Giulia Sissa, an "erotic rage." In Rome, twenty-nine-year-old Ciro has an expression of grim satisfaction when he tells me his plan to shorten his girlfriend's night with her hot lover by slashing her tires. "At least now I don't have to imagine her in his arms; I just see them waiting for the tow truck in the rain."

In the United States, however, and other Anglo-Saxon cultures (which tend to be Protestant), people are remarkably silent on the subject of this perennial malady of love. Instead, they want to talk about betrayal, violated trust, and lying. Jealousy is denied in order to protect the victim's moral superiority. We take pride in being above such a petty sentiment that reeks of dependency and weakness. "Me, jealous? Never! I'm just angry!" Stuart, whom I meet on a flight from Chicago, admits that it irked him to see his girlfriend flirting with some guy, in plain sight. "But I would never let her know that I felt jealous," he says. "I don't want her to think that she has that much power over me." FYI, what Stuart doesn't realize is that we may try to hide our jealous feelings, but the one who inspires them always knows—and sometimes even enjoys stoking the embers into maddening flames.

Jealousy wasn't always disavowed. Sociologist Gordon Clanton surveyed popular American magazine articles on the topic over a forty-five-year period. Until the 1970s, it was generally seen as a natural emotion intrinsic to love. Advice on the topic, not surprisingly, was exclusively directed to women, who were encouraged to control it (in themselves) and avoid provoking it (in their husbands). After 1970, jealousy fell out of favor, and became increasingly viewed as an inappropriate remnant of an old marriage model in which ownership was central (for men) and dependency inevitable (for women).

In the new age of free choice and egalitarianism, jealousy lost legitimacy and became something to be ashamed of. "If I have freely chosen you as the one, forsaking all others, and you have freely chosen me, I shouldn't need to feel possessive."

As Sissa points out in her refreshing book on the subject, jealousy has a built-in paradox—we need to love in order to be jealous, but if we love, we should not be jealous. And still, we are. Everybody speaks ill of jealousy. Therefore, we experience it as an "inadmissible passion." We are not only forbidden to admit we are jealous, we are not allowed to *feel* jealous. These days, Sissa warns us, jealousy is politically incorrect.

While our societal rebalancing around jealousy was part of an important shift beyond patriarchal privilege, perhaps it has gone too far. Our cultural ideals are sometimes too impatient with our human insecurities. They may fail to account for the vulnerability inherent in love and for the heart's need to defend itself. When we put all of our hopes in one person, our dependence soars. Every couple lives in the shadow of the third, whether they admit it or not, and in some sense, it is the lurking presence of potential others that consolidates their bond. In his book *Monogamy*, Adam Phillips writes, "Two's company, but three's a couple." Knowing this, I am more sympathetic toward the intransigent feelings that modern lovers seek to suppress.

Jealousy is riddled with contradictions. As captured by the incisive pen of Roland Barthes, the jealous one "suffer[s] four times over: because I am jealous, because I blame myself for being so, because I fear that my jealousy will wound the other, because I allow myself to be subject to a banality: I suffer from being excluded, from being aggressive, from being crazy, and from being common."

And furthermore, while we hesitate to admit our own jealousy, we may worry if our partners are free of jealousy. "He that is not jealous is not in love," says an old Latin proverb, and when it comes to other people, we tend to agree with him, even if we do not apply the same logic to ourselves. I'm reminded of the scene in *Butch Cassidy and the Sundance Kid*, when Paul Newman's Butch takes his buddy Sundance's girl, Etta Place (Katharine Ross), for a bicycle ride one morning. He drops her off at her place, and they embrace. Sundance (Robert Redford) appears on the porch and inquires, "What are you doing?" "Stealing your woman," Butch replies. "Take her," says Redford in his trademark deadpan style. I remember watching this scene as a young girl, and while everyone seemed to enjoy this brotherly display of trust, I found myself wondering, Would she have felt more loved if he had put up more resistance?

The Quandary of Possessiveness

Polly reached out to me across the Atlantic. Convinced of her husband Nigel's unfailing morality for almost three decades, she had been stunned to discover that even he could succumb to a midlife tonic, in the form of a young woman named Clarissa. "I would have staked my life on his fidelity!" she told me. But this proud father of four didn't see himself as having an affair—he was in love and was seriously considering leaving Polly for a new life. To his great chagrin, his dark-eyed mistress decided he came with too much baggage, preferring to travel lighter. Nigel was crestfallen but also a little relieved. He decided to return home and end what he now terms his "temporary insanity."

In my first session with this British couple on the verge of turning fifty, I learn more about the other woman than I learn about them. Polly can't stop talking about her.

"I wish I could get *that woman* out of my head," she tells me. "But

I keep having flashbacks of the scenes he described in his emails to her. I want him to tell her it was just a foolish physical infatuation. I imagine her feeling smug about what they shared, convinced that it was more meaningful than his connection with me. I think he should set the record straight—that he loves me and doesn't love her. Maybe that would free me from the trauma." I hear her pain, but in her demands I also hear the unmistakable voice of jealousy.

Polly feels exposed when I point this out. She doesn't deny it, but clearly she is churning inside. The jealous person knows that she is not a sympathetic character and that her torment is likely to invite more criticism than compassion. Consequently, what Proust called "the demon that cannot be exorcised" has simply gone in search of a socially acceptable vocabulary. "Trauma," "intrusive thoughts," "flashbacks," "obsessiveness," "vigilance," and "attachment injury" are the modern vocabulary for betrayed love. This PTSD framework legitimizes our romantic affliction, but it also denudes it of its romantic essence.

I reassure Polly that her jealousy is a natural response, not something to be ashamed of. To acknowledge jealousy is to admit love, competition, and comparison—all of which expose vulnerability. And even more so when you expose yourself to the one who hurt you.

The green-eyed monster taunts us at our most defenseless and puts us directly in touch with our insecurities, our fear of loss, and our lack of self-worth. This is not delusional or pathological jealousy (sometimes called the black-eyed monster), where unfounded suspicion is fed more by childhood trauma than by any current cause. It is the type of jealousy that is intrinsic to love and therefore to infidelity. Contained within this simple word are a host of intense feelings and reactions, which can run the spectrum from mourning, self-doubt, and humiliation to possessiveness and rivalry, arousal and excitement, vindictiveness and vengeance, and all the way to violence.

I ask Polly to tell me more about how she feels. "Sometimes it's like I'm the consolation prize," she concedes. A woman of her time, she wants more. "I need her to know that he came back because he loves *me*, not out of guilt or duty or because she dumped him."

Here we are, caught in the quandary of possessiveness. The desire to own and control is at once an intrinsic part of the hunger in love and also a perversion of love. On the one hand, we want to compel our partners to come back to us. But we don't want them to come back just out of obligation; we want to feel chosen. And we know that love that is deprived of its freedom and willing surrender is not love. Yet it is scary to make space for that freedom.

If I had seen Polly and Nigel just a few years earlier, I too might have tilted my attention toward trauma and betrayal and failed to absorb the liturgy of jealous love. I am grateful to the work of Scheinkman for shedding new light on this exiled emotion and for reminding me that, after all, infidelity is not just about broken contracts, it is about broken hearts.

Trauma or Drama?

Given the cultural zeitgeist, it's important to acknowledge the centrality of love in today's narrative of infidelity, and jealousy is a doorway into this conversation. Of course, jealousy can sometimes go too far—consuming and undermining us, and in extreme cases, leading to aggression or even blows. But in other cases, it may in fact be the last glowing ember of eros in an otherwise burned-out relationship—and therefore, it is also the means of relighting the fire.

"Jealousy is the shadow of love," writes Ayala Malach Pines in

Romantic Jealousy: Causes, Symptoms, Cures, because it affirms to us that we value our partner and our relationship. By introducing this idea in a session, I remind couples like Polly and Nigel that an affair is not only a breach of contract; it is also an experience of thwarted love.

Sissa describes jealousy as "an honest feeling" because it cannot disguise itself. "It courageously carries its suffering and it has the humble dignity of being able to recognize its vulnerability," she writes. Interestingly, when we trace the origins of the term, they lead us back to the Greek word *zelos*, which means zeal. I like this concept because then I can give people something to fight for, rather than staying in the grip of victimization.

Many couples welcome this reframe—they would rather see themselves as protagonists in a forlorn love story than as parties in a failed institution. The breach-of-contract script—"you're my husband and you owe me loyalty"—no longer cuts it in the age of personal happiness. The "I love you and I want you back" script is risky, but it carries emotional and erotic energy and dignifies the hurt.

"Is It Fucked Up That His Affair Turns Me On?"

"Sometimes when we make love, I imagine I am her—a voluptuous thirty-five-year-old Spanish bartender with big boobs and an accent." Once Polly gets over her initial hesitation, she speaks freely about her jealous imagination. "We are naked behind the counter after closing, in the bushes in the park, in the moonlit ocean late at night. It's exciting. I always wanted him to do those things with me—to want me so much he had to risk getting caught. Now I feel like they stole my fantasy. Is it fucked up that his affair turns me on? Afterward I feel humiliated. But I can't stop thinking about her."

She tells me she wants Nigel to make love to her as he did to Clarissa. "I want to know how she felt," she says. But I wonder, is that really it? I tell Polly, "It seems to me that you'd like to know if he can feel with *you* the way he felt with *her*."

I inquire about how their sex life has been since the unraveling of the affair. Somewhat embarrassed, Polly tells me, "Our sex has been the most erotic we have ever had—frantic, ardent, and urgent."

Many couples I see are ashamed to admit the intense erotic charge that sometimes follows the discovery of an affair. "How can I lust for someone who betrayed my trust? I'm so mad at you, but I want you to hold me." And yet, the need to connect physically with the one who just abandoned us is surprisingly common.

Eros does not conform to our rationalizations. In *The Erotic Mind*, sexologist Jack Morin identifies the "Four Cornerstones of Eroticism." Longing—the desire for what is not present—is number one.* Hence we can understand why the fear of loss triggered by infidelity can rekindle flames that have in some cases been dormant for years. Moreover, for some, like Polly, obsessively imagining the lovers' entwined bodies is itself an unexpected aphrodisiac. Jealousy has been known to work wonders. Nigel dropped a steamy novella in the middle of their relationship, and it acted as a sexual infusion. His confession that it was more than just a fling also cranked up Polly's arousal. Jealousy is indeed an erotic wrath, and her survival-of-the-fittest combat readiness is not just a symptom of trauma, it is a declaration of love. In Polly's case, I intuit that it may prove central to the resurrection of her marriage.

---

* Morin's other three cornerstones are violating prohibitions, searching for power, and overcoming ambivalence.

"It Tastes Like You, but Sweeter"

Of course, infidelity is not always a turn-on—frequently, it's quite the opposite. The jealous heart is insatiable with questions. And the more we mine for each sexual detail, the more it can confirm the unfavorable comparisons. In Mike Nichols's 2004 movie *Closer*, Larry (Clive Owen) interrogates his wife, Anna (Julia Roberts), after learning about her affair with Dan (Jude Law). "Did you do it here?" he demands. "When? Did you come? How many times? How? Who was where?"

He follows her around the apartment as she puts on her coat, his crescendo of increasingly explicit queries building as her answers drive him to greater rage. Finally, on the doorstep, she turns to face him. "We do everything that people who have sex do!"

He's not satisfied. "Do you enjoy sucking him off? Do you like his cock? Do you like him coming in your face? What does it taste like?"

Exasperated, she yells back at him, "It tastes like you, but sweeter!"

His ire deflates into bitter sarcasm. "That's the spirit. Now fuck off and die." As François de La Rochefoucauld writes, "Jealousy feeds on doubts, and as soon as doubt turns into certainty it becomes a frenzy or ceases to exist."

It's not just men who want the physical details. I've heard jealous women compare themselves to their rivals in terms every bit as graphic as men do. Her double Ds; my average breasts. Her multiple orgasms; my inconsistent ones. Her squirting; my need for lubricant. Her generous blow jobs; my distaste for the smell. We've all heard Alanis Morissette belt out the unforgettable line "Is she perverted like me?/Would she go down on you in a theater?"

Where Envy and Jealousy Mesh

People often ask, What is the difference between envy and jealousy? A definition I have found helpful is that envy relates to something you want but do not have, whereas jealousy relates to something you have but are afraid of losing. Therefore, envy is a tango between two people, yet the dance of jealousy requires three. Envy and jealousy are close cousins and often become intertwined.

My friend Morgan, an accomplished, smart, fifty-something journalist, found it hard to separate her jealousy of her husband Ethan's lover, Cleo, from her envy of what they were sharing. At first Ethan merely confessed to his affair. Then Morgan discovered his electronic archive of bliss. "How did I cope? I retreated into an alternate reality of obsession," she recalls. If she couldn't have Ethan, at least she could spy on his love affair from across the digital street. In "an orgy of masochism," she pored over his paramour's Instagram feed and her website.

"Cleo was the very portrait of an earth goddess. The shine of adoration in her eyes; her taut bod; that knowing smile—so natural, so youthful, and so seductive. This perfection of all creation was an independent filmmaker. A yogini. A champion of progressive causes. An adventurer. A wearer of toe rings. A most playful sprite with the kind of bright inner happiness that effervesces from deep within and elucidates everyone around her." Each layer of idealization was shadowed by a layer of self-abnegation. "If the lesson of it all was that I wasn't enough as a woman, at least I could live vicariously through this superwoman. How many times did I hear the oceanic conversations they must have had? I died and went to heaven a thousand times on his imagined behalf."

When I ask her why she focuses more on Cleo than on Ethan's betrayal, she says, "It's not so much that he transgressed as that he transcended. I was surpassed by his new and improved lover. Each captioned photo seared another layer of evidence in my fevered mind that he'd found the great love of his life and I was fucked. That's why terms like 'betrayal' or 'transgression' miss the point for me: They're loaded with all the condemnation to avenge me as a victim, but they dodge how I felt at the blurry edge of self, inadequate to sustain fascination." The violence of Morgan's self-inflicted pain is born of the poisonous alchemy of envy and jealousy. Beneath her fixation lurk shame and self-doubt. In further self-flagellation, she imagines Ethan and Cleo talking about her as "the dark succubus whose clutches he thankfully escaped."

How naked we feel when we imagine our partner talking about us with the lover—exposing our private world, our secrets, our weaknesses. We obsess: "What did he say about me?" "Did she make herself out to be a victim of an unhappy marriage?" "Did he slander me, in order to come out looking good?" We can't control the partner who leaves us, and even less so, the stories they choose to tell about us.

Looking back on a full year of mourning, like a widow, Morgan tells me, "The images and sensations played over and over like a crypt of dreams. At first they commandeered my thoughts every instant. With time, this stretched to every thirty seconds. Eventually I could make it through a full minute, then hours, then days. Do you know what it's like not to have freedom of thought?"

Morgan's eloquent description of the loss of her sovereign self calls to mind the voice of French author Annie Ernaux. In her novel *L'occupation*, she describes a state of being utterly consumed by the other woman. She compares jealousy to being an occupied territory—where one's entire being is invaded by a person one may never have met. "I was, in both senses of the word, occupied . . . on one side there was the suffering; on the other, my thoughts, incapable of focusing on anything else than the fact and the analysis of this suffering."

Morgan found solace in the support of her friends, in books, and in movies. Feeling like she was "addicted," she wanted to know how others loosened the grip of the snake. She needed to know she wasn't crazy. And she wasn't. Anthropologist Helen Fisher, who has done fMRI studies of the brain in love, tells us that romantic love literally is an addiction, lighting up the same areas of the brain as cocaine or nicotine. And when a lover has been rejected, the addiction remains—those same areas of the brain continue to light up when they look at images of their partner. Weaning oneself off of obsessive thinking about a lost love, she concludes, is akin to breaking a dependency on drugs. Lovers have always known this, and the metaphor has captured our imaginations long before we had fMRI machines.

Besides these activated biological circuits, Morgan was also caught in the psychological circuitry of early childhood losses. She was reliving multiple abandonments, some of which occurred even before she could remember, yet her body "kept the score," as psychiatrist Bessel van der Kolk puts it. Injured love sits on top of other injured loves. Like a ricochet effect across time, one breach in the present can trigger the resonance of all the breaches of the past.

Over time, Morgan recalls, "the neurons started to cool" and she "outgrew the madness." Two years later, Ethan popped up in her inbox asking for a second chance. And her survival instinct said no. "I'd invested too much effort in rebuilding myself from the wreckage. But one question I have yet to answer: What will it take to trust again?"

Reclaiming Love

For Morgan, the competition with her rival took her to the brink of self-annihilation. She needed to break the grip of the other woman to reclaim her self-confidence. For Polly, however, the competition was arousing. Seeing Nigel coveted by another woman yanked her out of her marital torpor and reinstated him once again as an object of sexual desire and herself as a woman in pursuit. There is nothing like the eroticized gaze of the third to challenge our domesticated perceptions of each other.

A year after the unraveling, I have the opportunity to check in with Polly and Nigel. They tell me they are doing well. Nigel has expressed sincere remorse and has been fully committed to the reconstruction of their relationship. There's only one sore point. Polly *still* can't stop thinking about "that woman."

She tells me that she has been seeing a local therapist who has diagnosed her with PTSD. She has been working on her intrusive thoughts with mindfulness, breathing exercises, and long gazing sessions with Nigel to restore bonding and trust. "I am hoping that as I feel safer, I won't have these thoughts anymore."

"Of course you would feel tremendous relief if that particular slate were wiped clean," I say to her. But remembering my earlier conversations with Polly, I propose another way of looking at this. "Why lose the thoughts? They seem perfectly natural. And besides, they appear to have done you a lot of good!" She looks less like a trauma victim than a woman invigorated by love and jealousy. "Allow me to suggest that 'that woman' has been quite a source of inspiration. You are glowing—more alive, more engaged, more physically active, and more sexually adventurous—and all to the good of your relationship."

Nigel looks at me with trepidation, not sure how Polly is going to take this. But she smiles. I have often found that for couples in this situation, it can be a relief to finally step out of the helpless narrative of trauma and back into good old drama—the perennial story of fractured love. It's actually a more empowering stance, more human than pathological.

Emboldened by Polly's smile of recognition, I smile in return. An idea occurs to me—one that is unconventional, to say the least, but might just give Polly the kind of relief she is seeking. "Let's take this a step further," I tell them. "Maybe, instead of banishing Clarissa, you should memorialize her. Imagine building an altar to this woman to express your gratitude for all the good she did for you. And every morning, before you leave the house, take a moment to bow and give thanks for your most improbable benefactor."

I have no way of knowing if this rather subversive suggestion will free Polly from her predicament. But I know what I am after: giving her back her power. In clinical parlance, this kind of homeopathic intervention is called prescribing the symptom. Since symptoms are involuntary, we can't erase them, but if we prescribe them, we can take control. In addition, staging a ritual gives new meaning to an old suffering. And the twist here is that the perpetrator becomes the liberator. A brief check-in with Polly some months later confirms that the playfulness did the trick. Clearly, this kind of approach is not for everyone. But I have seen it work more often than I ever expected.

Can We—and Should We— Evolve Beyond Jealousy?

No conversation about jealousy can bypass the ongoing debate between nature and nurture. Is jealousy hardwired, forged deep in the recesses of our evolutionary past? Or is it a learned response, a socialized construct born of outdated ideas about monogamy? This argument is at the forefront of most contemporary discourse on the topic.

Evolutionary psychologists recognize the universality of jealousy in all societies. They posit that it must be an innate feeling, genetically programmed, "an exquisitely tailored adaptive mechanism that served the interests of our ancestors well and likely continues to serve our interests today," in the words of researcher David Buss.

Developmental psychologists tell us that jealousy appears early in a baby's life, at around eighteen months, but long after joy, sadness, anger, or fear. Why so late? Like shame and guilt, it is a feeling that requires a level of cognitive development that can acknowledge a self and an other.

Another major point of contention in the jealousy debate is gender. The classic map has men anchoring it in the risk of uncertainty about paternity, and women, in the loss of commitment and resources needed to care for children. Hence, popular theory holds that women's jealousy is primarily emotional, whereas men's is sexual. Interestingly, the research shows the reverse among homosexuals: lesbian women tend to express more sexual jealousy than gay men, and gay men cop to more emotional jealousy than lesbians. Arguably, this reversal highlights that we feel most threatened where we feel least secure.

In the past few years, I've met many people determined to explode conventional ideas and attitudes about jealousy, particularly among those who practice consensual nonmonogamy. Some take Polly's experience to a new level, intentionally using jealousy as an erotic enhancer. Others work hard to transcend it altogether. Many of those who identify as polyamorous claim that they've developed a new emotional response called compersion—a feeling of happiness at seeing one's partner enjoy sexual contact with someone else. In their commitment to plural love, they actively work to overcome jealousy, seeing it as part and parcel of the possessive relationship paradigm they are trying to best.

"Sometimes when I see her with one of her other girlfriends, I do feel jealous," Anna told me. "But I remind myself that these are my feelings and it's up to me to deal with them. I don't blame her for inciting them, nor do I give myself license to act on them in a way that restricts her freedom. I know she's careful not to intentionally trigger those responses in me, and I do the same for her, but we're not responsible for each other's feelings." That's not the kind of attitude I typically hear from more traditional couples, who tend to expect each other to prevent the unwanted stirrings from ever arising. That being said, however, I've met plenty of nonmonogamous couples who struggle with intense bouts of jealousy.

It remains to be seen whether we can—or should—evolve beyond this all-too-human trait. Certainly, jealousy that is rooted in patriarchal notions of possession could use some reexamination. And relationships in which couples seek to claim ownership of each other's every thought can often be strengthened through loosening the grip. But before we consign the jealous heart to the pages of history, let us also listen for the whispers of eros. In a world where so many long-term relationships suffer much more from monotony and habituation than from unsettling feelings like jealousy, this erotic wrath may serve a purpose, if we are willing to bear the attendant vulnerability.

CHAPTER 7

SELF-BLAME OR VENGEANCE

The Dagger Cuts Both Ways

My tongue will tell the anger of my heart, or else my heart,
concealing it, will break.
—Shakespeare, *The Taming of the Shrew*

The dagger of romantic betrayal is sharp at both ends. We can use it to slash ourselves, to pinpoint our shortcomings, to underscore our self-loathing. Or we can use it to hurt back, to have the slayer experience the same excruciating pain they inflicted on us. Some people turn the dagger inward; others direct the blade toward the culprits, in real life or in fantasy. We swing from depression to indignation, from lifelessness to roaring rage, from collapse to counterattack.

"One day I think we can get past this and the next I am so full of hate for her that I don't think I will be able to look at her again," Gaia tells me. "I get mad at myself for being too easy in all of this, too understanding, and then I get so riled up thinking I'm a sucker, and I want to take my keys back and tell our daughter what she did. I hate the roller coaster she has caused in my head. I resent her for rocking my world, all because she needed to 'feel better about herself.' Her selfishness burns me."

For Buddy, self-contempt and resentment toward his unfaithful wife culminated in a moment of despair: "I found myself lying on my bed, crying horribly, with a shotgun in my mouth and flicking the trigger with my finger. This was my lowest point," he tells me. But his next sentence reveals the dagger's other edge. "When my wife texted me asking if I was okay, I responded, 'Sure, if you count having a shotgun in my mouth as okay.'" On the brink of suicide, which he never saw through, Buddy mixes self-destruction with blame. "You see what you made me do?"

Often our reactions are unpredictable, even to ourselves. Ming is a mild-mannered woman, a consummate caretaker who never raises her voice. She has perfected the art of self-reproach. She can't remember a time in her life when she didn't think that if something was wrong, it was because of her. "My childhood can be summed up in three words," she recalls. "It's my fault." But the roar that came out of her when she discovered her husband's online prowls surprised her almost more than it did him. She had not exploded like that in years. "Every time he tried to defend himself, I just told him to shut the fuck up. It was like an alter ego came out to defend me. I've been letting him act like a jerk for a long time, blaming me for everything, and my response was always to try harder. He actually tried to put his affair on me. He told me that all his friends feel sorry for him because he only has sex twice a week. I tore him apart."

The Cruel Logic of Self-Blame

"The shower was running so I went in to let her know I was home, and there she was, naked, with my best friend." Dylan shudders at the memory. "What still amazes me is that when she told me it was nothing, that they had just gone for a run and were taking a shower, I believed her. How stupid can a person be?"

Dylan and Naomi recovered from this incident, and it looked like things were back to normal. And then one day, as he was walking the dog, "I got this intuitive hit that she was having an affair with him." He found her diaries, and everything unraveled from there. "She kept on lying and I kept on sniping. We had bad therapy, bad advice from friends. The worst part was that I always felt like she didn't love me as much as I loved her, but she kept telling me I was just being insecure. Now I know I wasn't insecure, I was right. Or at least I was right to be insecure."

In the wake of a betrayal, we often feel deeply unworthy, our feared inadequacies finally confirmed. That old familiar voice may rise from the muddle to remind us that, actually, it's probably our own fault. A part of us suspects we got what we deserved.

One person chooses to have an affair, but in most cases, both people are responsible for the relational context in which it occurs. When the time is right, in the course of therapy, couples need to engage in a two-way examination. But in this process, one distinction must always be made: taking responsibility for creating conditions that may have contributed to the affair is very different from blaming oneself for the affair. In a state of shock, it's too easy to confuse the two. Your disproportionate self-condemnation can quickly summon up everything you don't like about yourself as being the reasons your partner strayed.

Dylan is susceptible to this kind of negative grandiosity. His self-pity quickly spirals into self-censure. "I guess I drove her into his arms. She complained that I sucked the life out of her. She said she wanted a guy with the killer instinct, not one of those needy new age sensitive boys."

Compounding his lack of confidence is Dylan's realization that most people around him knew what was going on for almost a year. The discovery that one is "the last to know" delivers a humiliating blow and makes one feel contemptible—as if to say, "no one values or respects you enough to tell you." Not only has he been betrayed by his girlfriend and his best buddy; he's lost social status in the eyes of his friends. He imagines them gossiping behind his back, pitying him at best, laughing at him at worst.

"You've Made Me Suffer, Now You'll Pay!"

Dylan piled it up on himself. I kept waiting for his anger toward Naomi to emerge. He knew that there is agency in righteous indignation, but it took him a long year to access it. However, for many of the people I see, the opposite happens: rage first, grief and self-examination later. And rage sparks the mortal urge for retaliation—that ancient rite of the injured.

The vengeful heart is wickedly imaginative. "I dug up the court records on him and sent them to her parents. I thought they should know whom their daughter was fucking." "One day I boiled his favorite clothes with the sheets. Oops." "I told the women in her parenting group what she did to me. I wouldn't want my kids to come to the house of a mother like that." "I had a yard sale and sold all his stuff while he was away on some dirty weekend with that whore." "I uploaded our sex tape to PornHub." Jilted love seeks retribution. "You're not getting off scot-free. I'm going to make you pay for this."

Revenge implies an attempt to "get even," often colored by vindictiveness and anticipated satisfaction. Avenging heroes strut through the Greek myths, the Old Testament, and countless great love stories, and while contemporary culture might claim to be less brutish, we have our own celebrations of payback, especially when the offense is infidelity. We relish seeing a cad get his comeuppance. We amp up the volume and sing along as Carrie Underwood describes how she took a Louisville Slugger to the headlights of her boyfriend's car while he danced with a "bleached blond tramp" inside the bar. Even in their most deadly form, so-called crimes of passion are often treated more leniently than cold-blooded murder, especially in Latin cultures.

Settling the Score

With the revelation of an affair, suddenly the scoreboard of a marriage is lit up: the giving and the taking, the concessions and the demands, the allocation of money, sex, time, in-laws, children, chores. All the things we never really wanted to do but did in the name of love are now stripped of the context that gave them meaning. "Of course I'll move to Singapore so you can take your dream job. I'm sure I can make new friends." "I'll have my son circumcised because your religion believes that's the right thing." "I'm willing to put my career on hold for you and raise our family." "I'll let your mother come live with us even though that means I will be her caregiver." "If it means that much to you, let's have another child." When infidelity robs us of the future we were working for, it invalidates our past sacrifices.

When things are good in a relationship, there's a spirit of abundance and love that breeds generosity. "I did it for us" makes sense as long as there is trust in that basic unit called "us." But intimate betrayal turns these graceful accommodations into a farce. The compromises that worked so well yesterday become sacrifices we will no longer stand for today. Healthy boundaries become insurmountable walls. Yesterday's harmonious sharing of power is today's all-out tug-of-war. Now, looking back, we add up every time we took one for the team. Heaps of regrets and contained resentments come crashing down, demanding redress.

When Shaun found out that Jenny had been sleeping with a fellow PhD student, he felt like years of unconditional support had been repaid with a slap in the face. "I managed to stop myself from kicking the shit out of the guy, but just barely." Instead he called her parents (less dangerous, more damaging) because he felt they needed to know who their daughter *really* was. "I worked so hard to give her everything she wanted—to let her leave her full-time job to get that expensive and useless PhD in medieval history—and this is what I get? That motherfucker understands her? He *inspires* her? The $100,000 education wasn't inspiring enough?" Shaun feels robbed. And now he wants to ransack her life like she's ransacked his. They have broken up, but his hatred keeps him glued to her, even more than when they were together.

Revenge often looks petty, but I have come to respect the depth of hurt it conceals. Unable to reclaim the feelings we've lavished, we grab the engagement ring instead. And if that's not enough, we can always change the wills. All are desperate attempts to repossess power, to exact compensation, to destroy the one who destroyed us as a means of self-preservation. Each dollar, each gift, each treasured book we extract from the rubble is meant to match a broken piece inside. But in the end, it's a zero-sum game. The urge to settle the score corresponds to the intensity of the shame that eats us up. And the deepest shame is that we were stupid enough to trust all along.

Trying to reason with Shaun is useless. Intellectually, he grasps the futility of his retaliation, but emotionally he's seething. At this stage my focus is twofold. First, containment. I ask him to send me his list of "the worst things you want to do to her" for safe storage. Second, challenging the revisionism. The edited story of the relationship that he's now telling leaves out much of the context for the decisions that both he and Jenny made. It misses the fact that she once supported him through school, for instance, and myriad other shared responsibilities. As we deconstruct the one-sided view, we reveal the pain behind the rage.

Cheating on the Cheater

The vengeful heart is not always ready to listen to reason. Sometimes nothing less than inflicting equal pain will suffice. In the age-old tradition of mirror punishment, retaliatory infidelity ranks high among the common strategies for chastisement. Two women taught me a lot about this dark art.

Jess fell for Bart, twenty years her senior, and was ecstatic when he left his wife for her. His adult kids were anything but ecstatic. Furious that this "gold digger" had usurped their mother's place, they cleverly leaked some information to Jess about the even younger women who kept Bart company on his so-called business trips. "How could he do that to me?!" she demands. Jess was no saint herself when it came to fidelity in her own prior relationships; in fact, she has always relied on the triangle to protect against the vulnerability of two. But with Bart, it was different, she explains. She was "all in."

Now she's immersed in rejection. "Not only did he lie to me, but he did it during the honeymoon phase! I can understand if people get bored after years, but right in the beginning, when we were at it like rabbits?"

Jess seeks to reclaim her power. Wanting Bart to feel exactly what she felt, she decides to give him an eye for an eye. Her old boyfriend Rob is more than happy to see her show up on his doorstep. "How does that help?" I ask her. "I needed a friend," she says defensively. It's clear to me, however, that Jess isn't just looking for sympathy; she's looking for leverage. "You're telling me honesty is so important to you," I say. "Can we acknowledge that Rob is an insurance policy?"

To her credit, she quickly concedes. "I don't think what I'm doing is okay, I know it's not good for me. But this is one way to get to him, and he deserves it after what he did to me." The fact that Bart strayed first makes Jess feel fully justified in her own corrective cheating.

We often hear that revenge is sweet, but research and life prove otherwise. Behavioral scientists have observed that instead of quenching hostility, delivering justice, or bringing closure, revenge can in fact keep the unpleasantness of an offense alive. The exultation of self-righteousness is a shallow pleasure that traps us in an obsession with the past. In fact, when we don't have the opportunity to exact a penalty, we move on to other things faster.

Jess and I discuss the meaning of her calculated return to her ex-boyfriend. I suggest that she values the relationship she had with him too much to make him an instrument of her scheming. Her hope is to be with Bart, whereas Rob still hopes to get back together with her. There are better ways to heal her heart than breaking his.

Lailani is a decade younger than Jess, but her strategies come from the same time-honored playbook. A self-described hoodrat girl from a rough neighborhood in Oakland, California, she had always used her body to get what she wanted, starting with a "boyfriend with a car who did my homework at age thirteen."

Lailani learned early on to best men at their own game. "I expected them to dump me, so to get ahead I dumped them first."

But at the age of twenty-nine, she decided it was time to look for something else. She met Cameron on OKCupid and instantly felt he was different from the guys she'd known. "He was trustworthy, responsible, *and* good looking."

For two years, it seemed perfect. Like Jess, she gave up her old ways and allowed herself to trust. "For the first time, I wasn't looking for an exit. Then one day, in my unsuspecting bliss, I got a Facebook message from a woman I had never met: 'I don't know you, but you should know that your boyfriend and I have been seeing each other. He never mentioned you, but I found your pictures online. I want you to know that from here on, I'll have nothing to do with him. I'm sorry.'"

When Lailani went online to check, Cameron had removed his entire digital presence. She confronted him, and he flat out denied it. But she was not deterred. "It takes a liar to know a liar," she says. "I decided to wait until I had my ducks in a row. I gave him a window to come clean, and he repeatedly lied to my face. That's the thing that still blows my mind." She wrote back to the other woman on Facebook and asked her to send some proof. His spurned lover, who felt equally cheated, was happy to oblige. Lailani was not surprised. "Rule one: If you're going to have a side chick, she needs to know she's a side chick! She was pissed." With the digital evidence in hand—texts, sexts, and chats—she finally cornered him.

The moment Cameron was forced to admit the truth, "I went from awestruck to shattered," Lailani says. "All my life I had been the bitch, using guys to get what I could and then leaving them. This was the first relationship I took seriously, and I gave it a real chance. I thought I had actually met a good one, and he turned out to be proof that all men are hopeless. Here *I* was played. What bad karma."

In a moment of reckoning, Lailani wondered, "Was I being

punished for all the shit I had pulled with other guys?" But then she talked to her girlfriends and some guy friends too, and they fanned the flames. "They all said the same thing—teach him a lesson, otherwise he'll keep pulling this shit."

Lailani agreed—and she has a plan: "He deserves some bad karma, too. I've always wanted to have a threesome, and now I feel that I have license to go for it. And if he finds out, I'll be happy. It would feel good to hurt him. He deserves it."

With both Lailani and Jess, one would think that their own transgressive behaviors would make them more empathic toward their cheating partners. But people often have their own inner scales of justice, convinced that what was done to them was worse than what they did—an interesting double standard.

I listen to Lailani and Jess, and I feel sad for them. Their responses are understandable, but their battle plans are ultimately ineffective. They are stuck in a rut of one-upmanship. Like many women striving for parity in what is still a man's world, they struggle to reconcile "soft" and "powerful." They are each conflicted between "I want you to come back to me" and "I won't let you come back to me; it's too dangerous."

They each took a chance and believed in the redemptive quality of a relationship that seemed different from all the rest. They both feel it blew up in their face. Now they are in danger of letting a single betrayal send them back behind the walls of self-protection. No woman should ever give one man all the power to shatter her romantic ideals. There is a big difference between saying, "That one person let me down and I'm hurt," and saying, "I'll never love again." But these two women are not ready to make that distinction. They see the world as offering two options—hurt or be hurt. As Lailani puts it, "I should've stayed the bitch. Nobody hurts the bitch."

Wrestling with Retribution

Even for the most enlightened among us, the desire for vengeance can strike unexpectedly. My friend Alexander, with whom I have shared many deep conversations about these matters, saw himself as an evolved, nonmonogamous man. He and his girlfriend, Erin, are professional dancers who have toured and performed together and apart on all continents. They have been a couple for the past five years—navigating the challenges of long-distance love across multiple time zones. They quickly figured out that with their lifestyle, it was likely that temptation would beckon, so they opted to have an open relationship from the beginning. Their commitment lies with each other; their bodies are free to lie elsewhere. Alexander sums up their "don't ask, don't tell" arrangement: "I know she sleeps with other men, but I don't really want to hear about it."

Furthermore, in the close-knit dancing community, neither of them savors the thought of unknowingly sharing a stage, dressing room, or hotel room with their partner's lovers. "I told her, 'I never want to come and visit you on tour and be at a dinner party where everyone there knows you were fucking someone else, maybe someone at the party, and I look like a fool. In return, you will never visit me on tour and have to worry that I was fucking one of the girls in my company, and everyone knows and pities you and thinks you're being played.'" They have set clear boundaries: no lovers within the small and incestuous world of dance, and no falling in love. "If that starts to happen, we'll talk."

"Micah was the one guy I always used as an example of someone who was off-limits," Alexander tells me. A longtime fellow dancer and rival, Micah keeps landing roles that Alexander feels should have been his. While he had to swallow these defeats onstage, there was no way that he would tolerate Micah in the real-life role of Erin's lover.

Until now their "ethical nonmonogamy" has worked. Like many couples or groups that choose more open configurations, they do not subscribe to the evolutionary psychologists' view of jealousy as innate and inevitable. They believe that it is a learned response that can be unlearned. However, they were not naive about the challenges of this process. Ayala Pines, who studied romantic jealousy among those with open marriages, as well as polyamorous groups and swingers, concluded that "it is difficult to unlearn the jealous response, especially if you live in a society that encourages possessiveness and jealousy." Alex and Erin understood the need to negotiate boundaries and lay down agreements to deter these all-too-human emotions.

Erin broke the agreement. On her last tour, she shared the stage and more with Micah. "How did I know she had sex with him? Like I said, we work in a small world. People talk," Alex says with a wry smile. His incensed imagination is graphic. "Not only do I know the guy, but I've spent hours watching him dress, undress, and dance. I know how he moves. So I can picture exactly how they look together. The images swoop around my head, like vultures circling their prey."

Feeling defeated, Alexander wants to lash out. He mocks her poor choice. "Is that really the best you could do? Or were you deliberately trying to hurt me?" Then he plots his counteroffensive. He imagines walking up to Micah and sucker-punching him, spitting well-rehearsed insults in his face. "I am always seeking that perfect balance between contempt and revenge—showing that he didn't really hurt me, but still bloodying his nose and making him look like a sniveling, crying weasel on the street. I pace around my table, trapped in that violent fantasy, my heart pounding, breathing hard, fists clenched."

Anger is an analgesic that temporarily numbs the pain and an amphetamine that provides a surge of energy and confidence. More biology than psychology, anger temporarily eases loss, self-doubt, and powerlessness. While it can at times be a positive motivator, more often, as psychologist Steven Stosny cautions, "Bouts of anger and resentment always drop you down lower than the point at which they picked you up."

Alexander tells me, "I literally see red. It's a physical, reptilian thing. I'm trying to respond in a more evolved fashion, but it's been a rough ride."

The feelings and thoughts he's describing are not crazy; they're human. However, if we act on them, in a fit of indignation, often they leave us no more powerful and no less vulnerable. Too often, acts of romantic reprisal are ultimately self-defeating. To get back at the other is not a way to get the other back.

Alexander needs to find a safe outlet for his all-consuming fury and the palpable pain that lies just beneath. First, he needs to know how to stay with his feelings when he has no other choice, and to get away from them when he can.

In moments when one is flooded with emotion, it's important to know how to self-regulate. Breathing exercises, soothing hot showers, bracing cold lakes, walks in nature, singing and dancing to music, and active sports can all be helpful. Stillness and movement can both be sources of relief.

But the desire for vengeance runs deep. Like jealousy, it is hard to banish completely, so I prefer to help people learn to metabolize it in a healthy manner. As psychoanalyst Stephen Mitchell points out, there is no love without hate, and we must befriend our aggression, rather than eradicate it. One means of doing this is to make space for the urge but not the action. The fantasy of reprisal can be extremely cathartic. Lodged within the sanctuary of our minds or written in a private journal, fantasies can be a way to purge the slanderous thoughts and the murderous rage that fill us up. Let your imagination run wild. Buy a little notebook and label it "My Revenge," and between its covers, do your worst. But give yourself a time limit. Seven minutes a day, max. And then when you put down your notebook, put aside the thoughts.

Creative revenge fantasies can be surprisingly satisfying. Ask yourself: What will it take for you to feel better? Five years of tiny daily doses of Chinese water torture? Or would you like to come up with a once-and-for-all perfect punishment?

If the fantasy is not enough, sometimes acts of revenge are appropriate. I've helped many couples strike an agreement on a measure of payback that feels fair to both, and then carry it out—stratagems that would make Machiavelli blush. And don't forget humor. One time, the husband, who was in politics, had to send a hefty check from his 401(k) account to his most despised rival in the local elections. "I'd rather see it go to him than to the hooker," his wife said gleefully. She was sated. There is an art to taking just enough revenge.

Alexander finds a reprieve in his fantasies, but he is in standby mode while Erin figures out what she wants. "It feels utterly weak to wait," he rants. "She has all the power. While she weighs all of her options, I sit here like a hostage."

His quandary echoes the legacies of masculinity. What kind of man lets a woman call the shots? It's no accident that the cuckolded heroes of the great dramas and operas tend to kill their beloved rather than give her the freedom not to choose them. Death—of her, of him, or of them both—is the only honorable way out. "The heart that bleeds wants blood to wash away the shame," croons Canio in Leoncavallo's *Pagliacci*.

I ask Alexander to consider that waiting for Erin to make up her mind isn't an abdication of pride or power—it is an expression of love. Slowly he moves from hurtfulness to hurt. He stops trying to get back at Erin, and instead tells her how devastated he is. They have reengaged and are ever more invested in creating an arrangement that will work for them. He tells me that recently he saw Micah perform with Erin, "and that dark place beckoned me. But I consciously decided to let it go."

The Art of Restorative Justice

Revenge may not always be sweet, but occasionally it hits a sweet spot that empowers the hurt party and allows a couple to put the past behind them. We all have a need for justice. However, it is important to distinguish between retributive justice and restorative justice. The former seeks only punishment; the latter engages in repair.

I've observed an interesting connection between my patients' responses to betrayal and the type of justice they are likely to seek. Some mourn the loss of the connection. "I'm hurt because I lost you." Others mourn the loss of face. "I can't believe you made such an idiot of me." One is a relational injury; the second, a narcissistic one. Wounded hearts; wounded pride. Not surprisingly, the person who focuses on the relationship is more able to experience compassion and curiosity around the partner's affair, which allows for a reparative response whether they decide to stay together or not. The person who homes in on the narcissistic injury is much less conciliatory. It is hard for them to muster much interest in what impelled their partner to stray, as they are caught up in vindictiveness.

Restorative justice can be quite creative. Whenever I think about the pleasures of meting out just deserts, the artfulness of a young Frenchwoman, Camille, comes to mind. She wrote to me after attending a lecture to share the story of "my husband's infidelity, my reaction, and the good that came from it all."

Camille, thirty-six, is from an old Bordeaux family. She has been married for ten years to Amadou, forty-five, who grew up in Mali and moved to France in his twenties. They have three children. The trouble began five years ago. Camille remembers the moment vividly. "I was sitting at the breakfast table with my boys when a friend called to tell me my husband was involved with a colleague of hers. At first I didn't believe her, so she put the woman on the phone."

Despite her hurt and anger, Camille really didn't want to lose her man. She had fought to marry him, in the face of her parents' disapproval. She confronted him, calmly but firmly, and then turned to her girlfriends for moral support. "I fell in a deep hole, going through all the typical feelings. I took a week of sick leave. I cried on my girlfriends' shoulders, pounded the floor, and drank a lot of coffee and pastis. And they comforted me, listened to me, shared my misery."

Then she felt ready for the challenge of explaining to her husband that in her culture, his behavior was not acceptable. "He grew up in a context where polygamy was normal," she explains. "So he listened and felt bad about how sad I was, but I could see he felt no guilt for what he had done." Camille also knew something else about her husband's background: he'd grown up in a deeply superstitious, animistic culture. With this knowledge, she understood what was needed. "I decided to enter *his* world and to speak to him in his language. I promptly switched from victim to actor, which totally changed how I felt. Seeing that I could take action helped me lighten up."

Camille's revenge tale is delightful in its creativity. "First, I contacted one of my husband's friends, an older man who is widely respected in the African community. He came to visit and chastised

Amadou for his choice—not the fact of having two women, but the fact that the other was someone in our circle." She knew she would not persuade him against the idea of multiple wives, but she also knew that the condition for polygamy in his culture is that a man must be able to take care of both women—materially and sexually. So she made a point of complaining about his inadequate sexual performance, an embarrassing revelation, to say the least.

The next day Camille went to the halal slaughterhouse. "I bought two legs of lamb, delivered one to the wife of my husband's older friend, and brought the other home to prepare for Amadou to eat. I knew that by the time he came home, he would already have heard from his friend about my gift, and sure enough, he asked about it as soon as he came through the door. I told him that I had gone with the imam to slaughter a lamb as a sacrifice to save our marriage. I am vegetarian, but hey, he believed it. Better yet, he was impressed."

Next, she wanted an insurance policy. "I took some shea butter [a natural product that is used in Africa for many things, but also as a lubricant] and mixed it with a very hot pili pili pepper. I hid it in my bedroom closet. I decided that if I ever discovered that he was with her again, I would happily massage him with this mixture on the place where he so enjoys heat."

Her interventions did not stop there. She also went to speak with the other woman. "I told her that if she dared come near him again, I would show up at her workplace and make one big scandal. Sorry for my choice of words, but like a dog I marked my territory."

Camille still wasn't done. "Finally, I hid a bottle of blood, also from the slaughterhouse, in our garden, in a spot where I thought he would likely one day discover it. According to African tradition, this can either be for a hex or for good fortune." The bottle has still not been discovered.

These rituals of justice came from a very different culture from her own, but they brought Camille peace, and something even more potent. Rather than simply punishing him, they empowered her and significantly improved their relationship. "I had to learn to live without the certainty that he will never do it again, but ultimately I gained another kind of certainty: trust and confidence in myself."

The desire for blood had not yet burned itself out—it was merely dormant. Last year, when picking up her kids from music class, Camille ran into the other woman, whose son was attending the same program. A surge of anger shot through her. "I still had so much aggression—I wanted to practice some of my karate moves on her. But then, as I thought about it, I realized that what I wanted to show her was that I am happy: with myself, with Amadou, and with the kids." Camille intuited one of the most important lessons about vengeance: If in the process of getting even you end up hurting yourself more than you punish the other, you gain nothing. The art of restorative justice is to elevate yourself rather than simply denigrating those who hurt you.

The next week, before going to the music school, Camille dressed up in a vibrant African dress, lipstick, perfume, and all. She walked past the woman's car holding her head high. "To be happy was a much better revenge than any karate moves could ever be."

CHAPTER 8

TO TELL OR NOT TO TELL?

The Politics of Secrecy and Revelation

A Truth that's told with bad intent
Beats all the Lies you can invent.
—William Blake, "Auguries of Innocence"

Secrets and lies emerge in my office in all shades. Often, a couple arrives with an affair freshly exposed, a raw wound that cannot be ignored. But others sit on my couch with the secret between them—obvious to me but unmentioned. Neither partner wants to tell or find out. I've also sat in countless sessions where one person asks the other, "Are you having an affair?" and it is flat out denied, even though the inquirer has irrefutable proof. Sometimes the unfaithful partner will drop hint upon hint, but the spouse does not seem to want to connect the dots. Other times the suspicious one is hot on the trail, with a damning dossier of evidence in hand, but waiting for the right moment to confront.

I've seen the full spectrum of dishonesty, from simple omissions to partial truths and white lies to blatant obfuscation and mental hijacking. I've seen secrecy in its cruel version and its benevolent one. Some lie to protect themselves; others lie to protect their partners; and then there is the ironic role reversal where the betrayed ends up lying to protect the one who deceived them.

The twists and tangles of lying are endless. Many unfaithful spouses tell me that their love affairs represent the first time they've stopped lying to themselves. Paradoxically, while engaged in a relationship built on deceit, they often feel that for the first time they are touching truth, connecting with something more essential, authentic, and sincere than their so-called real life.

During her two-year affair with the owner of the local bike shop, Megan got tired of hiding from everyone around her. But after having ended the double life, she now feels worse. "Now I'm lying inwardly. I'm deluding myself, pretending it's okay to live without him."

It's not just couples who struggle with issues of secrecy. Secrets litter the social landscape of infidelity. A woman borrows her married friend's phone and finds flirty texts from an unknown man. A mother knows her son wasn't with her last Saturday, as he told his wife, but isn't sure she wants to know where he actually was. And of course there is the "other woman" and the "other man." They don't just have a secret, they are the secret.

Secrets and lies are at the heart of every affair, and they heighten both the excitement of the lovers and the pain of the betrayed. They throw us into a web of quandaries. Must they be revealed? And if so, how? Revelation lies on a continuum, from "don't ask, don't tell" to a detailed postmortem autopsy. Honesty requires careful calibration. Is there such a thing as too much? Is it ever better to keep the affair concealed? What about the old saying that what you don't know can't hurt you?

For some, the answer is simple: Secrecy is lying, lying is wrong. The only acceptable course of action is confession, complete transparency, repentance, and punishment. The dominant view seems to be that revelation is the sine qua non for restoring intimacy and trust after an affair. Lying, these days, is seen as a human rights violation. We all deserve the truth, and there is no circumstance where withholding it can be justified.

I wish it were so simple—that we could use such categorical principles to neatly organize our messy human lives. But therapists don't work with principles—they work with real people and real-life situations.

Dilemmas of Disclosure

"This grad student I've been sleeping with is pregnant, and she's determined to have the baby," says Jeremy, a college professor who'd thought he was doing a good job of keeping his fling strictly casual. "I have no intention of ruining my marriage, but I don't want my child to grow up as a secret."

"A guy I hooked up with just told me he has herpes," says Lou, looking embarrassed. "My boyfriend is at risk. Do I have to tell him?"

"This girl I fooled around with tagged me in a picture on Instagram after I told her I could no longer see her," says Annie. "We only kissed, but my girlfriend won't see it that way. She has been checking my social media obsessively—she's bound to see the picture."

Many of you may conclude that in such situations the right decision is disclosure. But not all situations are so clear-cut.

"It was a momentary lapse in judgment—I was drunk and I deeply regret it," says Lina, who'd been engaged only a few months when a night of partying after her college reunion ended in an ex's bed. "If I tell my fiancé, I know it will destroy him. His first wife left with his best friend, and he always said if I cheated on him, it was over." Yes, she should have thought of that before. But should her slipup derail their whole life?

"Why would I tell my wife?" Yuri asks. "Since I met Anat, we don't fight about sex anymore. I don't beg her and I don't bug her, and my family is doing well."

In an act of defiance, Holly has fallen madly in love with a fellow Yorkie owner she met at the dog park. She'd like nothing more than to tell her "nasty, controlling" husband. "It would serve him right." But the price of honesty would be high. "With the prenup that he made me sign, I'd lose the kids."

Nancy's ongoing flirtation with a dad at her son's football games reignited her long-dormant sensuality. "I feel gratitude for the awakening of that part of me that is not just a mother, wife, or servant. I feel even more gratitude that I didn't act on it," she says. Her husband is delighted with her newfound erotic energy. But she's wondering, does she have to tell him about her "affair of the mind"? Nancy is of the firm belief that honesty means complete transparency.

In circumstances like these, might it be wiser for the involved partner to stay quiet and to handle matters alone? Truth can be healing, and sometimes fessing up is the only appropriate response. When counseling her patients about the wisdom of truth-telling, my colleague Lisa Spiegel uses a simple and effective formula: Ask yourself, is it honest, is it helpful, and is it kind?

Truth can also be irrevocably destructive and even aggressive, delivered with sadistic pleasure. On more than one occasion, I've seen honesty do more harm than good, leaving me to ask, Can lying sometimes be protective? To many, this notion seems unfathomable. But then again, I've also heard informed spouses scream, "I wish you'd never told me!"

At a training for therapists, a participant working in hospice care asked me for advice. "What can I say to the terminally ill patient who wants to confess to his wife a lifetime of infidelity before he dies?" I replied, "While I understand that to him, 'coming clean' after all these years may seem like a genuine expression of deep love and respect, he needs to know that he may die in relief but she will live in turmoil. While he's resting in peace, she'll be tossing and turning, sleepless for months as she replays movies in her head that are probably far more torrid than the affairs ever were. Is that the legacy he wants to leave?"

Sometimes silence is caring. Before you unload your guilt onto an unsuspecting partner, consider, whose well-being are you really thinking of? Is your soul-cleansing as selfless as it appears? And what is your partner supposed to do with this information?

I have seen the other side of this situation in my office, where I've tried to help a widow deal with the double bereavement of losing her husband to cancer and losing her image of their happy marriage to his deathbed confessions. Respect is not necessarily about telling all, but about considering what it will be like for the other to receive the knowledge. When exploring the pros and cons of revelation, don't think just in either-or terms or in the abstract, but try to imagine yourself in the actual situation with the other person. Enact the conversation: Where are you? What do you say? What do you read on the other person's face? How do they respond?

The question "to tell or not to tell?" becomes even weightier when social norms render people particularly vulnerable. As long as there are countries in the world where women only suspected of glancing elsewhere can be stoned and burned alive, or where homosexuals can be barred from seeing their own children, honesty and transparency should always be thought of in context and on a case-by-case basis.

Should Therapists Keep Secrets?

Therapists working with infidelity must grapple with the thorny issue of secrets. The conventional approach stipulates that clinicians in couples therapy cannot keep things under wraps; and that in order for therapy to be productive, the unfaithful must end the affair or come clean. Otherwise they are to be referred to individual therapy. I often hear American colleagues say that there is nothing you can do with a secret in the middle of the room. Interestingly, my international counterparts say something quite different—there is a lot you can do so long as the secret is not revealed. Once you have raised the curtain, there is no going back. They caution against gratuitous revelation, citing the unnecessary pain inflicted on one's partner and the harm to the relationship.

In recent years, a small minority of therapists, including Janis Abrahms Spring and Michele Scheinkman, have begun to challenge the American orthodoxy around secrets, finding the traditional approach to be unhelpful, limiting, and even damaging. I have chosen to adopt what Spring calls an open-secrets policy. When I first meet a couple, I let them know that I will see them apart as well as together, and our individual sessions are confidential. Each is guaranteed a private space to work through their issues. Both people have to sign off on this. Like Spring, I see the decision to reveal or not to reveal as part of the therapy itself, not as a precondition for therapy.

This approach is not without its complications, and I constantly grapple with it. I have on occasion had to answer yes to the question "Did you know all along?" when a partner finds out they have been deceived. While this situation is painful for all involved, it is not an ethical breach under the terms of our agreement. And for the time being, I find it to be the more productive stance. As Scheinkman writes, "A no-secrets policy holds the therapist hostage, unable to help in possibly one of the most critical moments in a couple's relationship."

This policy does not apply just to affairs. In fact, the turning point for me was a session in which a woman told me that for the past twenty years she couldn't wait for sex with her husband to be over. She didn't like his smell and faked her orgasms. Knowing that this wouldn't change and not considering it a marital dealbreaker, she didn't see the point of telling him. I was willing to proceed with therapy cognizant of her pretense. So I had to ask myself, How is this secret fundamentally different from others?

Was it any less grave than a clandestine affair? Would her husband be less hurt to learn that she had been lying to him all along than to learn she was sleeping with someone else? Should I insist that she reveal her distaste in order for us to continue therapy? Sexual secrets come in many forms. Yet therapists tend to struggle more with lies about extramarital sex than with decades of lying about intramarital sex. We hold many confidences without experiencing an ethical conflict. Infidelity may not always take the gold medal in the hierarchy of essential disclosures.

Truth-Telling in Many Languages

"We live in a culture whose messages about secrecy are truly confounding," writes Evan Imber-Black in her book *The Secret Life of Families*. "If cultural norms once made shameful secrets out of too many events in human life, we are now struggling with the reverse: the assumption that telling secrets—no matter how, when, or to whom—is morally superior to keeping them and that it is automatically healing."

To understand America's views on secrecy and truth-telling, we need to examine the current definition of intimacy. Modern intimacy is bathed in self-disclosure, the trustful sharing of our most personal and private material—our feelings. From an early age, our best friend is the one to whom we tell our secrets. And since our partner today is assumed to be our best friend, we believe, "I should be able to tell you anything, and I have a right to immediate and constant access to your thoughts and feelings." This entitlement to know, and the assumption that knowing equals closeness, is a feature of modern love.

Ours is a culture that reveres the ethos of absolute frankness and elevates truth-telling to moral perfection. Other cultures believe that when everything is out in the open and ambiguity is done away with, it may not increase intimacy, but compromise it.

As a cultural hybrid, I practice in many languages. In the realm of communication, many of my American patients prefer explicit meanings, candor, and "plain speech" over opaqueness and allusion. My patients from West Africa, the Philippines, and Belgium are more likely to linger in ambiguity than to opt for stark revelation. They seek the detours rather than the direct route.

As we consider these contrasts, we also have to take into account the difference between privacy and secrecy. As psychiatrist Stephen Levine explains, privacy is a functional boundary that we agree on by social convention. There are matters that we know exist but choose not to discuss, like menstruation, masturbation, or fantasies. Secrets are matters we will deliberately mislead others about. The same erotic longings and temptations that are private in one couple are a secret in another. In some cultures, infidelity is commonly treated as a private matter (at least for men), but in our culture, it is usually a secret.

It's almost impossible to discuss cultural differences without taking a moment to observe America's favorite point of sexual comparison: *les Français*. Debra Ollivier describes how the French "favor the implicit over the explicit, the subtext over context, discretion over indiscretion, and the hidden over the obvious—in that, they're exactly the opposite of Americans." Pamela Druckerman, a journalist who interviewed people around the globe for her book *Lust in Translation*, expands on how these predilections shape French attitudes about infidelity. "Discretion seems to be the cornerstone of adultery in France," she writes, noting that many of the people she spoke with seemed to prefer not to tell, and not to know. "French affairs can seem like Cold War conflicts in which neither side ever draws its guns."

Back at the ranch, the guns are blazing. While Americans have little tolerance for extramarital sex, deception is often condemned more harshly than the transgression it seeks to conceal. The hiding, the dissimulation, and all the tall tales are the main ingredients of the affront and are seen as a fundamental lack of respect. The implication is that we only lie to those beneath us—children, constituents, and employees. Hence, the refrain echoes from private bedrooms to public hearings: "It's not that you cheated, it's that you lied to me!" But would we really feel better if our partners gave us advance notice of their indiscretions?

Translating Secrets

Amira, a thirty-three-year-old Pakistani American social work grad student, still vividly remembers the day she began to unravel her father's secret. "Dad was teaching me to drive. He had this weird Japanese trinket hanging from his rearview mirror. One day I tried to take it down, but he stopped me and told me it was a gift from

Yumi, his secretary. That name came back to me immediately seven years later, when Dad asked me to look for an address in his phone, and I found a string of texts from someone called Y. Then I knew."

"Does he know that you know?" I ask her. She shakes her head.

"Will you ever tell him?"

"What I really want to tell him is 'Learn to delete your text messages!' Maybe one day I'll show him how. I just wish he had covered his tracks. I don't like feeling complicit in his deception of my mother."

"Have you considered telling her?" I inquire. Immediately, she says no.

A second-generation immigrant whose parents came to America before she was born, Amira has a foot in two worlds. She knows her silence is unconventional here. "My American friends would have gone immediately to their mothers. They would see exposing the secret as the right and caring thing to do." But while she went to school in suburban Kansas, when it comes to family matters, Amira's code is rooted in Karachi. "Yes, we value honesty and trust," she says, "but we value the preservation of the family even more."

Amira's decision came almost as a given. Here's how the logic went: "If I tell her, what then? Break up the home? Divide all that we've worked to build? Conduct ourselves like Americans—impulsively and selfishly—and end up spending weekends with one parent and weekdays with another?"

She did feel anger and resentment on her mother's behalf. "But my parents love each other," she adds, "and you should know, they were an arranged marriage. I know that my mother is massively uncomfortable with the topic of sex, but it's not like my father is much better. My gut told me that he chose the path that allowed our family to stay together. Maybe my mother would rather not be bothered. It felt fair, so I was able to make peace with it. Besides this one stain, Dad is the most upstanding father, husband, and citizen. Why would I want to ruin all these great things about him?"

"What about the disrespect to your mother?" I ask.

"The way I see it, my father considered it to be most respectful to not shake the core of our family by being open with us about something that we couldn't weather. And as for me, I found it to be most respectful to keep whatever facts I came across to myself. I wouldn't dare shame my parents by thrusting this truth into the daylight. For what? So that we can be 'honest'?"

Clearly, the conviction that telling the truth is a mark of respect isn't universal. In many cultures, respect is more likely expressed with gentle untruths that aim at preserving face and peace of mind. This protective opacity is seen as preferable to disclosure that might result in public humiliation.

Amira's reasoning is part of a long-standing cultural legacy that extends beyond Pakistan to all family-oriented societies. Her framework is a collectivist one, where family loyalty mandates compromising around infidelity—and secrets. Of course, we could look at her situation through the lens of gender politics and see her elucidations as a sad but ingenious apology for patriarchy. Furthermore, we cannot afford to minimize the damaging effects that secret-keeping may have on children. As my colleague Harriet Lerner highlights, secrecy "puts a crack in the foundation of the relationship with both parents and operates like an underground river of confusion and pain that affects everything. It not infrequently leads to symptomatic behavior and acting out by kids and teens who are then put in therapy where the real source of anxiety and distress is never identified."

But is Amira's choice any more distressing than that of her fellow student Marnie? The twenty-four-year-old New Yorker is still haunted by the day she grabbed her mother's "secret phone" and threw it down the stairs into her father's hands. "He deserved to know she was cheating!"

Marnie had known about her mom's affair with her chiropractor for several years. "She used to hide her secret phone in the laundry hamper and would spend hours 'doing ironing.' Yeah, right. She wasn't that domestically inclined." On that fateful day, "My mom started crying frantically and saying, 'Oh my god, what did you do? What did you do?' My world came crashing down in a matter of hours. Now our family is completely splintered. No more dinner for four at TGI Fridays, no more big family parties on holidays. The last time I saw my mom and dad in a room together, I was fifteen."

Marnie still agonizes over the painful and irreversible consequences of the tumbling phone, but it would never occur to her to question the moral platform from which she threw it. Her value system, while dramatically different from Amira's, is just as instinctive. In her individualistic framework, the personal "right to know" trumps the harmony of the family. For Marnie, lying is categorically wrong; for Amira, it depends on the particular situation.

I have often witnessed the tension between these two world views. One accuses the other of duplicity and lack of transparency. The other is repelled by the destructive spilling of secrets in the name of honesty. One is shocked by the distance that the other seems to establish between men and women. The other sees unvarnished directness as damaging to love and antithetical to desire. Collectivist and individualistic cultures both manage the overt and the covert, with pros and cons on all sides. Since we tend to get stuck within our own paradigm, it is instructive to know how a neighbor from another country addresses the same situation with a very different ethical and relational logic. That said, in our global world, many of us are children of multiple cultures, and these dialogues take place within our own hearts and minds.

What to Tell, What Not to Tell?

The disclosive dilemmas do not end when an affair is revealed. At every step, the questions continue to arise: What to confess? How much? And how to do it? Furthermore, what we tell others depends on what we are willing to admit to ourselves. Very few people I meet are lying to their loved ones in cold blood. More often than not, they have constructed elaborate scaffolds to legitimize their actions, otherwise known as rationalizations.

"The tendency toward infidelity depends to a great extent on being able to justify it to ourselves," writes behavioral economics expert Dan Ariely. We all want to be able to look in the mirror and feel good about the person we see, he explains, but we also want to do things that we know aren't quite honest. So we internally rationalize our various forms of cheating in order to maintain a positive self-image—an ethical sleight of hand that Ariely calls the "fudge factor."

When dealing with the fallout of infidelity, it's important to unpack these rationalizations; otherwise we risk simply dumping them on our partner in the name of truth. Kathleen had her antennae out for years, but when she could no longer tolerate her husband Don's emotional and sexual absence, she took a closer look at his iPad. Her suspicions confirmed, she now wants the truth, the whole truth, and nothing but the truth. Don has come to meet me for advice on how to answer her questions.

A youthful sixty-something Chicago native, Don grew up poor, with a father who struggled to keep a job and a much-revered mother who managed two jobs. He's worked hard to create a life of comfort and refinement, and has dedicated himself to serving his constituency as a community leader. Kathleen is his second wife— they have been married twenty-two years. From the moment Don comes into my office, it is clear that this is a man with deep contradictions. He loves his wife, has always been devoted to her, but he has never been faithful to her.

To begin, I ask him to bring me up to speed. Kathleen is aware of his two mistresses, Lydia and Cheryl. She also knows that they have been in his life for decades, conveniently located on opposite coasts at a safe distance from his family home. As he lays out the logistics of his triple life, I sense a slight irritation with the fact that he was discovered. After all, he had handled his triptych with such care and discretion. The pleasure of his affairs, he admits, was the sense of control it gave him when he had a personal world that eluded the eyes of society.

Now Kathleen knows the basic facts. What she is asking him is, Why did this happen?

"So what will you tell her?" I ask.

"Well, the truth is, I had these other women because I wasn't getting satisfying intimacy at home."

Of the hundreds of truths he hasn't told his wife, this is the one he chooses to start with? Clearly we've got some work to do. I ask Don to consider how that will make her feel. And more important, is it even as true as he believes it to be? Or is this simply one of his rationalizations?

"Do you really think that if you had better sex with your wife, you wouldn't have your mistresses?" I ask semi-rhetorically.

"I do," he insists. He tells me a long, involved story about menopause, hormones, her increased self-consciousness, his difficulty sustaining erections. With his ladies, he has no such trouble. That doesn't surprise me in the least. But before he goes telling his wife that he did this because something was missing with her, he needs to ask himself, to what extent was he missing in action? I suspect that if I were to ask Kathleen, she would probably agree that, given his long-standing emotional retreat, it's little surprise that their sex life became dull and unimaginative. Don looks uncomfortable, so I press ahead.

"Imagination—that's the key word here. With your affairs, the arousal starts on your flight over there. You don't need the blue pill because what turns you on is the plot, the planning, the carefully chosen clothes. All the anticipation is what fuels the desire. When you come home and the first thing you do is take off your nice clothes and put on old sweatpants, nobody's going to get turned on."

Don seems a little taken aback at my bluntness, but he's listening attentively. He's by no means the first man or woman to come to me to carp about sexual ennui at home. I don't deny the erotically muting effects of domesticity. But sex with his wife stands no chance when all his energy is devoted to his wanderings. Rather than blaming the lackluster sex at home for his affairs, maybe he should fault the affairs for the sexual dullness with his wife. Furthermore, he's been roaming for a very long time, in his first marriage and in every relationship since. This isn't about hormones, age, or arousal. It's about him.

"Do you see now that what you wanted to say to your wife is anything but true? These are your rationalizations—stories you've told to yourself to justify continuing to do what you want. Now, let's try to find something more honest to tell her."

In the course of our conversations, I get to know and like Don. He is not a Don Juan who revels in the conquest. It seems strange to say, but he is a man with a genuine love and respect for women. They raised him and they shaped him—his mother, his sisters, his aunts, his mentors. As a teenager and as a boy, he lacked confidence, acutely aware of his poor education and humble beginnings. He figured out that one of the ways to feel more manly was by surrounding himself with strong, accomplished women. Both his long-term loves have advanced degrees (as does his wife), are "age appropriate," have had children of their own, and are not looking for more—a perfect fit, since he's always been clear with them that he will never leave his wife. He's careful, respectful, and loyal. Some would call him a true gentleman.

Did they know about each other? I ask him. He admits that Mistress 1 knows about Mistress 2, but Mistress 2 knows only about the wife. And he promised Mistress 1 that he'd stop sleeping with Mistress 2, a promise he did not keep. Meanwhile, he told both of them the same half-truth he told me: that his sexual needs are unmet at home. Slowly, as we unravel the intricate web of his affairs, he realizes that he's been lying to all three.

Living in triplicate has taken a tremendous toll. In the early days, Don had a life with a little secret on the side. But as time wore on, the obfuscation increasingly structured his entire life. Secrets have a tendency to mushroom. You can't tell your partner where you were between six and eight, because then you may have to tell her where you were between four and five. You think you're keeping it all together, but in fact you are becoming more fragmented. As his pieces come back together into a cohesive whole, Don is less dissociated and has become more open both with himself and with his wife.

"What else has Kathleen been asking?" I inquire.

"I've promised her that I will never do this again, but she asks me, 'What will stop you if you have the opportunity?' I've told her that I won't do it again because I know that if she were to find out, there would be no hope of repairing our relationship."

Don is emphasizing the fear of getting caught. It's honest, but there's more. What would happen if he were actually straight with Kathleen about the fact that he's not by nature a one-woman guy?

He looks surprised at the idea. "No, I've never said that. I was always fearful of what her reaction would be. I think she would say she didn't sign up for that."

"Fair enough. And I'm not suggesting you impose a harem on her. But the point is, she didn't sign up for the lying either. You never gave her a choice. By definition, if you go behind someone's back, you're acting in a unilateral fashion."

Don's surprise is giving way to relief. "I love my wife, but I also love other women. That's who I've always been. Just to admit that is so helpful. I've never said any of that, not to Kathleen, not even to myself." Now we are reaching a new level of truth. So often, in the wake of an infidelity, I hear repentant partners promise never to be attracted to another again. This simply engenders more fibs. It would be more realistic to say, "Yes, I may feel attractions, but because I love you and I respect you, and I don't want to hurt you again, I will choose not to act on it." That's a more honest—and more trustworthy—statement.

Now that we are clear on what Don wants to tell his wife, we turn our attention to how. I suggest that he begin with a letter. Handwritten, because it's more personal that way, and hand-delivered.

The goal is threefold. First, take responsibility for his hurtful behavior, in particular, the way he rationed his closeness by giving her only a fragment of his divided self. Second, be vulnerable with her about his own proclivities and how, for years, he justified it to himself at her expense. And third, pour out his love for her and fight for their relationship.

Over the years I have come to find love letters a lot more conducive to healing than the more common therapeutic practice of having the unfaithful partner create an exhaustive inventory of offenses—hotels, dates, trips, gifts. I thought that Don needed to acknowledge that he was a master of deception. I didn't think it would help his wife to know the details of every lie.

When Don returns the following week, he tells me that Kathleen was moved by the effort and sincerity he had put into his letter, but also was cautious—wanting to believe but afraid to trust. I am hopeful for this couple. Despite granting himself hidden and selfish privileges, Don always loved his wife. From the very first session, I could hear it in the way he spoke about her—with reverence, fondness, and admiration. Kathleen was deeply hurt, but Don's hidden lives had not fractured her love and regard for him—or her respect for herself. She was determined not to let the crisis rewrite their whole history.

Over the next few months, I guide Don as he ends his long-standing relationships with Cheryl and Lydia with as much care and integrity as possible, and continues to rebuild his connection with his wife. More than once, he succumbs to the knee-jerk response to lie when Kathleen asks about his comings and goings. This bad habit is going to take some hard work to break, but he is committed to the task. And every time he gives her a straight answer, he is amazed by the simplicity of the transaction. Their ordeal is not over, but I have a sense they will come out of this crisis stronger and closer.

How Much Do You Want to Know?

I work on both sides of the dishonesty divide—coaching habitual liars like Don, but also counseling those who have been deceived. We commonly assume that people want to know everything, and we are quick to judge the self-delusion of those who opt for voluntary ignorance.

Carol has always known her husband is an alcoholic. What she didn't know until now is that he liked to mix his drinks with escorts.

While contemplating her options, she tells me that she's not sure she wants to know more. "That's your choice," I tell her. "It's okay if you don't want all the details. Let him carry the burden of that knowledge and take responsibility for figuring out who he wants to be as a man, as a person."

Others feel a need to gorge themselves on detail. In an effort to protect them from information overload, I remind them that once we know, we have to deal with the consequences of knowing. I often ask, Do you really want the answer to your question, or do you want your partner to know that you have the question?

I make a distinction between two kinds of inquiry—the detective questions, which mine the sordid details, and the investigative questions, which mine the meanings and the motives.

Detective questions include: How many times did you sleep with him? Did you do it in our bed? Does she scream when she comes? How old did you say she was? Did you suck his cock? Was she shaved? Did she let you do anal? Detective questions add further scarring and are often retraumatizing, inviting comparisons in which you are always the loser. Yes, you need to know if he protected himself or if you should get tested. You need to know if you should worry about your bank account. But maybe you don't need to know if she was blond or brunette, if her breasts were real, if he had a bigger penis. The interrogations, the injunctions, and even the forensic evidence fail to assuage your fundamental fears. Moreover, they make reconciliation much more difficult, and if you choose to separate, they will be fodder for the legal proceedings. Another line of inquiry may be more conducive to rebuilding trust.

Investigative questions recognize that the truth often lies beyond the facts. They include: Help me understand what the affair has meant for you. Were you looking for it, or did it just happen? Why now? What was it like when you would come home? What did you experience there that you don't have with me? Did you feel entitled to your affair? Did you want me to find out? Would you have ended it if I hadn't found out? Are you relieved it's all in the open, or would you have preferred if it stayed hush-hush? Were you trying to leave me? Do you think that you should be forgiven? Would you respect me less if I were to forgive you? Did you hope I would leave so you wouldn't have to feel responsible for breaking up the family? The investigative approach asks more enlightening questions that probe the meaning of the affair, and focuses on analysis rather than facts.

Sometimes we ask one question while the real question hides behind it. "What kind of sex did you have with him?" is often a stand-in for "Don't you like the sex we have?" What you want to know is legitimate, but how you go about asking it makes all the difference to your peace of mind. My colleague Steven Andreas suggests that to transform a detective into an investigative question, it is helpful to ask yourself: If I knew all the answers to all my questions, what would that do for me? This can bring you to a more useful line of inquiry that respects the intent of the original question but avoids the pitfalls of unnecessary information.

My patient Marcus feels that to trust again, he needs to know everything. He is obsessively grilling Pavel to give him a precise account of his Grindr activities. "I ask you a question; I want an answer." While I understand Marcus's need to reorient himself, I suggest that this scavenger hunt, rather than being reassuring, is likely to trigger more rage, less intimacy, and more policing.

It is only reasonable, in the immediate aftermath, for couples to agree on certain limits to preserve peace of mind—for example, ceasing to see and communicate with the affair partner or coming right home after work rather than stopping at the bar. But too often, there is an assumption that a cheater has forfeited all rights to privacy. In the digital age, in the name of rebuilding trust, it is common for a duped partner to demand access to cellphones, email passwords, social media log-ins, and so on. Psychologist and author Marty Klein points out that rather than enhancing trust, this actually thwarts it. "You can't 'prevent' someone from betraying you again. They either choose to be faithful or they don't. If they want to be unfaithful, all the monitoring in the world won't stop them."

Trust and truth are intimate companions, but we must also acknowledge that there are many kinds of truth. What are the useful truths, for us as individuals and as couples, in light of the choices we are likely to make? Some kinds of knowledge bring clarity; others just give us visions to torture ourselves with. Steering our questions toward what the affair means—the longings, the fears, the lusts, the hopes—offers an alternative role to that of the victim turned police officer. Authentic curiosity creates a bridge—a first step toward renewed intimacy. We become collaborators in understanding and mending. Affairs are solo enterprises; making meaning is a joint venture.

PART III

MEANINGS
AND
MOTIVES

CHAPTER 9

EVEN HAPPY PEOPLE CHEAT

Mining the Meanings of Affairs

Sometimes I can feel my bones straining under the
weight of all the lives I'm not living.
—Jonathan Safran Foer, *Extremely Loud and Incredibly Close*

Sex trades on the thrill of discovering, over and over again,
that we are unknown to ourselves. . . . What makes for
adventure is not only the novelty of the Other, although that helps,
but the Otherness of the self.
—Virginia Goldner, "Ironic Gender, Authentic Sex"

What if the affair had nothing to do with you?

That question often seems ludicrous to a partner who has been
cast aside for a secret lover, lied to, two-timed by their one and
only. Intimate betrayal feels intensely personal—a direct attack
in the most vulnerable place. However, looking through the lens
of the damage it caused the aggrieved partner, we see only one
side of the story. Cheating is what they did to their partner, but
what were they doing for themselves? And why?

Holding the dual perspective—the meaning and the consequences—is a central part of my work. Phase 1 focuses primarily on the what: the crisis, the fallout, the hurt, and the duplicity. Phase 2 turns to the why: the meaning, the motives, the demons, the experience on its own terms. Listening to these revelations with an open mind is an essential part of the recovery process, for all parties involved.

"Why do people stray?" is a question I have been asking continuously for the past few years. Whereas in literature, we are invited to eavesdrop on the complex yearnings of married miscreants, in my field their motives tend to be reduced to one of two options: either there is a problem with the marriage or there is a problem with the individual. Hence, as Michele Scheinkman has pointed out, "What was once for Madame Bovary a search for romantic love is today . . . encased in a framework of 'betrayal' that is less about love and desire and more about symptoms in need of a cure."

The "symptom" theory goes as follows: An affair simply alerts us to a preexisting condition, either a troubled relationship or a troubled person. And in many cases, this holds true. Plenty of relationships culminate in an affair to compensate for a lack, to fill a void, or to set up an exit. Insecure attachment, conflict avoidance, prolonged lack of sex, loneliness, or just years of being stuck rehashing the same old arguments—many adulterers are motivated by marital dysfunction. And plenty has been written about trouble leading to trouble. However, therapists are confronted on a daily basis with situations that defy these well-documented reasons. How are we to interpret these?

The idea that infidelity can happen in the absence of serious marital problems is hard to accept. Our culture does not believe in no-fault affairs. So when we can't blame the relationship, we tend to blame the individual instead. The clinical literature is rife with typologies for cheaters—as if character always trumps circumstance.

Psychological jargon has replaced religious cant, and sin has been eclipsed by pathology. We are no longer sinners; we are sick. Ironically, it was much easier to cleanse ourselves of our sins than it is to get rid of a diagnosis.

Strangely, clinical conditions have become a much-coveted currency in the recovery-from-adultery market. Some couples arrive in my office with a diagnosis in hand. Brent is eager to don the mantle of pathology if it means finding an excuse for twenty years of gallivanting. His wife, Joan, is less enthusiastic and lets me know what she thinks about it: "His therapist told him he has an attachment disorder because his father abandoned him and left him alone to take care of his mother and his sister. But I tell him, 'You can't just be a pig anymore? You need a diagnosis?'"

Jeff's wife, Sheryl, just discovered a slew of evidence that he has been cruising BDSM* sites and meeting strangers for sex. After many sessions with a therapist, Jeff is now convinced he is a "sex addict" who self-medicates his depression in the dungeon. His wife agrees, and indeed, it may be true. But medicalizing his behavior should not be used as a deflection from honestly exploring the uneasy territory of his kinky predilections. It's easier to label than to delve.

If psychological diagnoses are not convincing enough, there's always the booming world of popular neuroscience. Nicholas, whose wife, Zoe, had been having an affair for more than a year, looked visibly brighter when he arrived for our last session brandishing the *New York Times*. "Look!" He pointed to the headline: "'Infidelity Lurks in Your Genes.' I knew that because of her parents' open marriage, her sense of morality is weaker. It's hereditary!"

There is no doubt that many renegade spouses do display signs of

---

* An overlapping abbreviation of bondage and discipline (BD), dominance and submission (DS), sadism and masochism (SM).

depression, compulsion, narcissism, attachment disorder, or plain sociopathy. Thus, at times, the right diagnosis finally lends clarity to an inexplicable and distressing behavior, both for the person enacting it and for the person suffering the consequences. In those situations, it is a useful tool that helps to lay out a path to insight and recovery. But too often, when we jump to diagnosis too quickly, we short-circuit the meaning-making process.

My experience has compelled me to look further, beyond the widespread view that infidelity is always a symptom of a flawed relationship or individual. The most readily apparent causality isn't always the accurate one. I learned this lesson when I wrote *Mating in Captivity*. I had always been told that sexual problems are the consequence of relationship problems, and that if you fix the relationship, the sex will follow. While that was indeed the case for lots of couples, I was seeing countless others who kept telling me, "We love each other very much. We have a great relationship. Except for the fact that we have no sex." Clearly, their sexual impasse was not merely a symptom of a romance gone awry. We had to look in less obvious places for the roots of their erotic demise—which meant talking directly about sex, something couples therapists often prefer to avoid.

Similarly, conventional wisdom would hold that good intimacy guarantees fidelity. Our model of romantic love assumes that if a union is healthy, there is no need to go looking elsewhere. If home is the place where you feel safe, seen, appreciated, respected, and desired, why would you roam? In this view, an affair is de facto a product of a deficit. Accordingly, successful therapy aims to identify and heal the problems that caused the affair in the first place so that the couple can leave with a certificate of immunization in hand. But can this problem-solving approach neutralize the limits and intricacies of love?

I don't think so. First, because it suggests that there is such a thing as a perfect marriage that will inoculate us against wanderlust. And second, because in session after session, I meet people who assure me, "I love my wife/my husband. We are best friends and happy together. But I am having an affair."

Many of these individuals have been faithful for years, sometimes decades. They seem to be well-balanced, mature, caring men and women who are deeply invested in their relationships. Yet one day they cross a line they never imagined they would cross, risking everything they had built. For a glimmer of what?

The more I listen to these tales of improbable transgression—from one-night stands to passionate love affairs—the more I find myself drawn to seek less obvious explanations. Why do happy people cheat?

To this end, I encourage the unfaithful to tell me their stories. I want to understand what the affairs mean for them. Why did you do it? Why him? Why her? Why now? Was this the first time? Did you initiate? Did you try to resist? How did it feel? Were you looking for something? What did you find? All of these questions help me to probe the meanings and motives for the infidelities.

People stray for a multitude of reasons, and every time I think I have heard them all, a new variation emerges. But one theme comes up repeatedly: affairs as a form of self-discovery, a quest for a new (or a lost) identity. For these seekers, infidelity is less likely to be a symptom of a problem, and is more often described as an expansive experience that involves growth, exploration, and transformation.

"Expansive?!" I can hear some people exclaiming. "Self-discovery, my ass! Sure, that sounds better than screwing around in a highway motel. Cheating is cheating, whatever fancy new age labels you want to put on it! It's cruel, it's selfish, it's dishonest, and it's abusive." Indeed, to the one who was betrayed, it can be all of these things. But what did it mean to the other?

Once the initial crisis subsides, it's important to make space for exploring the subjective experience of affairs alongside the pain they can inflict. What for Partner A may have been agonizing betrayal was transformative for Partner B. Understanding why the infidelity happened and what it signified is critical, both for couples who choose to end their relationship and for those who want to stay together, rebuild, and revitalize theirs.

In Search of a New Self

Sometimes, when we seek the gaze of another, it isn't our partner we are turning away from, but the person we have become. We are not looking for another lover so much as another version of ourselves. Mexican essayist Octavio Paz describes eroticism as a thirst for otherness. So often, the most intoxicating *other* that people discover in the affair is not a new partner; it's a new self.

Priya's first letter was filled with confusion and distress. "Most descriptions of troubled marriages don't seem to fit my situation," she began. "Colin and I have a wonderful relationship. Three great kids, no financial stresses, careers we love, great friends. He is a phenom at work, fucking handsome, an attentive lover, fit, and generous to everyone including my parents. My life is *good*."

Yet Priya is having an affair with the arborist who removed the tree that went through her neighbor's garage after Hurricane Sandy. "Not someone I would ever date—ever, ever, ever. He drives a truck and has tattoos. It's so clichéd, it pains me to say it out loud—like the middle-aged boss and the hot young secretary. And it's dangerous. It could ruin everything I've built, which I don't want to do. My therapist is the only one who knows, and she told me to block his number and never talk to him again. I know she's right and I've tried, but I keep coming back."

She tells me about her experience, half fascinated and half horrified. "We have nowhere to go, so we are always hiding in his truck or my car, in movie theaters, on park benches—his hands down my pants. I feel like a teenager with a boyfriend." She can't emphasize enough the high school quality of it all. They have had sex only half a dozen times during the whole relationship; it's more about feeling sexy than having sex. And she is stuck in an all-too-common adulterer's dilemma: "This cannot go on. But I can't stop it."

Priya can't figure out why she's in this mess. She too has bought into the idea that this stuff happens only when there's something missing in the marriage. As she vaunts the merits of her conjugal life, however, I start to suspect that her affair is not about her husband or their relationship.

To doggedly look for marital causes in cases like these is an example of what's known as the "streetlight effect," where the drunken man is searching for his missing keys not where he dropped them but where the light is. Human beings have a tendency to look for things in the places where it is easiest to search for them rather than in the places where the truth is more likely to be found. Perhaps this explains why many couples therapists overwhelmingly subscribe to the symptom theory. This way, they can focus on the familiar territory of the relationship rather than submerge themselves in the quagmire of transgression. It's easier to put the blame on a failed marriage than to grapple with the existential imponderables of our ambitions, our longings, and our ennui. The problem is that unlike the drunkard, whose search is futile, therapists can always find problems in a marriage. These just may not be the right keys to unlock the meaning of the affair.

A forensic examination of Priya's marriage would surely yield something: her disempowered position as the person who earns less; her tendency to repress anger and avoid conflict; the claustrophobia she sometimes feels; the gradual merging of two individuals into a "we," so succinctly summarized in the phrase "Did we like that restaurant?" If she and I had taken that route, we might have had an interesting chat, but not the one we needed to have. The fact that a couple has "issues" doesn't mean that these issues led to the affair.

"I think this is about you, not your marriage," I suggest to Priya. "So tell me about yourself."

"I've always been good. Good daughter, good wife, good mother. Dutiful. Straight As." Priya comes from an Indian immigrant family of modest means. For her, "what do I want?" has never been separated from "what do they want from me?" She never partied, drank, or stayed out late, and she had her first joint at twenty-two. After medical school, she married the right guy and even welcomed her parents into their home before buying them a retirement condo. At forty-seven, she is left with the nagging question, "If I'm not perfect, will they still love me?" In the back of her mind there is a voice that wonders what life is like for those who are not so "good." Are they more lonely? More free? Do they have more fun?

Priya's affair is neither a symptom nor a pathology; it's a crisis of identity, an internal rearrangement of her personality. In our sessions, we talk about duty and desire, about age and youth. Her daughters are becoming teenagers and enjoying a freedom she never knew. Priya is at once supportive and envious. As she nears the mid-century mark, she is having her own belated adolescent rebellion.

These introspections may seem superficial—petty first-world problems. Priya has said as much herself. We both agree that her life is enviable. And yet she is risking it all. That's enough to convince me to not make light of it. My role is to help her make sense of her actions. It's clear that this is not a love story that was meant to become a life story (which some affairs truly are). This is an affair that started and will end as such—hopefully without destroying her marriage in the process.

Secluded from the responsibilities of everyday life, the parallel universe of the affair is often idealized, infused with the promise of transcendence. For some, it is a world of possibility—an alternate reality in which we can reimagine and reinvent ourselves. Then again, it is experienced as limitless precisely because it is contained within the limits of its clandestine structure. It is a radiant parenthesis, a poetic interlude in the prose of life.

Hence, forbidden love stories are utopian by nature, especially in contrast with the mundane constraints of marriage and family. A prime characteristic of this liminal universe—and the key to its irresistible power—is that it is unattainable. Affairs are, by definition, precarious, elusive, and ambiguous. The indeterminacy, the uncertainty, the not knowing when I'll see you again—feelings we would never tolerate in our primary relationship—become kindling for anticipation in a hidden romance. Because we cannot *have* the lover, it ensures that we keep wanting, for we always want that which we cannot have. It is this just-out-of-reach quality that lends affairs their erotic mystique and ensures that the flame of desire keeps burning.

Reinforcing this segregation of the affair from reality is the fact that many, like Priya, choose lovers who either could not or would not become a life partner. By falling for someone from a very different class, culture, or generation, we play with possibilities that we would not entertain as actualities.

Infidelity promises "lives that could never be mine," as journalist Anna Pulley writes in a beautiful essay about her affair with a married woman. "I was," she writes, "a road she would never take.... Ours was a love that hinged on possibility—what we could offer each other was infinite potential. Reality never stood a chance against that kind of promise.... She represented a singular perfection, she had to because she contained none of the trappings of a real relationship.... She was perfect in part because she was an escape, she seemed always to offer more."

Interestingly, very few such affairs actually survive discovery. One would think that a relationship for which so much was risked would endure the transition into daylight. Under the spell of passion, lovers speak longingly of all the things they will be able to do when they are finally together. Yet when the prohibition is lifted, when the divorce comes through, when the sublime mixes with the ordinary and the affair enters the real world, what then? Some settle into happy legitimacy, but many more do not. In my experience, most affairs end, even if the marriage ends as well. However authentic the feelings of love, the dalliance was only ever meant to be a beautiful fiction.

The affair lives in the shadow of the marriage, but the marriage also lives in the center of the affair. Without its delicious illegitimacy, can the relationship with the lover remain enticing? If Priya and her tattooed beau had their own bedroom, would they be as giddy as in the back of his truck?

I have met countless women (and men) like Priya. I acknowledge the power of their experience. I do not belittle it as petty, selfish, or immature. Yet at the same time, I challenge the arrogance of lovers who feel that the epiphany of their connection has rendered everything else in their life bland. Falling in love, as Francesco Alberoni writes, "rearranges all our priorities, throws the superfluous overboard, projects a glaring light onto what is superficial and instantly discards it." As I warn Priya, when the poetic flight comes crashing down, she is likely to realize that her prosaic life matters to her a great deal.

The Seductive Power of Transgression

No conversation about relationships can avoid the thorny topic of rules and our all-too-human desire to break them. Bucking the rules is an assertion of freedom over convention, of possibility over constraints, and of self over society. Priya may be mystified and mortified by how she is putting her marriage on the line. But that's precisely where the power of transgression lies: in risking the very things that are most dear to us. Acutely aware of the law of gravity, we dream of flying. The consequences can be transformative or destructive, and sometimes you cannot pull the two apart.

Priya often feels like she's a walking contradiction: alternately dismayed by her reckless behavior, enchanted by her daredevil attitude, tormented by fear of discovery, and unable (or unwilling) to put a stop to it. Neuroscientists would no doubt explain that in her everyday life, she is following the rational commands of her frontal cortex, while in her affair, her limbic system is firmly in charge.

From a psychological perspective, our relationship to the forbidden sheds a light on the darker and less straightforward aspects of our humanity. Transgression is at the heart of human nature. Moreover, as many of us remember from our childhood, there is a thrill in hiding, sneaking, being bad, being afraid of being discovered, and getting away with it. As adults, we can find this a powerful aphrodisiac. The risk of being caught doing something naughty or dirty, the breaking of taboos, the pushing of boundaries—all of these are titillating experiences. As sexologist Jack Morin observes, most of us retain an urge from childhood to demonstrate our superiority over the rules. "Perhaps," he suggests, "this is why encounters and fantasies with a flavor of violation so often leave the violators with a sense of self-validation or even pride."

Morin's now-famous "erotic equation" states that "attraction plus obstacles equal excitement." High states of arousal, he explains, flow from the tension between persistent problems and triumphant solutions. We are most intensely excited when we are a little off-balance, uncertain, "poised on the perilous edge between ecstasy and disaster."

This insight into our human propensities helps to shed light on why people in happy, stable relationships are lured by the charge of transgression. For Priya, the question is bewitching: What if just this once I act as if the rules don't apply to me?

While for some, breaking the rules is a long-deferred dream, for others, entitlement is a way of life. They simply assume they are above the rules. Their narcissism gives them license to breach all conventions. For them, infidelity is opportunism—they cheat with impunity, simply because they can. Their grandiosity is the master narrative.

All affairs are plots of entitlement, but I am particularly interested in the meaning of entitlement for those who have lived responsible, dutiful, committed lives. What does rebellion represent for these upstanding citizens? What are we to make of the self-contradictory nature of their trespasses, when the constraints they are defying are the very ones they themselves created?

Our conversations help Priya bring clarity to her confusing picture. She is relieved that we don't have to pick apart her relationship with Colin. But having to assume full responsibility leaves her heavy with guilt. "The last thing I've ever wanted to do is hurt him. If he knew, he would be crushed. And knowing that it had nothing to do with him wouldn't make a difference. He would never believe it."

Priya is at a crossroads. She could tell her husband about the affair, something many people would advise her to do, and then deal with the consequences. She could keep it a secret and end it, hoping he would never find out. Or she could continue skating on parallel tracks for the time being. My concern with the first option is that, while I don't condone deception, I know that the moment the affair is revealed, the narrative will irrevocably switch. It will no longer be a story of self-discovery, but one of betrayal. I am not sure what they have to gain from that.

So what about the second option, quietly ending it? She has tried that several times: deleted his phone number, driven a different route back from dropping the kids at school, told herself how wrong this entire thing is. But the self-imposed cutoffs become new and electrifying rules to break. Three days later, the fake name is back in her phone.

As for the third option, Priya's torment is mounting in proportion to the risks she is taking. She's beginning to feel the corrosive effects of the secret and getting sloppier by the day. Danger follows her to every movie theater and secluded parking lot.

Taking all of this into account, I hope to guide her toward a fourth option. What she is telling me, in effect, is: I need to end this, but I don't want to. What I can see, and she has not yet grasped, is that the thing she is really afraid to lose is not him—it's the part of herself that he awakened. "You think you had a relationship with Truck Man," I tell her. "Actually, you had an intimate encounter with yourself, mediated by him."

This distinction between the person and the experience is crucial in helping people to extricate themselves from their affairs. The extramarital excursion will end, but their souvenirs will go on traveling with them. "I don't expect you to believe me right now, but you can terminate your relationship and keep what it gave you," I tell her. "You reconnected with an energy, a youthfulness. I know that it feels as if in leaving him, you are severing a lifeline to all of that, but I want you to know that over time you will find that some of this also lives inside of you."

We discuss how to go about saying goodbye. The clean break hasn't worked because it emphasizes only the negative aspects and does not acknowledge the depth of the experience. Priya and her lover have also tried the slow and gentle approach, spending hours discussing how they should end it. I know how that kind of conversation goes: Couples spend entire nights planning their farewells, but wind up feeling closer and more connected in the face of their impending separation.

I introduce a different kind of conversation: a proper goodbye that does not deny all the positives, but holds the contradiction: "I don't want to end this, yet that's what I came to do." She should express her gratitude for what their relationship has given her and tell him she will always cherish the memory of their time together.

She asks me, "I need to do it today, right?"

"You'll have to do it many days," I tell her. "You'll have to learn to extract yourself from him. And it won't be easy. Sometimes it will feel like a root canal. He's become such a presence in your life that when you don't see him, at first you'll walk around numb and empty. This is to be expected and it may take time."

In some situations, this process can be a matter of a single enlightening conversation; in others, it can take weeks or months before the meaning is metabolized and the affair can die a natural death, having served its purpose. For Priya, I suspect it will be the latter. "You'll have to force yourself not to text, call, follow, or drive by his house. You may slip on occasion, but one day it will stick. You will feel loss, you'll mourn, and gradually you'll come to accept it. You'll experience the relief of not being fragmented. And on occasion, when you think of him, you'll feel young again."

Perhaps what I am saying is true, and Priya will remember Truck Man fondly. But I know it's equally possible that a year from now, she will look back at this episode and wonder, "What the hell was I thinking? Was I mad?" He may remain a beautiful flower in her secret garden, or she may see him as a weed. For now, suffice to say that giving her the permission to internalize him will help her let him go.

People often ask me, "Can a couple really experience an authentic, secure connection while one of them keeps such a secret? Doesn't it render the whole relationship false?" I have no tidy answer to these questions. In many instances, I have worked toward revelation, hopeful that it will open up new channels of communication for the couple. But I've also seen a carelessly divulged secret leave unfading scars. When I am working with Priya, my focus is on getting her to own her experience and to deal with it in the most caring way possible. These days, my messages have replaced those of her lover on her WhatsApp thread. I act as something of a sponsor as she weans herself off his daily affirmation and gradually pursues her goal, which is to reintegrate her life.

The Lure of Unlived Lives

The quest for the unexplored self is a powerful theme of the adulterous narrative. Priya's parallel universe transported her to the teenager she never was. Others find themselves drawn by the memory of the person they once were. And then there are those whose reveries take them back to the missed opportunities, the ones that got away, and the person they could have been. As the eminent sociologist Zygmunt Bauman writes, in modern life, "there is always a suspicion . . . that one is living a lie or a mistake; that something crucially important has been overlooked, missed, neglected, left untried, and unexplored; that a vital obligation to one's own authentic self has not been met or that some chances of unknown happiness completely different from any happiness experienced before have not been taken up in time and are bound to be lost forever if they continue to be neglected." He speaks directly to our nostalgia for unlived lives, unexplored identities, and roads not taken.

As children we have the opportunity to play at other roles; as adults we often find ourselves confined by the ones we've been assigned or the ones we have chosen. When we select a partner, we commit to a story. Yet we remain forever curious: What other stories could we have been part of? Affairs offer us a window into those other lives, a peek at the stranger within. Adultery is often the revenge of the deserted possibilities.

Dwayne had always cherished memories of his college sweetheart, Keisha. She was the best sex he'd ever had, and she still featured prominently in his fantasy life. They'd both known they were too young to commit, and parted reluctantly. Over the years, he has often asked himself what would have happened had their timing been different.

Enter Facebook. The digital universe offers unprecedented opportunities to reconnect with people who exited our lives long ago. Never before have we had so much access to our exes and so much fodder for our curiosity. "Whatever happened to so-and-so? I wonder if she ever got married?" "I heard he was having difficulties in his relationship." "Is she still as cute as I remember?" The answers are a click away. One day Dwayne searched for Keisha's profile. Lo and behold, they were both in Austin. She, still hot, was divorced. He, on the other hand, was happily married, but his curiosity got the better of him and "add friend" soon turned into secret girlfriend.

In the past decade, it seems to me that affairs with exes have proliferated, thanks to social media. These retrospective encounters occupy a place somewhere between the known and the unknown—bringing together the familiarity of someone you once knew with the freshness created by the passage of time. The flicker with an old flame offers a unique combination of built-in trust, risk-taking, and vulnerability. In addition, it is a magnet for our lingering nostalgia. The person I once was, but lost, is the person you once knew.

We all have multiple selves, but in our intimate relationships, over time, we tend to reduce our complexity to a shrunken version of ourselves. One of the essential components of recovery is finding ways to reintroduce the many pieces that were abandoned or exiled along the way.

The Return of the Exiled Emotions

While some people are surprised to discover that there are many parts to who they are, Ayo is well acquainted with his multiple selves. He has always defined, redefined, and developed himself through relationships—with friends, mentors, and intimate partners. "I have layers or circles of friends corresponding to various stages of my life, in different parts of the world," he tells me, "Each one summons the person I was in the formative years of those relationships. I find it exhilarating to re-experience myself across life stages simply by choosing to spend time with one or the other circle of friends."

In the past two years, however, the most influential person in Ayo's ongoing project of personal growth has been Cynthia, a fellow international development consultant. He describes their two-year affair as "a vital developmental accelerator"—propelling him into a new experience of himself.

Ayo's infidelity tells a less well-known but not uncommon tale about men. There's a certain type of guy who has spent his life on the tough side of the emotional spectrum, fearless and always in control. For Ayo, who grew up in Kenya and moved around several times during a turbulent childhood, this strategy made sense. "I seemed to want many of the good bits of love—the warmth, the protection, the caring, the friendship, and the romance—but not the leaky parts—the vulnerability, the weakness, the fear, and the sadness," he reflects.

His wife, Julie, offered him just that. They met in London twenty-seven years ago, when both were embarking on careers in the same field. "She was beautiful, exceptionally smart, athletic, and neither overly introspective nor fragile, which suited me." Five children followed, with Julie deciding to leave her career and raise their brood while Ayo continued to travel the world.

Their marriage was a happy one. It was, as Ayo describes it, "premised on respectful extramarital liberty"—a liberty he had taken multiple times over the years, enjoying casual encounters in every time zone. Julie turned a blind eye to his "side steps," as she called them ("they took some of the pressure off of me"), and even had a brief affair herself, which she told her husband about.

Ayo first encountered Cynthia through her writings and thought them "brilliant"—her voice "enchanting, funny, genuine, and wise." When they met in person, she was all of that, and also elegant and graceful. "We tumbled in love," he says, "meeting through work and writing endless letters to each other—thousands of pages over the past two years." Their relationship had many facets—deep professional respect, creative partnership, intellectual camaraderie, erotic passion, and humor.

Initially, Ayo and Cynthia planned to tell their respective spouses, hoping that the flexible boundaries that characterized both marriages would stretch to include their connection. But they knew this relationship was more serious than any previous fling and was likely to "test the limits of our spouses' tolerance."

Before they could follow through with this plan, life intervened, in the form of a cancer diagnosis for Cynthia. The decision to tell went out the window, as did any remaining boundaries. "I jumped right into her life and spent as much time with her as I could," Ayo recalls. "I fell deeper and deeper in love. For the first time, I allowed myself to be afraid, to be sad."

Ayo describes getting in touch with emotions that had always been suppressed, finding a new curiosity, empathy, and tolerance for uncertainty. Always self-reflective, he sums it up as follows: "I acquired a level of literacy in the emotional space that I had lacked." This softer man appeared also in his lovemaking—"more playful, more balanced, and less driven by outcomes."

When Julie found out about Cynthia, Ayo still held out hope that she might "shrug it off" as she had his past adventures and accept it as part of a new polyamorous agreement. To his surprise and dismay, the opposite occurred. "She sank in agony." When he wrote asking for a couples session, he was trying to find a way out of their impasse.

"The fact is that I love Julie," he wrote, "her boundless physical energy, her unquestioned commitment to our marriage and family, her invulnerability, her thoughtfulness, her well-grounded certainties, and her rich bedrock of values. We have a lot in common that will keep us interested well into old age. And the fact is that I am in love with Cynthia—her grace, her exquisite emotional intelligence, her brilliance, her vulnerability, her ontological uncertainties, and her complexity of mind. I love the way I show up with her as my biggest self. So different parts of me pull in opposite directions. With both of them in my life, I have felt like the most fortunate man ever."

By the time we meet, Ayo has reluctantly ended the sexual side of his relationship with Cynthia, but he insists on continuing their creative collaboration—something Julie is deeply unhappy about. He tells me honestly that he is considering several options. Part of him hopes that I can convince Julie to allow him to have both his marriage and his affair. Another part of him hopes I will "straighten him up and shake him out of his delusions" so he can focus solely on his marriage. Yet another part wonders if this crossroads is meant to take him into a new life, and hopes I can help him face the implications. He doesn't know which outcome we should be working toward.

Julie, meanwhile, wants to make sense of the irresistible pull Cynthia exerts on Ayo and the intensity of her own response. "Why did this hit you differently than his previous flings?" I ask her. We are familiar with the story of the middle-aged man who takes up with a young beauty and the wife's feelings of inadequacy by comparison. For Julie, however, young beauties had never been a problem. "Not feeling threatened by them, I decided to ignore them," she says. But Cynthia was a kick in the gut. A professional, accomplished woman, she was the same age as Julie and had excelled in the field Julie had walked away from decades earlier to devote herself to motherhood.

As I listen to her, it begins to fall into place why this revelation plunged her into such despair. Her husband did not just fall in love with another woman—he fell for the woman Julie could have been. Cynthia does not just represent some new part of Ayo that he is discovering. She also represents everything his wife gave up. It could have been Julie working at his side, sharing his passions, and celebrating their successes together. She chose differently, and there is no going back for her. Meanwhile, he has the option of doing a take two.

For the first time in our session, contemplating her lost self, her reserve cracking, Julie begins to cry. When our meeting ends, both she and Ayo are facing very uncomfortable and new developmental thresholds, to use a term that Ayo would appreciate. Can he bring his newfound empathy to his wife, rather than just being surprised she is hurt? And can she go beyond her stoic attitude and show her underbelly? How can she create a new sense of purpose?

One of the options Ayo had not included in his menu of possible outcomes was the creation of a fresh emotional vocabulary between him and Julie. If fear, sadness, and vulnerability can be introduced into their sanctuary, they might encounter new selves in places they never expected. At the end of our single daylong session, I leave them considering this possibility.

It is real-life dramas like these that highlight for me the limitations of the symptom theory. Infidelity needs to be seen not simply as a pathology or a dysfunction. We must lend a careful ear to the emotional resonance of transgressive experiences as well as to their fallout; otherwise we perpetuate the compartmentalization that undergirded the affair itself. We leave the couple at risk of sinking back into the status quo. Untangling the meanings of the affair sets the stage for all the decisions that will follow. Too much is at stake to spend precious time searching for our keys in all the wrong places.

CHAPTER 10

AN ANTIDOTE TO DEADNESS

The Lure of the Forbidden

Today I am a woman torn between the terror that
everything might change and the equal terror that everything might
carry on exactly the same for the rest of my days.
—Paulo Coelho, *Adultery*

At its best monogamy may be the wish to find
someone to die with; at its worst it is a cure for the terrors of aliveness.
They are easily confused.
—Adam Phillips, *Monogamy*

"'Let's take the stairs,' he said as we waited for the elevator outside the office. Then his hand brushed against mine. The slightest touch and I felt electricity. I felt *alive*." Danica's eyes light up at the memory. "And you know, it shocked me, because I didn't even know I wanted to feel like that. Until that moment, I didn't realize I'd been missing that feeling for a very long time."

Danica's account doesn't shock me at all, nor does the fact that this conscientious wife and mother followed her younger Brazilian coworker Luiz not only up the stairs but into a full-blown affair. The one theme that I hear above all else from those who have bitten into the forbidden apple is this: It makes them feel *alive*.

Countless wanderers narrate their excursions in similar terms: reborn, rejuvenated, intensified, revitalized, renewed, vibrant, liberated. And many, like Danica, report that they didn't even recognize the absence of these feelings until they were caught unawares. The sense of aliveness is rarely the explicit motive for an affair—in many instances they don't quite know why it began—but it is often the unexpected meaning that is found there. In the decade I have been studying rebellious love, I have heard this sentiment expressed all over the world. Affairs are quintessential erotic plots in the ancient sense of eros as life energy.

"Everything with Cindy was intense," Karim tells me, reflecting on their three-year affair. "The planning to see each other was intense. The sex. The fights were intense—and the making up. I guess she was both what I craved and what I feared at the same time. In contrast, my marriage is just normal. Not bad, but sort of blah."

"I'd never even thought about falling in love with someone else," Keith tells me. "Joe and I have been together since art school. But then I met Noah at an artists' colony, and it was like waking up from a long winter hibernation. I didn't even know how asleep I'd been. He pushed me and inspired me. I felt completely energized; I was getting my best work done with him."

"My husband hadn't been able to get my juices flowing in more than a decade," Alison exclaims. "I was thirty-five and convinced there was something medically wrong with me. In all other ways, we share so much. He's my best friend, my copilot, and from the outside, we look perfect. Then Dino showed up, and with just a few words and suggestions, he did what all the lubricants and toys had not been able to do for me. It was an amazing feeling—as if he activated me."

When I ask people what "being alive" means, they lay out a multifaceted experience. Power, validation, confidence, and freedom are the most common flavors. Add to these the elixir of love, and you have an intoxicating cocktail. There is the sexual awakening or reawakening, of course, but it doesn't stop there. The awakened describe a sense of movement when they had felt constricted, an opening up of possibilities in a life that had narrowed down to a single predictable path, a surge of emotional intensity where everything seemed bland. I have come to think of encounters like these as existential affairs, because they cut deep to the essence of life itself.

However we may judge their consequences, these liaisons are not frivolous. Their power is often as mystifying to the person involved in the secret as they are to the spouse who uncovers it. But having heard the same story so many times, I know that there is a method to the madness—an underlying riddle of human nature that leads people to unexpected trespasses. I often feel like part therapist, part philosopher—explaining to couples the existential paradoxes that make what seems inconceivable also quite logical.

An Antidote to Death

In a surprising number of these cases, a direct line can be traced from an extramarital adventure back to our most basic human fear—the confrontation with mortality. I frequently witness affairs occurring on the heels of loss or tragedy. When the grim reaper knocks at the door—a parent passes, a friend goes too soon, a baby is lost—the jolt of love and sex delivers a vital affirmation of life.

Then there are other more symbolic losses. Bad news at the doctor can trample our sense of youth and robustness in an instant. I've seen quite a few men and women with a cancer diagnosis in hand who were escaping their death anxiety in the arms of a new love. Infertility puts us face-to-face with the inability to create life. Unyielding unemployment saps our confidence and makes us feel worthless. Depression robs us of hope and joy. Dangerous circumstances like wars or disaster zones incite us to take unusual emotional risks. In the face of the helplessness and vulnerability we feel at such moments, infidelity can be an act of defiance. Freud described eros as the life instinct, doing battle with thanatos, the death instinct.

Those same people may have previously felt tempted, but I wonder if it is the brusque confrontation with the brevity of life and its fragility that emboldens them to seize the day and act. Suddenly they are unwilling to settle for a life half-lived. "Is this all there is?" They hunger for more. Compromises that seemed reasonable yesterday become unbearable today. "Life is short, have an affair." AshleyMadison.com's infamous slogan may seem crude, but it is aptly targeted. Stories like this are so common that I now routinely ask my patients: "Have you suffered any losses, deaths, or tragedies in the past few years?"

Maybe it is death with a capital D, or maybe it is just the deadness that creeps up from dulling habit—whatever the case, I now see these affairs as a powerful antidote. "Love and Eros wake up the most tired person," writes Italian sociologist Francesco Alberoni. The thirst for life triggered in such an encounter topples us with an irresistible force. It is often neither planned nor sought. The unexpected boost of erotic desire galvanizes us beyond the mundane, abruptly breaking the rhythm and the routine of the quotidian. Time slows down. The inexorable advance of age seems to lose its momentum. Familiar places take on fresh beauty. New places beckon to our reawakened curiosity. People report that every sense feels amplified—food tastes better, music never sounded so sweet, colors are more vivid.

"It Can't All Be Bad"

When Danica's husband, Stefan, followed the trail of texts and uncovered her eighteen-month affair with the man who made her feel alive, he felt kicked in the gut. "I can still feel your hands all over me," she'd written. "Perhaps we can sneak out at lunch again? I dressed especially for you." But he also recognized in those missives the vital and playful woman he'd once fallen in love with—a woman he'd barely seen in years.

After he got over the initial shock, Stefan was "oddly positive," as he puts it, hopeful that there might be a silver lining. Danica had expressed deep regret and insisted the affair was over. Stefan came to see me and confided his wish that perhaps this crisis would rekindle their once passionate but now rather listless marriage. Perhaps he too would get to taste the woman who wrote those steamy messages to her office-mate.

After a couple of canceled appointments, I am finally meeting with Danica. An elegant, reserved woman in her early forties, she works as a consultant at the World Health Organization. I know from Stefan that she's skeptical and more than a little annoyed that he has been nagging her for weeks to watch my talks on YouTube. Her demeanor tells me in no uncertain terms that there are so many more important things she could be doing right now than meeting with me. So let's just say I don't feel very welcome. She's reluctant even to talk about what she calls her "mistake." "Why does it matter? It's over. I just want to move on."

I sense that she expects me to judge her as she judges herself. But she feels bad enough as it is, there is nothing for me to add. Her shame and discomfort are palpable, and she has written off the entire experience as "wrong."

In moments like this, I'm used to helping repentant adulterers express more authentic regret and remorse. With this woman, however, I find myself in the opposite situation. Her sweeping self-blame blocks all avenues for understanding and change, for her as well as for her marriage. We need to separate "wrong" from "hurtful," so that she can acknowledge the positive aspects of her experience, all the while taking responsibility for the pain it caused. Otherwise, there is little chance that she can bring that newfound energy home. Stefan recognizes that woman and wants her back; Danica, however, is so shocked by her own actions that she insists the woman who came alive in Luiz's arms "wasn't me."

"What happens inside an affair generally includes some enjoyable elements," I tell Danica. "You fell hard for this guy, so it can't have been all bad. Yes, you feel guilty, but nevertheless, you say he made you feel alive. Tell me more."

She begins hesitantly. "I wasn't looking for a fling. I've been approached many times, and I've never even bothered. Luiz was different. He wasn't just hitting on me. He'd say, 'You have a beautiful energy, but it's all blocked. There is a real woman somewhere deep inside, waiting to be released.' He would compliment me in a way that felt much deeper than a compliment. And he was persistent." Privately, I think that his words sound exactly like a come-on. But I know the effect that the simplest comment can have when it lands directly on a deep and unacknowledged yearning. Mere flattery turns into a dizzying tonic.

She continues: "There are so many things going on at home. If it's not the kids, it's my parents. I often feel it's all too much. I don't even have time to take my coat off when I walk through the door. I go from one thing to the next, and by the end I am exhausted. Things changed for me that fall. I would go to the office and I'd feel worthy, in my element, even a little giddy." Her encounter with Luiz infused her life with a renewed sense of joy and anticipation, both potent erotic ingredients that had long since disappeared from the marital home.

Too bad, because the home in question was once a dream come true. It is a lovely chalet overlooking Lake Zurich, with a red-tiled roof and wide bay windows. She and Stefan, a successful lawyer, have lived there for the past decade and a half, and Danica lovingly oversaw every detail of its remodeling. A refugee from the Balkan conflict who fled Bosnia as a child, she had yearned for that stable haven all her life. She is quick to assure me that she doesn't want to leave—this was not an exit affair. But she is struggling to understand how she ended up so divided. How did this idyllic place become so numbing that she sought escape? And she is even more bewildered by the fact that she hurt Stefan, "the first guy who ever made me feel safe."

The Conundrum of Security and Adventure

There is a painful irony to affairs in which people find themselves rebelling against the very things they value most deeply. And yet this is a common predicament that reflects an existential conflict within us. We seek stability and belonging, qualities that propel us toward committed relationships, but we also thrive on novelty and diversity. As psychoanalyst Stephen Mitchell has insightfully pointed out, we crave security *and* we crave adventure, but these two fundamental needs spring from different motives and pull us in different directions throughout our lives—played out in the tensions between separateness and togetherness, individuality and intimacy, freedom and commitment.

We straddle these opposing drives from the moment we come into this world—alternating between the safety of our mothers' laps and the risks we take in the playground. We carry this dichotomy into adulthood. One hand clings to the known and the familiar; the other reaches out for mystery and excitement. We seek connection, predictability, and dependability to root us firmly in place. But we also have a need for change, for the unexpected, for transcendence. The Greeks understood this, which is why they worshiped both Apollo (representative of the rational and self-disciplined) and Dionysus (representative of the spontaneous, sensuous, and emotional).

Modern romance makes a new and tantalizing promise: that we can satisfy both needs in one relationship. Our chosen one can be at once the steady, reliable rock and the one who can lift us beyond the mundane.

In the early stages of a relationship, this merger of contraries seems perfectly reasonable. Security and adventure rarely start out looking like an either-or proposition. The honeymoon phase is special in that it brings together the relief of reciprocated love with the excitement of a future still to be created. What we often don't realize is that the exuberance of the beginning is fueled by its undercurrent of uncertainty. We set out to make love more secure and dependable, but in the process, inevitably we dial down its intensity. On the path of commitment, we happily trade a little passion for a bit more certainty, some excitement for some stability. What we don't anticipate is that the hidden price we may pay is the erotic vitality of our relationships.

The permanence and stability that we seek in our intimate connections can stifle their sexual spark, leading to what Mitchell calls "expressions of exuberant defiance," otherwise known as affairs. Adulterers find themselves longing to untangle themselves from the constraints of security and conventions—the very security they so arduously sought to establish in their primary relationship.

This is not a predicament Danica ever thought she would find herself in. A man like Stefan, children, a solid job, and the reassurance that comes from making plans for next year were exactly what she had always wanted. But with children came a new dread—one that in her case was particularly acute. Her youngest boy had had heart surgery before his first birthday and required ongoing special care; her oldest boy decided it was time for him to get some attention at age twelve and has been particularly imaginative in instigating panic in his parents.

All the stresses notwithstanding, Danica and Stefan enjoyed a comfortable life. Stefan missed the fire in his wife's eyes, but he kept thinking that he couldn't ask for more, given how maxed out she was. He hurried home from work every day to be with her and the kids, and she was too absorbed in her responsibilities to even notice the growing numbness inside. "We don't have a bad marriage," she insists. "He never misses our weekly date nights. But how do you expect me to feel romantic when I'm worried about one kid's health and the other one's failing grades, and I know I've got to get up at six? To be honest, I'd rather just catch up on email before bed, so that's one less thing I have to do in the morning."

The historian and essayist Pamela Haag has written a whole book about marriages like Danica and Stefan's, which she calls "melancholy marriages." Analyzing the plight of these "semi-happy couples," she explains:

A marriage adds things to your life, and it also takes things away. Constancy kills joy; joy kills security; security kills desire; desire kills stability; stability kills lust. Something gives; some part of you recedes. It's something you can live without, or it's not. And maybe it's hard to know before the marriage which part of the self is expendable . . . and which is part of your spirit.

For Danica, like many others, it was not until someone outside of her marriage reminded her of that part of her spirit that she realized it was not expendable after all. Luiz's carefully worded flirtations tapped right into her unspoken melancholy and awoke a self that she no doubt feels is more authentic than the self-critical, frustrated, multitasking mom of today.

Affairs as a Both/And Solution

If we needed evidence of how challenging it is to consolidate our disharmonious drives, infidelity would be exhibit A. And perhaps, as Laura Kipnis suggests, it is not merely a by-product of the all-too-human desire for two things at once, but a kind of resolution. "The adulterous wish lodges itself in th[is] fundamental psychic split," she writes, and affairs offer "the elegant solution of externalizing the conflict through the competing agents of your custom-designed triangle."

It is a given that many people go outside to find things they *cannot* find at home. But what about those who go looking elsewhere for things they don't really *want* at home? For some, their snail mail address is not an appropriate venue for the kinds of messy emotions associated with romantic passion or unbridled sex. As Mitchell suggests, it is much more risky to unleash those forces with the person upon whom we depend for so much. In such cases, people's extramarital adventures are not motivated by a disregard for what they have at home; quite the contrary, they value it so much that they don't want to tamper with it. They are loath to disturb the stability of their domestic lives with the intemperate energy of eros. They may want to escape the cozy nest temporarily, but they sure don't want to lose it. Infidelity beckons as a neatly segmented solution: the risk and the rush in the lover's bower; the comfort and closeness in the marital abode.

At least in theory, an affair solves the dilemma of reconciling security and adventure by promising both. In outsourcing the need for passion and risk to a third party, the unfaithful gets to transcend the tedium of domesticity without giving it up entirely. After all, the adulterous bed is not necessarily the place we want to take up residence—we just want the freedom to visit it when we choose. So long as we are successful in keeping the secret, there is a feeling that we can have it all. As sociologists Lise VanderVoort and Steve Duck write, "The transformative allure of an affair is heightened by this contradiction—everything changes yet nothing need change. An affair offers the seductive promise that both/and is possible—the either/or of monogamy can be defied."

A Woman's Desire, Lost and Reclaimed

Danica is hardly the first woman who shuts down at home and wakes up outside. Hers is an archetypal tale of the muting of eros. I see women like her all the time—usually dragged into therapy by their frustrated husbands who are tired of being rejected, night after night. The typical complaint is: she is totally absorbed with the kids and has zero interest in sex. "No matter how many dishes I wash, I can't get lucky." But it's those very same women, I've found, who "come alive" in a completely unexpected romance.

Many men struggle to understand how the woman who can't be bothered in the marital bed is suddenly having a torrid affair in which she can't get enough. For years, they've been thinking she's just not interested in sex, period; now, with new evidence in hand, they reconsider—"she must not be interested in sex with me." In some cases, a woman's roaming desires may indeed be a reaction to an unimaginative husband, but not always. In fact, Stefan is a romantic who loves to set the stage for his wife's pleasure, but her typical reaction is "let's not make a production out of this. Shall we?" With Luiz, however, she reveled in the many-act play of languorous lovemaking—and made it last even longer in the multiple texts that followed.

The wife can't wait for sex to be over. The lover wishes it would never end. It's easy to think that it's the men who make the difference. But the context matters more. And by context I mean the story she weaves for herself and the character she gets to play within it. Home, marriage, and motherhood have forever been the pursuit of many women, but also the place where women cease to feel like women.

The writings of prominent researcher Marta Meana are particularly illuminating about the enigma of female desire. She challenges the common assumption that women's sexuality is primarily dependent on relational connectedness—love, commitment, and security. After all, if these assumptions were true, then sex should be thriving in marriages like Danica's. Meana suggests that women are not just "touchy-feely" but also "saucy-sexy"—in fact, "women may be just as turned on as men by the novel, the illicit, the raw, the anonymous, but the arousal value of these may not be important enough to women to trade in things they value more (i.e., emotional connectedness)."

As I have often said, our emotional needs and our erotic needs do not always neatly align. For some, the security they find in the relationship gives them the necessary trust to play, to take risks, and to safely lust. But for many others, the nesting qualities that nurture love are the same ones that slowly stifle desire. When forced to choose, what do women do? Meana posits that "women choose good relationships over sexual pleasure."

In other words, since time immemorial, women have put their emotional needs ahead of their erotic needs. She knows what turns her on, but she also knows what is more important than being turned on. She knows what she likes, and she knows what she needs. The choice is already made for her.

Stefan, understandably, has not deciphered this puzzle of the feminine senses. Like many men, when his wife withdrew, he concluded that she didn't like sex. This leads us to another common misunderstanding that Meana's work has highlighted: We interpret the lack of sexual interest as proof that women's sexual drive is inherently less strong. Perhaps it would be more accurate to think that it is a drive that needs to be stoked more intensely and more imaginatively—and first and foremost by her, not only by her partner.

In the transition to marriage, too many women experience their sexuality as shifting from desire to duty. When it becomes something she *should* do, it no longer is something she wants to do. By contrast, when a woman has an affair, she brings a self-determination to her pleasure. What is activated in the affair is her will—she pursues her own satisfaction.

Stefan feels bad that he didn't notice the depth of Danica's decline, and he even went so far as to seek out her lover in an attempt to figure out why. He asked, "How did you know she was dead inside? What did you see?" Luiz told him, "She reminded me of a tree in winter. Although it has no leaves, you can imagine its true natural state of glory in the summertime." Upon hearing this poetic rendering of his wife's predicament, Stefan felt sad and jealous. Why was Luiz able to make her bloom again while he was not?

I tell him, "With Luiz, she doesn't have to think about the kids, the bills, the dinner—all things that make her feel erotically drab. Put him in your place, and he'd soon have the same fate."

"Erotic silence" is the term psychotherapist and author Dalma

Heyn uses to describe this predicament—an "unexpected, inarticulable deadening of pleasure and vitality" that happens to some women after they tie the knot. "A woman's sexuality depends on her authenticity and self-nurturance," she writes. Yet marriage and motherhood demand a level of selflessness that is at odds with the inherent selfishness of desire. Being responsible for others makes it harder for women to focus on their own needs, to feel spontaneous, sexually expressive, and carefree. For many, finding at home the kind of self-absorption that is essential to erotic pleasure proves a challenge. The burdens of caretaking are indeed a powerful anti-aphrodisiac.

When a woman struggles to stay connected to herself, an affair is often a venue for self-reclamation. Like the heroes of ancient mythology, she leaves home to find herself. Her secret liaison becomes one thing in her life that is for her alone—a stamp of autonomy. When you have an affair, you know for a fact that you're not doing it to take care of anyone else. Heyn's subjects confirm the self-realization that is inherent in this kind of romance. "Whereas before their affairs these women experienced their bodies as fragmented, their voices muted, some vital organ or aspect of their personality missing, during the affair and after it they became changed. They let go of those muffled feelings and entered a clear reality, one filled with color and vibrancy, in which they felt alive and awake and strong and focused."

In my experience, this theme of autonomy is more pronounced in female infidelity, but it is by no means exclusive to women, nor is it limited to heterosexual couples. Women are more likely to say, "I lost myself"; men complain that "I lost my woman." They too begin to roam not just in search of more, or more exciting, sex but in search of connection, intensity, aliveness. Ironically, as the adulterous wheel turns, they will often end up meeting a woman who at home feels just like their wife and is seeking her own awakening elsewhere.

Meana's research with fellow psychologist Karen E. Sims confirms the erotic fate of so many otherwise happily married women. Their findings identify three core themes that "represent dragging forces on sexual desire." First, the institutionalization of relationships—a passage from freedom and independence to commitment and responsibility. Second, the overfamiliarity that develops when intimacy and closeness replace individuality and mystery. And lastly, the desexualizing nature of certain roles—mother, wife, and house manager all promote the de-eroticization of the self.

These findings support my clinical observation that the challenge of sustaining desire lies in navigating these fundamental polarities within us. And again, they challenge conventional thinking about female desire, in particular the assumption that women rely exclusively on security in order to feel sexually open. "Rather than being anchored in the 'safe side' of the continuum," they conclude, "female sexual desire requires a balance between opposing impulses . . . of comfort and freedom, of security and risk, of intimacy and individuality."

For those who struggle to maintain this delicate balance between opposites, it is easy to see why infidelity offers an enticing proposition. The structure of the affair is anything but institutionalized, a sure pathway to freedom and independence. It is, as Sims and Meana put it, a zone of "liminality"—an abdication of rules and responsibilities, an active pursuit of pleasure, a transcendence of the limits of reality. There is certainly no risk of the overfamiliarity that comes from sharing a bathroom for decades. Mystery, novelty, and the unknown are built in. And the role of lover is quintessentially sexual, while the mother, the wife, and the housekeeper are left safely locked up at home.

"Who Are You When You Are Not with Me?"

When I meet with Stefan and Danica together, he reiterates that he wants nothing more than for his wife to reclaim her erotic self with him. "I don't like how she sacrifices herself constantly for the kids, leaving nothing for herself or for us. I want to support her in changing that." He is full of ideas for how he can help her take more time and space for herself—to pick up all the things that used to make her feel happy. Volleyball. Yoga. Girl time. "But so far, it hasn't happened," he tells me.

Danica, I notice, is silent.

"That's all great," I tell him. "But there is only so much you can do." If he keeps trying to solve the problem for her, every suggestion will add to the feeling of pressure and paradoxically reinforce her resistance. She needs to go after what she wants herself, not what he wants from her.

I often say to my patients that if they could bring into their relationships even a tenth of the boldness, the playfulness, and the verve that they bring to their affairs, their home life would feel quite different. Our creative imagination seems to be richer when it comes to our transgressions than to our commitments. Yet while I say this, I also think back to a poignant scene in the movie *A Walk on the Moon*. Pearl (Diane Lane) has been having an affair with a free-spirited blouse salesman. Alison, her teenage daughter, asks, "Do you love the blouseman more than all of us?" "No," her mother replies. "But sometimes it's easier to be different with a different person."

If this marriage is to recover, not just emotionally but erotically, Danica needs to find a way to be different with the same person she has lived with for so long. And while there's no doubt that's a challenge, it's not impossible. I have seen quite a few women, armed with fresh erotic entitlements and confidence, bring their new-found selves back to their partners, who may not even know what sparked the change, but certainly appreciated it. Close encounters with the third can bring to life (or bring back to life) a dormant sexuality. So while infidelity often delivers a devaluation of a couple's sexual stock, at other times it can be an economy of addition.

Danica needs to embrace her inner contradiction and make peace with the woman who enthusiastically pursued her own pleasure even when it meant betraying her marriage. "If you disavow her, make the affair only ugly and shameful, you will cut off a lifeline to your aliveness," I explain. But she still seems reluctant, and Stefan's frustration is palpable.

For him, the deepest wound is not that she went elsewhere—it's that she showed him what was possible and then seems unable or unwilling to share it with him. As long as he thought she simply didn't have it in her anymore, he was resigned. Now he too is feeling entitled to more ardor, and the idea of going back to the tepidity is terrifying for him.

Sadly, bringing lust home proves more difficult than he imagined. When he writes to me, eighteen months later, he is still waiting to meet the flowering summer tree, and his hopes are fading.

Given our dialectical desires, is the inner conflict that leads to infidelity inevitable? Are we predisposed to cherish habit and safety at home and then escape it to find adventure elsewhere? Is it possible to stay alive with a life partner? Can we experience the otherness we crave in the midst of familiarity, and what does it take? Danica and Stefan's story does not provide much encouragement, and you might be forgiven for feeling rather demoralized at this point. But it is illustrative of human realities that we cannot afford to avoid. Love and desire do not have to be mutually exclusive. Many couples find a way to integrate their contradictions without resorting to compartmentalization. But it starts with the understanding that we can never eliminate the dilemma. Reconciling the erotic and the domestic is not a problem to solve; it is a paradox to manage.

CHAPTER 11

IS SEX EVER JUST SEX?

The Emotional Economics of Adultery

In London alone, there are 80,000 prostitutes. What are they but . . . human sacrifices offered up on the altar of monogamy?
—Arthur Schopenhauer, *Studies in Pessimism*

A guy walks into a bar, takes off his wedding ring, pulls out a wad of cash, and motions a pretty girl to come dance for him . . .

I can imagine what you're thinking. Perhaps you are getting turned on; perhaps you are disgusted. You may be quick to judge or justify. "Men are pigs!" "Guys need sex. Maybe his wife doesn't put out." "Asshole." "Horndog." "Addict." "Prick." One word you're probably not thinking is "love." Women cheat for love, the common assumption goes, but men? They cheat for sex. And this assumption is all the more strongly reinforced when the sex in question is anonymous, transactional, or commercial. Such encounters are designed to be free of emotion. Isn't the fact that he'd rather not remember her name proof that sex is the exclusive commodity being traded?

In the twisting tale of adultery, however, things are not always what they seem. Plenty of women's affairs are driven by physical desire. And plenty of men's escapades are fueled by complex emotional needs—including many whose brand of infidelity tends toward casual or commercial conquests.

Garth, fifty-five, has had chronic erectile dysfunction with his wife, Valerie, for years. "I didn't want him to feel bad, so we stopped even trying," she tells me. "Then I find out he's been going to strip clubs, sex parties, and prostitutes, throughout our marriage!" Valerie, also in her fifties, is beside herself. "I believe he loves me. But how can he be two people—a loving if ED-damaged husband at home and a compulsive seeker of anonymous sex outside? And to think that I gave up my sexuality for that?"

Scott, twenty years younger than Garth, is in a fairly new relationship with Kristen, thirty-one. They used to have sex every day, he says, but then about six months in, he just couldn't get into it anymore. It wasn't that he didn't feel horny—he just preferred to retreat to his man cave and satisfy himself with porn. Kristen was worried by the drop-off in their sex life, but she knew he'd been going through a tough time, as his business was struggling and his mother had just passed away. Her empathy turned to horror, however, when a girlfriend told her that she'd seen Scott getting into a hotel elevator with two girls. "He admitted he found them on Tinder looking for a threesome. One of them gave him an STD." As Kristen began to dig, she was broadsided by the extent of Scott's porn habit, his Tinder matches, and his occasional splurge on thousand-dollar-a-night escorts. "If I had been shaming him, nagging him, or rejecting him, I would understand, but this makes no sense to me."

And then there is Jonah, also in his thirties, married to Danielle, his college girlfriend. They have two kids and their sex life just seemed to have faded out, when Danielle discovered Jonah's weekly massages were of the "happy ending" variety, and his hours on the computer were not spent playing World of Warcraft.

Jonah, Scott, and Garth are three among many men who've shown up in my office with their confused, shocked, and often disgusted wives. This particular breed of adulterer is almost always male and heterosexual. They are usually married or in a committed relationship, and want to stay that way. They are responsible, loving fathers, sons, boyfriends, or husbands, the kind everyone turns to when they need help, cash, or advice. They could have an affair without opening their wallets if they were so inclined. And contrary to popular belief, there is often an attractive woman waiting at home, eager to sleep with them. Yet they are outsourcing their sex lives to hookers or hookups, strippers and online sex workers, erotic gaming or porn.

Why do these men export their lust, and why do they do so in transactional encounters? How can their wives reconcile the gentle man they know at home with the guy who slinks out of the gentleman's club?

In the past, going to a prostitute was often considered less egregious than cavorting with the neighbor's wife. It hurt, but it didn't endanger the marriage because he wasn't going to leave his wife for her. In fact, many people didn't even count sex workers as cheating, and some went so far as to declare that hookers exist so that men won't stray.

Today, however, many women view cheating with a prostitute as worse than a noncommercial affair. It immediately raises much broader and more distressing questions about the kind of men they are married to. What does it say about him that he would pay for sex or seek it in what they perceive to be such a degraded and degrading form?

It's easy to condemn these men, both for abandoning their wives and for participating in an industry that, in its darker forms, traffics, exploits, and subjugates women. There is an urge to write them off as entitled, misogynistic, hypersexed boys. And some of them are. But working with men like Garth, Scott, and Jonah has compelled me to delve deeper into the insecurities, fantasies, and emotional turmoil that can drive nice guys to moonlight in a shady world. What are they seeking in their fleeting trysts? If they pay, what are they really paying for? Clearly, there's sex sans strings. It's fun, it's different, it's exciting, it won't be interrupted by a crying baby. But is that the whole story? These men strike me as an interesting subsection of the unfaithful with something to teach us about the intersection of masculinity, infidelity, economics, and culture.

A Man's Desire: When Love and Lust Part Ways

"You're going to think I'm a complete jerk." It is my first session alone with Garth. He proceeds to tell me a "sordid" tale of the assorted infidelities that have played out, not just with Valerie, but in each of his two prior marriages.

"The same thing has happened each time," he notes. "It starts out hot and heavy. But after about a year, I lose all interest. I can't even get it up. This may sound strange, but it almost feels wrong to touch her."

His last comment is not so strange to me—it's an important clue to his impasse. It's one thing to lose interest; there are plenty of people for whom voraciousness mellows into tenderness. But what he describes is more visceral—an aversive sexual response to his partner, almost as though it would mean crossing a forbidden line. This sense of taboo alerts me to the possible presence of what therapist Jack Morin calls a "love-lust split."

"One of the key challenges of erotic life is to develop a comfortable interaction between our lusty urges and our desire for an affection-ate bond with a lover," Morin writes. I suspect that Garth's quest for sex on the outside is a manifestation of his inability to integrate closeness and sexual passion. Men in his predicament are not just bored, looking for novelty, ready to move on. "Believe me, I don't like it this way," Garth tells me. "I don't want to be the kind of guy who cheats. Plus, I feel very bad that I'm not able to satisfy Valerie, and I try to make up for it by taking care of her in all other ways. She thinks the ED is because of my diabetes, but this happened to me long before." Furthermore, he has no problem getting hard when he seeks pleasure on the lam.

Garth is not proud of his dalliances, but he had resigned himself to the idea that for him, love and lust could not exist under one roof, and he'd always been discreet. It was only Valerie's discovery that prompted further self-reflection. By the time we meet, he has already figured out that it has nothing to do with either his wife's attractiveness or the intensity of his love for her.

I affirm the conclusions he's come to so far. "For the record, I don't think you're a complete jerk. But clearly, there is a pattern here that has caused a lot of pain—both to your wives and to your-self. Listening to Valerie, I believe you know how to love. But some-thing in the way you love makes it hard for you to make love to the woman you love." Helping Garth to put a stop to his extramarital forays will have limited value unless I can also help him to under-stand what drives his inner split.

I ask him to tell me more about his childhood. Where there is a repeated sexual shutdown, like his, it generally indicates the pres-ence of underlying trauma. Our erotic proclivities and inhibitions originate in our early experiences and develop throughout our lives. Sometimes it takes a bit of psychological sleuthing to uncover sex-ual blocks, but very little in the erotic psyche is happenstance.

Garth's is a long, sad tale in which his father played a central role. An alcoholic and a violent man prone to bursts of wrath, he left both visible and invisible marks on his firstborn son. More often than not, Garth chose to take the blows to protect his helpless mother and his younger brother.

Terry Real, who has written extensively about men in relationships, describes a particular "unholy triangle" between "the powerful, irresponsible, and/or abusive father, the codependent, downtrodden wife, and the sweet son caught in the middle." These sons, he expands, become unhealthily enmeshed with their mothers, and as adults, they "become afraid of their own range of emotions." They are kind souls who feel they must curtail their own feelings and take responsibility for the happiness of Mom and the women who follow. Real calls this "intrusion trauma," which lives not just in the psyche but in the body—hence its power to inhibit physical intimacy. Garth fits this pattern well, and it goes some way toward explaining why he feels so beholden to the women he loves, yet is unable to be aroused by them.

The emotional resonance between his relationship with his parents and his relationship with his wife is so strong that it leads to an unfortunate cross-wiring. Hence, the feeling that sex is "wrong," almost incestuous. When a partner starts to feel too familial, sex will inevitably be the casualty. Ironic as it may seem, at that moment the taboo of infidelity feels less transgressive than sex at home.

Love always entails a feeling of responsibility and worry about the well-being of our beloved. But for some of us, these natural feelings can take on an extra weight, especially when a child has had to parent his parents. Finely attuned to the fragility and brittleness of the one he loves, he carries a sense of burden that impedes the letting go necessary for erotic intimacy and pleasure. Think of the trust game we play as kids, where we let ourselves fall back onto someone who catches us. So too in sex, you can let go only if you trust that the other is sturdy and will be able to receive the force of your desire.

For people like Garth, their outer behavior reflects this inner divide. There are many variations on the love-lust split, for men and women alike, but in Garth's case, it is an extension of his childhood wounds. Many boys who were beaten by their fathers promise themselves they will never be like that and try very hard to repress any form of aggression. The problem is that in attempting to control this disavowed emotion, they end up stifling their ability to be sexual with the ones they love.

I explain to Garth that desire needs a certain degree of aggression—not violence, but an assertive, striving energy. It's what allows you to pursue, to want, to take, and even to sexualize your partner. The prominent sexuality researcher Robert Stoller describes this kind of objectification as an essential ingredient of sexuality—not treating the other as an object, but seeing the other as an independent sexual being. It creates the healthy distance that allows you to eroticize your partner, which is essential if you want to remain sexual with a person who becomes family.

For men who are afraid of their own aggression and seek to segregate it, desire becomes alienated from love. For them, the greater the emotional intimacy, the greater the sexual reticence. Men with extreme versions of this split often end up affectionate but sexless with their partners, while avidly consuming hard-core porn or engaging in various forms of transactional sex. In these emotionless contexts, their desire can manifest freely without the fear of hurting a loved one.

Some may associate the love-lust split with Freud's madonna-whore complex, and they are certainly related. However, the way I conceptualize the divide is not only about how the woman is perceived but also about a split in the man's identity. The part that loves, that feels intensely attached and responsible, is the good boy. The part that lusts becomes the bad boy—ruthless, subversive, irresponsible. I could sum it up as follows: They can say "fuck me" sexually only when they have said "fuck you" emotionally. Callous as that may sound, every man who has lived with this relational framework recognizes it on the spot.

When I talk with the partners of these men, I often find myself unpacking the appeal of the girl on the stage, on the street corner, or on the screen. The obvious explanation is that he's after her physical assets. But is this really the primary draw? What they highlight in our conversations is not her looks but her attitude. Her act presents a woman who is anything but fragile. She is sexually assertive, even demanding, and never reminds him of his victimized mother or his overwhelmed wife. Her confidence and availability are a turn-on that frees him from any caretaking responsibilities. As psychoanalyst Michael Bader has written, her lustfulness allays the fear that he's imposing his primitive, even predatory, urges on her. Hence, his inner conflict around his own aggression is temporarily lifted. He can safely let go in ways that he is unable to do with the wife that he loves and respects.

Love-lust splits come in many forms. For some, it occurs when the partner is enlisted—willingly or not—in a parental role. This may be the classic "I married someone like my mommy/daddy," or it may be quite the opposite: "I married someone who could be the mommy/daddy I never had." It may simply be the role of motherhood. One woman told me that with baby number one, her partner didn't touch her from the moment she started showing till the moment she lost the weight. With baby number two, same thing. She hungered for touch, let alone for sex, but he seemed repulsed. By the time baby number three came along, she filled the vacancy with a lover who delighted in the erotics of fertility.

However it occurs, the over-familialization of an intimate part-ner spells disaster for sex. The person becomes divested of his or her erotic identity. The relationship may be very loving, affectionate, and tender, but it is devoid of desire.

The love-lust split is one of the most challenging infidelity scenar-ios I confront. It's easy to think that if these men didn't have their side action, they would simply bring their libidos home. But I've seen many who extinguish their parallel flames only to find themselves shut down and unable to reignite the home fires. For some, the divide is so vast that it's difficult to help them find a way out.

More often, there's a lurking trap. One of the roving husband's flings turns more serious. He falls in love and thinks he's found the holy grail: for the first time in a long while, he loves and de-sires the same woman. Convinced that he must have just been with the wrong person, he leaves his family and his marriage for his new sweetie, only to find himself back in the same predicament a short while later. Garth is on his third time around.

His wife, Valerie, knows the odds are stacked against her. She saw this happen before in the role of his last lover. Now she's the wife, and she'll be damned if she sits by and waits for him to divorce her. First she takes a pragmatic approach. "If you're going to have a lover, I'll have one, too! I don't want to spend the last thirty years of my life home alone eating Chocolate Cherry Garcia. I intend to have a great third act." But Garth won't hear of it.

"That's not a marriage!" he counters. So often, the same man who won't touch his wife can't bear the thought that someone else might do so. There is a little boy inside, terrified he might lose his mommy.

"I won't live with him constantly blowing smoke up my ass," Valerie fumes. "It's so demeaning, and it weakens him! He's just a skeevy little lying fuck. How am I to build intimacy with someone

I can't respect?" She files for divorce, hopeful that next time she'll find a man in whom love and lust have come to a better understanding.

Dispelling the Masculine Mystique

Scott comes to see me alone. Kristin has told him flat out that none of his explanations make any sense, and he'd better "deal with his shit fast." My task is to help this young man understand why he lost interest in his beautiful, accomplished girlfriend, and instead is spending hours every day swiping and watching porn.

Scott grew up in Houston, Texas. A popular football player in high school and college, he's always had plenty of girlfriends and has always supplemented his sanctioned engagements with plenty of extracurricular flings. He and Kristen, a model turned physical therapist, have been dating for almost two years.

"Tell me about the beginning of your relationship. You didn't have any trouble making love to her at first?"

"Not at all. We had sex every day—sometimes a few times in a day."

"Really?" I ask.

"Yeah, well, that's what I'm supposed to do, isn't it? If I don't have sex with her every day, she'll think I'm not into her."

"But did you want to have sex every day?" I probe.

"To be honest, I didn't always feel like it, but I did it anyway. I'm not saying I didn't enjoy it, but sometimes I would worry that I wasn't going to last very long. I didn't know if she came or if she enjoyed it as much as she had with other guys. So I got a prescription for Viagra, which Kristen didn't know about. Sometimes I would take it even when I was naturally aroused, just to impress her."

I inquire as to whether he had ever asked Kristen what she wanted, or was he just assuming she was looking for some kind of stallion? He admits he never asked.

"So what happened when the stallion got tired?" I ask. "How did it stop?"

He tells me it was gradual at first, but over time, he found himself spending more time on his phone than in his bed. At first he was not even concerned—after all, he'd been watching porn since he was twelve.

Scott's sex ed started in the locker room. "One of my older teammates showed me some good sites." Girls were plentiful, but he wasn't too confident, so he got into drinking "to feel less tense." In college, he pledged to a fraternity—full of guys who bragged about scoring every night. "I've always had a sense of not really measuring up," he confesses.

For Scott, masculinity is equated with sexual performance, and he carries a whole set of expectations about love, men, and women that are impossible for him to live up to. Meanwhile, his girlfriend has her own expectations: She wants him to be more tender, communicative, and open about his feelings. But he doesn't want to be a puddle, either. This leaves him with a bunch of competing ideologies about what it means to be a man.

New definitions of masculinity are fast emerging, and modern men are encouraged to embrace a whole new suite of emotional skills that were not traditionally part of their repertoire. At the same time, the old definitions die hard. Too many men are ensnared in outdated and self-defeating ideals of male sexual prowess, which sire shame and humiliation. Advice columnist Irma Kurtz sums up this predicament: "Men are finding it ever more difficult to squeeze themselves and their erections into the shrinking maneuvering space between being a wimp or being a rapist."

A guy like Scott has grown up in a macho culture, where all he heard from his frat brothers was that dudes always want sex. He's also read a bunch of articles that make the same case. I inform him that most of these studies are done on young college students; hence we actually know very little about the sexuality of mature men. No wonder so many men are confused about themselves and each other. Most men don't know what the next guy is dealing with sexually, and there's a huge pressure to boast. The day a group of guys in a locker room start talking about how they feign headaches when their girlfriends are jumping them, the world will have changed.

In the meantime, it's little wonder that men like Scott are obsessed with performance—so are all the researchers. Studies of sexual desire are vastly skewed toward women. Why study male desire if we assume that it is always in ample supply? Hence, if the erection isn't there, it's a mechanical issue. We think of women's arousal as being on a spectrum, but for men it's all or nothing, hard or soft. None of these stereotypes is good for men's self-esteem or their relationships.

Scott is impatient to get to the bottom of things. "So what about the cheating?" he asks.

"We'll get there," I reply. But digging deeper into his ideas about masculinity will help us more accurately decode his sexual acting out. On the surface, his behavior plays out the stereotype of the "man on the hunt." But if we take it at face value, we end up reinforcing the very image of masculinity that has contributed to his erotic block in the first place.

Scott has bought into the oversold definition of male sexuality as being biologically driven, uncomplicated, ever ready, and always in search of novelty. The late psychoanalyst Ethel Person captures it perfectly: "This macho view depicts a large, powerful, untiring phallus attached to a very cool male, long on self-control, experienced, competent, and knowledgeable enough to make women crazy with desire."

Much good research has come out in recent years to highlight the multidimensionality of women's sexuality—its subjectivity, its relational character, its contextual nature, and its reliance on a delicate balance of conditions. However, an unintended by-product is that by contrast it has served to oversimplify and reinforce the reductionist notions about men. Once we grace both men and women with a more nuanced understanding of their sexuality, we will have a better grasp of their infidelity.

When it comes to desire, men and women are in fact more similar than they are different. Nothing in Scott's sexual blueprint makes me think that his sexuality is any less complicated or less emotional than the female version. Nor is it less relational. When I hear the pressure Scott puts on himself to please his girlfriend, the way he grades himself by the number of her orgasms, and his fear that she liked it better with previous boyfriends, I hear shame, performance anxiety, and fear of rejection. "What else should we call these emotions if not relational?" I ask him.

I help Scott to make the connection between his bedroom troubles and these unacknowledged feelings. The sadness and depression that he felt upon losing his mother no doubt play a role. We also talk about his anxiety, and in particular, the feeling he has of being a fraud—projecting a confidence that is only an act. He admits that he's not told Kristen or any of his entrepreneurial friends that his business is teetering. "I don't want them to think I'm a loser."

Men's sexuality is dependent on their inner life. It's more than just a biological urge. Sex, gender, and identity are deeply interrelated for men. If a man has low self-esteem or feels depressed, anxious, insecure, ashamed, guilty, or alone, it has a direct effect on how he feels about himself sexually. If he feels dissed in his job, too small, too short, too fat, too poor, it can directly impact his ability to become aroused.

I let Scott ponder these new thoughts for a while. It helps him make sense, he tells me, of why he lost interest in Kristen, especially after his mother's death and during the tough months with his company. "But how come I was still interested in sex anywhere but with my girlfriend?"

This is where men and women differ. Men are much more likely to soothe their inner rumblings by turning to less emotionally complicated forms of sex, including solitary pleasures and paid ones. In fact, I can imagine that the level of dissociation that they bring to their sexual fixes is a direct response to all these uncomfortable emotional pulls. I would suggest that precisely because male sexuality is so relational, many guys seek sexual spaces that are the exact opposite, where they don't have to confront the litany of fears, anxieties, and insecurities that would render the biggest stallion limp. The degree of freedom and control they seek in their anonymous encounters is often proportional to the depth of their relational entanglements.

Perhaps it should not be surprising at all that in a world where men are receiving such conflicting messages about who they are and who they should be, so many of them prefer porn, paid sex, or anonymous hookups over relational intimacy. I don't think it's an accident that I've observed an increase in emotionally disengaged acts of infidelity in tandem with the rise of the emotionally engaged man. Sitting in a strip club, hiring a hooker, swiping right, or watching porn, guys can take a break from the tightrope of modern masculinity.

Part of the appeal of paid sex in particular is the promise that, at least for the sixty minutes the hooker is on the clock, she'll take away these complexities. And the girl on the screen is irresistible because he never has to seduce her and she never rejects him. Neither does she make him feel inadequate, and her moans assure him that she is having the best of times. Porn entices with a momentary promise to shield men from their basic sexual vulnerabilities.

A lot can be said about the differences between prostitutes, strip clubs, full body massage, and porn, but in this sense they all yield common emotional dividends. They put men at the center of the woman's attention, relieved of any pressure to perform and in a position where they can fully receive.

After listening to the stories of men, I've come to understand the following: In light of the multiple emotional transactions involved in marital lovemaking, the simple equation of a few bucks for an anonymous fuck starts to seem like a better deal. When he prefers to pay to play or opts for a solo porn session, he buys simplicity and a seemingly uncomplicated identity. He purchases the right to be selfish—a brief hour of psychological freedom before hopping on the commuter train home. As more than one man has said to me, you don't pay the hooker to come—you pay her to leave.

Even so, can we really call it "just sex" when the entire enterprise is set up to avoid certain emotional pitfalls and fulfill a host of unspoken emotional needs? When a man feels lonely or unloved; when he's depressed, stressed, or disabled; when he's caged by intimacy or unable to connect, is it sex he buys or is it kindness, warmth, friendship, escape, control, and validation all delivered in a sexual transaction?

Sexuality is the sanctioned language through which men can access a range of forbidden emotions. Tenderness, softness, vulnerability, and nurturance have not traditionally been encouraged for men. The body is the place where they have sought to satisfy these needs disguised in a sexualized language. When we say about men that all they want is sex, maybe we shouldn't take this literally. Sex is the entrance to their emotional antechamber.

Interestingly, the opposite may be true of women. Their sexual needs have not been culturally sanctioned, but their emotional needs are well acknowledged. Perhaps hidden in women's pursuit of love lies a host of physical yearnings that can be justified only when wrapped in an emotional package. This turns the old adage that "men use love to get sex, while women use sex to get love" on its head.

Both men and women turn up in the therapist's office when their disavowed desires lead them to the wrong bed. But if we take their behavior at face value and label them with the old tags—men as cheaters, sex addicts, or worse; women as lonely and love-starved—their true motives and longings are driven deeper underground.

Sex and the Sensitive Guy

"It was only a hand job," Jonah told himself, "so it wasn't technically cheating." This was how he justified his penchant for full body sensual massage, or FBSM, otherwise known as massage with a happy ending. Like Scott, he's in his early thirties, lives with a woman he loves, and procures his orgasms with a click or a credit card. But that's where the resemblance ends. While Scott's gender template is based on machismo, Jonah is the quintessential "new man." Raised by a single mom, he has been drilled in the arts of empathy, emotional literacy, consent, and equity—which makes it all the more interesting that these two young men have ended up in such similar predicaments.

After a few months of visiting the masseuse, it was no longer enough for Jonah to lie on the table. He initiated oral sex with his favorite practitioner, Renée, and she gladly reciprocated. Jonah continued to rationalize. "I was paying for it, so it wasn't an affair. There was no risk of falling in love. I was getting release that I wasn't getting elsewhere, so I was preserving my marriage."

The marriage in question had become part of the growing phenomenon of professional wives and stay-at-home husbands. Danielle and Jonah, both in their thirties, have been together since their junior year in college. They have two young kids and live in North Carolina's Research Triangle. Danielle recently stumbled upon the evidence of her husband's alternative erotic portfolio.

Jonah's sexual escapades were inspired by a compendium of familiar insecurities. "I was a geek, didn't think of myself as very sexual, and couldn't last very long. I hadn't had many girlfriends before Danielle." He'd felt so lucky to be chosen by this outgoing, smart, pretty girl, but intimidated by the studly boyfriends who had come before him. "I knew she had been with jocks, and I was quite the opposite," he says.

Danielle tells me that she loved his sensitive side. While she admits to occasionally hankering after a more assertive lover, she felt she had picked the perfect guy in every other respect: loving, loyal, and emotionally available, and frankly, too insecure to pursue other women like her philandering father had done. Or so she thought.

I examine the emotional back end of their relationship. While to the rest of the world Danielle presented herself as a confident go-getter, she longed to not always have to be "on." With Jonah, she felt she could drop her guard, express her ups and downs, and even let herself fall apart, trusting that he would be there to pick up the pieces. His emotional reliability allowed her the luxury of vulnerability. It was well worth the sacrifice of any sexual mismatch.

For his part, Jonah had felt affirmed as a man by this powerful, sexy woman, and hoped she would redeem him from his geeky self-image. What a surprise, then, when he slowly realized that she wanted him to remain that guy. He had been recruited for a role he was all too good at—taking care of a woman's needs, which was exactly what he'd done when he supported his mom through her divorce. But secretly he resented the hegemony of her wants. To be clear, neither Danielle nor his mother had ever asked for such sacrifice, but this is what loving boys do.

For years Danielle and Jonah wished for more erotic zest, but both colluded in creating the vacancy. Danielle had a real stake in keeping Jonah in a caretaking role and assuming he was incapable of roaming. By desexualizing him, she made him safe. And Jonah's problem was not that he couldn't sexualize his wife, it was that he couldn't sexualize himself.

When I ask them to describe to me their erotic erosion, Jonah says, "I just wasn't that into it." Danielle took frequent business trips, and he started frequenting the growing world of Internet porn. He didn't even have to leave the house, but it was a journey nonetheless. "Twenty minutes of searching for thirty seconds of watching," he comments. It was that same sense of adventure that eventually led him away from the screen and into the massage parlors.

Why would a guy like Jonah rather go and jack off to porn or get himself a rub and tug than be with the wife he loves and once couldn't keep his hands off of? Just as I did with Garth and Scott, I seek to analyze the emotional economics of his erotic ventures and thus better understand his infidelity.

In his parallel lust life, Jonah found escape from the constraints of the nice, sensitive, domesticated guy. "I felt like I'd never fully developed sexually. For the first time, I could express myself unabashedly. I felt desirable, powerful, more than adequate, manly. I wasn't just a nice guy—I could be a womanizer and a cheater and a liar, and there was a major thrill in that. I felt bad—but in a good way."

And where does this leave his wife? Danielle too had been sexually unsatisfied in the marriage. The twist is that while her husband pursued his own sexual awakening in the socially condemned environment of the massage parlor, she had been lying at home reading the socially sanctioned *Fifty Shades of Grey*. I'm not making these a moral equivalent, but in the world of fantasy they have something in common, as I point out to the couple. She's reading about the guy that he is trying to be somewhere else—the guy she doesn't want him to be at home.

These are confounding times for couples. Eroticism is not always politically correct. The great gifts of contemporary Western culture—democracy, consensus building, egalitarianism, fairness, and mutual tolerance—can, when taken too punctiliously in the bedroom, result in very boring sex. The rebalancing of gender roles represents one of the greatest advances of modern society. It has improved our sexual rights immeasurably, but as Daphne Merkin writes in the *New York Times Magazine*, "No bill of sexual rights can hold its own against the lawless and untamable landscape of the erotic imagination." Sexual desire doesn't always play by the rules of good citizenship. That doesn't mean we should head back to the dark old days of siloed gender roles, patriarchal privilege, and female subjugation. But it's important to analyze our sexual choices—both sanctioned and illicit—within the frame of the culture of the day.

A Different Kind of Happy Ending

So what's a woman to do when she discovers that her seemingly vanilla husband has a hidden spice cabinet? In some instances, realizing that one's partner has an entire sexual self that one has never met is irreconcilable with the rest of one's reality. In others, it can be the beginning of a new shared space. Some partners cannot get over their repulsion at the form the infidelity has taken. Their finger is pointing directly to the door. But I've also seen times when the discovery of an unknown erotic being elicits curiosity. Jonah and Danielle were lucky enough to fall into this second category. His infidelity hurt, but it also showed her that he had it in him—he could be manly, after all. Her perception of him as "a relatively low-libido guy" changed dramatically. Their sex life boomed. And along with the increase in sex came something even more important: an increase in sexual honesty.

Sexual honesty isn't just about divulging the details of your infidelities. It's about communicating with your partner in an open and mature way—revealing core aspects of yourself through your sexuality. Sometimes it means bringing out of the closet secrets that have been hidden for a lifetime—for both partners. While emotional transparency is touted everywhere as the crux of modern intimacy, I am amazed at the paucity of real sexual communication between partners. Part of my work in post-infidelity involves direct coaching as to how, why, where, and when to talk about sex.

Jonah took this advice to heart. Once Danielle let him know that she was ready to hear, he told her what he had learned about himself as a man in his sexual explorations. They both invited each other into their personal red-light districts. "Things that I thought would spell disaster for our relationship—for example, telling her that I fantasize about having sex with someone we know—have instead opened up a new dimension," he says. "As I felt more accepted, I felt more attracted to her."

On her side, a greater understanding of the recesses of Jonah's erotic interiority helped to put his infidelity into a different light.

While it didn't take away the pain, what was once seen as sexual defiance became a portal for the disclosure of long-standing hidden wishes.

As their sex life became more engaged, they started to be more experimental. They watched "ethical porn." They went to a strip club together and Danielle got a lap dance. She told him she had always fantasized about being with another woman. "At some point we arrived at the idea of trying FBSM together," he says. "I wanted her to experience what I loved so much—the joy of being 100 percent at the center of someone's sexual attention and being able to just lay back and be pleasured."

Danielle chose the practitioner, and Jonah dealt with the logistics. That way, he says, "I was still able to experience the thrill of arranging and anticipating an FBSM session, and I could do this without risking my marriage and my family." They both found the experience to be quite a turn-on. What was once forbidden and hurtful has become "a joint, shared adventure."

Jonah feels more integrated, and as a result, is less likely to take his libidinal needs offshore. For this couple, it was true that, as Janis Abrahms Spring provocatively suggests, "You may eventually discover that you needed a nuclear explosion like an affair to blow your previous construction apart and allow a healthier, more conscious and mature version to take its place."

To be clear, I am not prescribing infidelity as a solution to marital gridlock. Nor am I suggesting that a threesome is the healing balm for every broken heart. I could never have anticipated the innovative path that Jonah and Danielle took in reimagining their relationship. Although their choice is certainly not for everyone, it speaks to the resilience and the creativity of couples.

When Danielle asks him if he would ever do it again, Jonah confesses that he misses the exclusiveness he felt when he was the center of Renée's attention. And sometimes he longs for the bad boy he had just gotten to know. "I miss whatever part of me was stimulated by the secrets, the danger, the thrill. But I have decided that the great place you and I have arrived at is too valuable to put at risk." His honesty, rather than scaring her, calms her. She understands him better now, and their trust is buttressed by a freedom to share their thoughts and desires truthfully, without shame. The growing sense of acceptance they both feel is one of the strongest protectors against future betrayal.

Sex Addiction: The Medicalization of Adultery

Each of these infidelity stories embraces a complex conundrum of personal, cultural, and physical factors. But in discussing these cases with my colleagues, they would often furnish a different explanation: sex addiction. Garth, Scott, and Jonah each fit most of the common criteria for this malady du jour—all organized around the notion of "excess" and lack of control.

Sex addiction is a hot topic in therapy circles, and it is not my intention to get entangled in the contentious debate. However, I could not complete a chapter focused on men who compulsively seek out sex without at least spending a moment on the matter.

While there is no official diagnosis for sex addiction, many researchers and clinicians have rushed to define the disorder, borrowing criteria from clinical definitions of chemical dependency. An entire industry has sprung up in response, including expensive rehab and treatment centers. Some clinicians welcome the label as evidence that what was once considered "men just being men" is no longer normal or acceptable. Others point out the lack of scientific evidence, and see the sex-addiction diagnosis as a medicalized mask for therapists' judgments about what kind of sex is or is not healthy.

Whatever we call it, sexually compulsive behavior is a real issue for many people, and both they and their loved ones suffer tremendous pain as a consequence. Lives, reputations, and families have been destroyed by it. For some men, being able to name their behavior as a disease is a positive step, lifting the shame enough to enable them to seek desperately needed help. But even if we call it a disease, it hasn't lost its stigma. I have sat with more than one mother who struggled to tell her children, "I'm leaving your father because he's a sex addict," whereas she wouldn't have faced the same mortification over an alcoholic spouse. Another wife insisted that she preferred the medical label of addict—rather than compulsive— because it meant that her husband had a bona fide condition. But the husband in question had his own preferred label: asshole. At least that way, he had agency over his behavior and wasn't just an out-of-control compulsive.

To be sure, the diagnosis of sex addiction has become the latest spin on an old culture war. The issue of what is too little or too much sex—what is normal or aberrant, natural or unnatural—has preoccupied and polarized humankind forever. Every religious or cultural system has regulated license and abstinence, permission and prohibition. Sexual norms and sexual pathologies have never existed apart from the morals of their time, and they are inextricably bound up with economics, gender ideals, and power structures. As a case in point, when female chastity was prized, women used to be diagnosed as nymphomaniacs; today we prize female sexual assertiveness, and we invest millions trying to fix the new curse, "hyposexual desire disorder." Similarly, the rise of the diagnosis of sex addiction is a fascinating study in the social construction of ills. It echoes an age-old fear that too much sex, especially for men, is a slippery slope to a life of deviance. (Interestingly, women are rarely diagnosed with sex addiction; we prefer to see them as being addicted to love—a no less slippery slope, I would say, but a more flattering one.)

When we medicalize behavior like Garth's, Scott's, and Jonah's, we should be mindful of the pitfall of "premature evaluation," as my colleague Douglas Braun-Harvey calls it. The broader range of their motives—personal, familial, and societal—needs to be taken into account if men are to better understand and integrate their own sexuality, and if their partners (and their therapists) are to respond constructively to their infidelity.

CHAPTER 12

THE MOTHER OF ALL BETRAYALS?

Affairs Among Other Marital Misdemeanors

The bonds of wedlock are so heavy that it takes
two to carry them, sometimes three.
—Alexandre Dumas, père

"At least I didn't go and fuck someone else," Dexter spits. No, he didn't. But for years, he has been routinely bullying his wife, Mona, patronizing her, and ridiculing her fear of flying. He even has made a habit of taking their kids on trips that involve several planes, leaving her stranded on the ground. While he has been a good father and a consistent provider, he has just as consistently made sure she is kept in the dark about their finances. She always has plenty in her account, he insists, but his tone makes it clear that he thinks she's inept. It's no surprise that she felt lonely and inferior—until, after twenty-two years of living under this benevolent dictator, she met Robert, ten years her junior. For the past six months, Mona has discovered kindness and realized that she actually has interesting things to say.

A trickle of confidence has begun to flow. Accustomed to a more brittle wife, Dexter noticed an unusual resilience to his put-downs, throwing him into an unfamiliar state of insecurity and suspicion. He put a GPS in her car, and the rest was obvious. Armed with new indignation, he appropriates her affair to his cause and feels justified in doubling the dose of insults, which now include "whore!" and "slut!"

The current zeitgeist in America is unequivocal: Infidelity is the worst thing that can happen in a marriage. The breach of trust it causes can surpass the severity of domestic violence, of gambling away all the family savings, and even of incest. In a 2013 Gallup poll, 91 percent of American adults responded that infidelity was "morally wrong." People condemn cheating at much higher rates than any of the other morally dubious behaviors listed in the poll, including polygamy (83 percent), human cloning (83 percent), suicide (77 percent), and, most interestingly, divorce (24 percent). In an analysis of the poll, *The Atlantic*'s Eleanor Barkhorn remarked, "It's difficult to think of any other relatively common and technically legal practice of which more of us disapprove." Situations like Mona's, however, have led me to question the assumption that unfaithfulness is the mother of all betrayals.

Working in the trenches of couples therapy has cautioned me not to impute moral superiority to a guy like Dexter just because he didn't stray. His brand of fidelity borders on vindictiveness and codependence, and his years of treating his wife so poorly also spell betrayal with a capital B. Indeed, too many partners whose behavior is subpar will eagerly vilify the one who cheats and claim victimhood, confident that the cultural bias is in their favor. Infidelity hurts. But when we grant it a special status in the hierarchy of marital misdemeanors, we risk allowing it to overshadow the egregious behaviors that may have preceded it or even led to it.

Betrayal comes in many forms, and sexual betrayal is just one of them. I regularly encounter those for whom sexual faithfulness is the easiest faithfulness to sustain, even as they break their vows daily in so many other ways. The victim of the affair is not always the victim of the marriage.

Why didn't Mona just leave? She thought about it, even voiced the idea many times. But Dexter just took it as new fodder for his scorn. "Where would you go? Who would want a useless, fifty-something washed-up woman like you?" Her bond with Robert nurtured the strength she needed to even know that there was an alternative to her cage. Now that Mona's filing for divorce, Dexter's intimidation tactics no longer dictate her every move. Her friend helped her find a shark of a lawyer who will expose the concealed finances behind his apparent magnanimity.

Bringing in a third party to disrupt an unhealthy relationship can be an act of cowardice, but it can also be a source of courage. Sometimes we need the actual experience of being with another person to taste a sweeter life and have the guts to go after it. For people who live in the swamp of emotional torments that signify common marital sadism—neglect, indifference, intimidation, contempt, rejection, and disdain—infidelity may be an expression of self-preservation and self-determination. Fidelity, in a destructive relationship, is sometimes more akin to weakness than virtue. Being stuck should not be confused with being faithful. For those who live with physical abuse, trading the hands that strike for hands that caress is a gesture of bold defiance. On a personal as well as on a political level, a breach is sometimes the necessary doorway into a new social order.

My point here is not to transfer the blame, but to highlight the multiple dynamics of power and powerlessness that permeate relationships. "Who betrayed whom first?" is a legitimate question that many are afraid to ask.

Rodrigo couldn't muster up an apology. He knew he hurt Alessandra when he extended a business trip for a more personal kind of business. But every time he began to say, "I'm sorry," he would think of the years of aggressive lack of interest his wife had perfected and a feeling of justification would surge inside of him. "Who should really apologize here?" he demands.

Julie wrote to me that her husband had been "emotionally unfaithful for twenty years." But she wasn't talking about another woman. "He stood me up for concerts, dinners, vacations—always putting his work first. My sister says, at least he didn't cheat on me, but his job was more demanding than any mistress. Now I met a man with plenty of time for me, and *I'm* the unfaithful one?"

Displaced intimacy comes in many forms. "Russ's primary relationship was with crystal meth," says Connor. "I begged him for years to cut back and get help, but the high was clearly more pleasurable than my company. And now he's upset that I found a guy who is actually into me."

Why is one form of diverted attention an indisputable violation of trust, while another gets couched in nicer words? While it appears that each of these seekers was looking for sex, they were also looking for depth, appreciation, lingering gazes—all the other forms of penetration that don't involve physical intercourse. Call it intimacy, call it human connection—it's what makes us feel that we matter.

If the first question that such scenarios typically provoke is "Why didn't they leave?" the next predictable question is "Did they try talking about it?" In the era of democratic couples communication, we believe in the talking cure. And to be sure, there's nothing like a good heart-to-heart to make us feel heard. But when our lamentations fall on deaf ears, the loneliness is worse than being alone. It's less painful to eat by ourselves than to sit across the table from someone who has tuned us out.

Many despondent partners have tried every variation of talking. They started out gentle and considerate; they ended angry and defeated. When they eventually stop begging, and take their battered hearts' desires elsewhere, their indifferent partners finally begin to take note. Could they have gone about it any other way? Of course. But the adulterous alarm system can shake up a calcified couple like nothing else.

The Rebellion of the Rejected

Being cheated on makes people feel insignificant, but feeling insignificant for years on end may lead people to cheat. When the kids are young and needy and their father is once more out at the sports bar watching a game with his buddies, extramarital appreciation can feel like a tonic. When your marriage has become Home Management Inc. and you talk only about logistics, the poetry of an affair is a spiritual uplifting from the mind-numbing prose of the everyday. When your partner disappears at six P.M. each day to the den with his six-pack, you have ample time to go online and look for a guy with a different kind of six-pack. When you're tired of fighting over every stupid thing, a colleague who appreciates your sense of humor reminds you that you were once more than just a bitch. The list of resentments, micro-aggressions, and dismissals that stoke our need to seek respite elsewhere is long and varied. Marital gloom cries for escape. And never more so than when the marriage in question is devoid of physical intimacy.

It may seem obvious that secretly transferring our desires outside the marital bed trespasses on our commitments. But how are we to think about those situations when the marital bed might as well have a No Entry sign on the headboard? I don't mean a general decline in frequency to once a week or even once a month. Some degree of waning desire is natural over the course of a relationship, and differences in libido are to be expected and managed. I'm talking about partners who have steadfastly been unresponsive to the sexual advances of their mates for years or even decades, even while they remain affectionate and close. Nobody wants to return to domestic rape or duty sex, but we also need to acknowledge that when one partner unilaterally decides there will be no (or very little) sex, that is not monogamy—it's enforced celibacy.

How should we deal with the loss of the erotic? It may seem reductionist to concentrate on sexual ills, but I have come to respect the power of sexual deprivation for what it is. Our culture tends to minimize the importance of sex for the well-being of a couple. It is seen as optional. Companionate coupledom has many merits, and there are plenty of people who nurture affectionate relationships without suffering sexual agony. But when sex is woefully lacking, and not by mutual agreement, it can leave a gap in an otherwise satisfying relationship that is unbearable. And when we haven't been touched in years, we are more vulnerable to the kindness of strangers.

Marlene tells me that for her, an affair would have been easier to bear than her husband's absolute rebuff of her sexual advances. "I didn't even have the cold comfort of knowing he lusted after someone else. There was no third party involved on whom to lay all the blame."

I have received countless letters from famished lovers across the globe who feel desperate, raging, sad, defeated, self-doubting, lonely, unseen, and untouched. And contrary to stereotypes, they're not all men. It isn't only women who feign headaches.

Isabelle can count on one hand the times she and Paul have had sex during their ten-year marriage, and she doesn't have to use all her fingers. "Within weeks of our wedding, he lost interest," she says. "I went through every imagined cause: Is he cheating, is he gay, was he one of those boys who was abused by a priest?" She's tried talking about it, going to counseling, and initiating sex in every adventurous way she can, but to no avail. Paul's silence is confounding. He's had his testosterone checked (normal) and tried Viagra (successful physically, but left him grossed out). Isabelle says she's hung in with him through all this because he is a good man and she takes the commitment of marriage seriously. But recently she met a man in church. "Nothing has happened yet," she tells me, "but I'm standing on the edge of a precipice."

Brad feels at the mercy of Pam's "I don't feel sexy" mood. "Every night, her iPad is there between us, like a sex shield. I bought her lingerie and asked her to wear it for me, but four weeks later it's sitting on the chair, still wrapped. She only wants to spoon, which means 'you soothe me, then we go to sleep.' I can't be in a relationship where I'm so sexually frustrated, but she tells me she can't do anything about it! She feels like she is not enough for me, although I tell her every day she is all I want."

"After the condom failed and Louise became pregnant for the fourth time, I wanted to terminate the pregnancy, but she refused," Christophe recounts. "I'm a responsible man, so I knew I had to stick around to take care of the kids and her. But in her wish to be the mom she never had, she completely forgot that she was a wife. She nursed for seven years altogether. That's a lot of oxytocin! I was completely out of the picture. No affection, no kisses, no sex. I had my first affair when my second daughter was eighteen months old. With or without sideshows, our sex life has been a drought for years. I find it outrageous that she insists my infidelity killed our marriage."

All Samantha wanted was a partner to grow old with. "I never imagined I would sit with my husband in a rocking chair and harbor guilt over cheating." But after ten years as a faithful wife, her marriage deteriorated. "I changed. He began sleeping in another bed—because he snored, couldn't sleep, his back hurt. I begged him to come back, but he said lots of married couples sleep in separate beds. Our sex life dwindled to five-minute drive-bys, which were completely unsatisfying for me. I was doing it all on my own—the money, the house, the kids. Sure, he was home every night, but absent."

On Craigslist, Samantha met Ken, also married and frustrated. Then she met Richard on Ashley Madison, same story. "So here I am. A married woman with a local married friend with benefits and a long-distance married boyfriend." Sometimes she's shocked at herself; sometimes she feels guilty. But she doesn't want to stop. "I can't go back to the deadness."

Commentators on sexless marriages have decided that fewer than ten times a year might as well be nothing. Who knows how they came up with that number? Fifteen to 20 percent of couples apparently belong to this category. So if you have sex eleven times a year, consider yourself blessed. If you want to see the fate you've narrowly escaped, check out the popular Reddit forum deadbedrooms (membership in the tens of thousands). Big data analyst Seth Stephens-Davidowitz reports in the *New York Times* that Google searches for "sexless marriage" outnumber searches related to any other marital issue.

Clearly, a lot of people are mourning the death of eros. And there are even more who may meet the requirements for sexual frequency but lack any satisfaction. Their lamentations land in my inbox daily.

"My partner shows little interest in my body other than intercourse. Foreplay feels like he is cranking a Model T. Within moments of getting in bed, he puts his knee between my legs and checks for wetness. I've tried so many times to talk to him, gently and with lots of praise, about what I like and what turns me on. Result: I am told no one ever complained before. After years of this, I worry that I am allowing my fear of being alone to be stronger than my self-respect."

Willa continued to have sex with Brian, but she felt little enjoyment or connection. "It was merely something I had to do, and less pleasant than most of the other household chores. Then one day it occurred to me that maybe I didn't hate sex; I just hated sex with my husband. I went outside the marriage to test the theory. And you can imagine, I wasn't wrong."

Gene says, "I'd love to play, go slow, but she just grabs my dick and puts it inside her. She makes me come to get it over with." What are all these languishing partners supposed to do?

I spend many hours working to reignite desire with couples who have lost the spark. We begin with the more common causes that can underlie sexual shutdown—parental violence, early sexual abuse, racism, poverty, illness, loss, unemployment, and so on. These multiple disempowerments leave people feeling that they live in a world where trust and pleasure are too dangerous. We explore their erotic templates, how their emotional history expresses itself in the physicality of sex. "Tell me how you were loved and I will know a lot about how you make love" is one of my guiding questions. Unearthing these issues helps to release the sexual blocks.

I intervene in couples' relational jams, helping them work through accumulated grievances. I teach them how to turn their criticisms into requests and their frustrations into feedback, and to be open and vulnerable with each other. As these knots are untied, couples can learn to use their imaginations to cultivate pleasure. I encourage them to stop taking sex so deadly seriously, and instead to tap into their playfulness, building anticipation and mystery in and out of the bedroom. In addition, I have a playbook of interventions to help people reconnect with the sensorial, the sensual, the sacredness of intimacy. They involve a lot more than just talking. I collaborate with sex educators, trauma therapists, Tantra practitioners, sexological body workers, dance teachers, fashion consultants, acupuncturists, nutritionists—anyone who can help. Sexuality intersects with all these modalities.

Some manage to turn the tide. But others, despite their best efforts, are unable to bring back the erotic rush. Are these couples just meant to accept that they can't have it all—that sometimes sex is the price of preserving a family? Or is sex such a fundamental part of life that its absence warrants dismantling an otherwise loving marriage?

How good can a relationship be when the sexual intimacy is gone? I'm not just talking about sex, the act: foreplay, penetration, orgasm, sleep. I mean the sensual, erotic energy that separates an adult romantic relationship from one among siblings or best friends. Does a sexless marriage inevitably set us up for infidelity?

As long as both partners are okay with the situation, love can flourish and stability abounds. But when one person is filled with unmet longings that stretch from one life stage to the next, they become like dry brush waiting for a spark. Given this dual mandate of sexual fidelity and sexual abstinence, we needn't be surprised when the lustful urge finally bursts free.

For Matt, it seems like it's been forever, although he can't pinpoint exactly when the sex disappeared. He and Mercedes, married ten years, met in their early thirties and married soon thereafter. In the beginning, they had sex because it felt nice. Then they had sex to make babies: Sasha, now seven, and Finn, four. Next they had no sex *because* of the babies. After that, they had perfunctory sex because a little was better than nothing. And then they simply had no sex. By the time I met them, Finn was sleeping with his mom in the king-size bed and Matt had scrunched up on the couch in the den. Mercedes wanted to want, but she didn't miss it that much. As a matter of fact, she'd never been particularly into sex. And she had other priorities now.

It was plain to see that they had organized around his desire and her refusal. In the beginning, he hotly pursued her and she was in the responsive role. She welcomed his advances. Gradually her interest gave way to resistance, and his wanting morphed into neediness. That was such a turnoff that it made her double down on her withdrawal. The more he begged, the more put off she was. And the more closed she was, the more clingy he became. In a classic pursuer-distancer dynamic, each of them would reinforce in the other the very behavior they abhorred.

On Monday, Matt stated his yearnings clearly. On Wednesday, he would merely hint, so as not to burden her or activate her sense of sexual inadequacy. By Friday, he would touch her so lightly that if she didn't respond, he could pretend he'd never asked.

On occasion, Mercedes engaged in reflection. "What's broken about me? You just flip a switch, while I'm scraping to get a flicker." At times Matt was encouraging. "Look!" he would say. "It was so nice last time! You'll get into it." Unfortunately, these well-meaning attempts backfired. "Don't patronize me—that's not sexy!" Next, he would try compassion. "I'm sorry you're feeling this way. I wish it were easier for you." She would thank him for his understanding, kiss him gently, and then roll over and switch off the lamp. Deflated, he'd retreat to the other room to relieve himself at the computer.

Inevitably his exasperation would build. Why was it all on her terms? Did she not know she was torturing him? Brooding and aching, he tried to contain his rage, but as another new year came and went, he would explode. "I'm tired of your bullshit! It's unfair and selfish!" He knew he wasn't going to get sex after that statement, but then again, he wasn't going to get laid anyway, so what did it matter? At least he was getting it off his chest. If Mercedes had ever felt guilty about enforcing abstinence, now she felt entitled. "How dare you!" she would fire back. "Is that supposed to turn me on?"

Twice annually, the intricate choreography of sexual refusal was interrupted, their anniversary and his birthday. "But she'd basically just lie there and do me a favor," he says. "Pity sex" was hardly what Matt had been wanting.

Mercedes was not untroubled by their predicament. She knew what the women in her Mexican family would say: "You're his wife, it's your role to satisfy his needs." But instead, she went to talk to her American girlfriends, and the advice she got was more to her liking: "You shouldn't have sex if you don't want to." "It's selfish of him to make you feel guilty about something you can't help." "And he'd better not be getting it anywhere else!"

Afraid that he might do just that, Mercedes initiated therapy on a number of occasions. Frankly, this couple tried hard. They ruled out past trauma, chronic pain, trust issues, and other explanations. But Mercedes valued sex only for its procreative purpose; beyond that, she didn't see the point. She was a sensual woman who loved many things—dancing in particular—but she never developed a taste for lovemaking, nor did she see why she should. "He's a vegetarian, and I accept that he doesn't like to eat meat. Why is this any different?"

For years Matt "just lived with it." He tried lowering his expectations, satisfying himself solo, taking up triathlons, and plunging into his work. All of these measures were too skimpy to fill the gulf of loneliness, or to counteract the creeping feelings of emasculation that are triggered by years of sexual brush-offs. And then he met Maggie, a mature, vivacious fellow triathlete, married for almost a decade to a man whose hands caressed only the remote control. Her matching desire brought back a sense of hope and vitality.

Matt didn't set out to betray his wife, but he could no longer bear the erotic lassitude. He is relishing the ardor, the hours of preliminaries, the feeling of timelessness. He assures me that his relationship with Maggie does not diminish his commitment to Mercedes. He is no longer faithful, but he is as loyal as ever. After fourteen months in this sexual haven, both lovers are happy that they have found a way to break out of their sexual incarceration without having to break up their respective families. This is not uncommon.

When the Affair Preserves the Marriage

As twisted as it may seem, Matt and Maggie's perspective has a logic. Many people have affairs not to exit their marriages, but in order to stay in them. "I have three more years till the kids leave," my patient Gina tells me. "This allows me to stay home with a smile on my face. It's not going to be an amicable divorce—he's far too proud and possessive. I want my kids out of the house before I take that step." At a recent conference in California, a woman told me that reality mandates that she and her husband stay together—they have a disabled child who needs both parents and both incomes. They're good friends, but little more. So she goes "dancing" twice a week. "He never asks," she said, "and it keeps me sane."

The last time Daphne caught Martin jerking off to porn, she reeled off a long list of shaming epithets. That didn't stop him; it just made him hide it better. Since they hadn't shared a bedroom in two years, this wasn't so hard. But he had to wait till she went out of town before he could go see the girls in Koreatown. "Visual aids," he called them. He knows she wouldn't approve, but his reasoning goes: "What would she prefer? That I stay home and fantasize about my twenty-year-old secretary bent over my desk? The dancers are doing their job. My secretary could become an actual seduction. To Daphne, it's all the same. But I think what I'm doing protects our marriage. What does she expect, that I'll just go without?"

Where Martin is bluntly pragmatic about his extramarital meanderings, Rachel Gray is poetic. In a twenty-three-year marriage to a man with whom she has little chemistry but many shared values, friends, and interests, she sent me a verse she composed about why she has had numerous affairs.

Through periods of doubt
When his lights are out,
Mine are flaming through the day.
You saw it right away.
Dance with me. I'm not confused,
Feeling taken for granted, and used.
Embrace me tightly, fill part of what's missing,
Like the rote lovemaking without kissing.
You want it too for reasons of your own.
Let's keep in touch. Call my cellphone.
I may spin away but I won't let go.
My heart says yes, but my head says no.
A gentle hug will pull me back in
For another dance. Is it such a sin?

Matt doesn't think it's such a sin, either. He feels torn about how Mercedes would feel if she knew, but he is not prepared to end either the affair or the marriage. Having found what he was missing, he no longer feels the need to choose. His affair is a stabilizer, a way to take the pressure off his primary relationship, not destroy it. The third party functions like a fulcrum that helps to keep the couple in balance. It allows him to avoid the Faustian bargain of losing his family or losing himself. As analyst Irwin Hirsch points out, "infidelity sometimes provides an emotional spacing that may allow imperfect love, sex, and family relationships to persist or endure over time."

Psychologists Janet Reibstein and Martin Richards describe this "segmented view" as "an understandable response to the real experience of marriage." Our inflated modern expectations of coupledom, they argue, make it inevitable that "a large portion of married people will feel that marriage has let them down in one way or another." When some parts of a marriage work very well while others do not, one response is to segment off those parts that do not work. And that often means sex. This eases the burden on one partner to fulfill all of our needs.

This kind of arrangement is particularly rife where one partner has a sexual preference or fetish that the other does not share or even finds repulsive, or when the age gap is in the double digits. It is also more common when one partner is disabled or living with a chronic illness. Unwilling to leave but not willing to go without, the unsatisfied quietly take their needs elsewhere.

Sonny is all too familiar with this strategy: "To put it bluntly, I love my wife, she's absolutely beautiful, but I have never felt that caveman desire to fuck her," he says. "We enjoy decent vanilla sex, but she won't join me in any kink—she even laughs at the idea of domination. I tried to be okay with that, but I've come to realize that BDSM isn't just something I like—it's part of who I am." So Sonny has taken his inner caveman elsewhere—to a "sugar daddy" website and the "sugar babe" who welcomes his most primal, unbridled fantasies. He didn't plan for this division of his identity— devoted dad to his family and dungeon master with his babe. But he's resigned himself to it as being the best solution.

Such arrangements are typically unspoken, particularly among heterosexual couples. People usually make secret deals with themselves, rather than opting for a more open discussion with their marital partners. They could learn a lot from their gay counterparts and from the polyamorous community, for whom a sexual standstill does not inevitably lead to a conversational standstill. Many of the gay couples I work with are more likely to have negotiated their monogamy or lack thereof, particularly if it has become de facto abstinence. Consensual nonmonogamy means that both partners have equal say in the decision to take unfulfilled hankerings elsewhere. In contrast, infidelity is a unilateral decision, in which *one* person secretly negotiates the best deal for themselves. They may imagine that it's the best deal for all involved—safeguarding the marriage and busting up the sexual gridlock—but it is nevertheless an exertion of power over the unsuspecting spouse. Of course, as one man countered, "When she says no every night, did I get a say in that? Who's been making unilateral decisions here?"

He has a point. Hence, when withholders tell me how distraught they feel at a partner's extramarital sex, I gently redirect their focus from what their partner *has* done to what they themselves have *not*. It's easy to see betrayal on the part of the person who takes thwarted desires elsewhere. It's more challenging to look at how the uninterested partner may have been an unwitting collaborator. A more honest conversation must include all sides of the story.

Divorce or Its Alternatives?

Matt's relationship with Maggie fulfilled its purpose as long as it was a secret, but when Mercedes found out, the rules changed. In therapy, we start by focusing on the wreckage of the revelation. Neither of them wants a divorce, so we engage in a dialogue on commitment and trust that expands the definition of loyalty and fidelity beyond the narrow frame of sexual exclusivity.

This couple illustrates a typical catch-22. They share years of rich history, happy and sad. They fondly remember moving into their first one-bedroom apartment and converting the utility closet into a nursery, and they're proud of having worked their way up to a little rented townhouse with a sunny yard. They've supported each other's careers, trading off sleep, chores, and child care so both could earn promotions. Three parents' deaths, two births, one miscarriage, and one cancer scare have come and gone while they remained steady. Hopes and dreams were woven together—a vacation cabin in the woods, a trip to Africa, a puppy for the kids to play with. Even today, sharing steaming java in the backyard is a daily pleasure. They love each other in all these ways. They just don't make love any more.

Should couples like this have to make a choice between dismantling the entire edifice of their marriage or never having sex again? In our marriage-is-for-everything culture, divorce or sucking it up tend to be framed as the only two legitimate ways to go—which makes it unsurprising that many opt for the unspoken but increasingly popular third alternative of infidelity. As Pamela Haag observes, "We'll break the marriage rules that don't work so well anymore before we'll condone revising them."

Marriage is in need of new options. We're quick to blame infidelity for the breakdown of relationships, but perhaps the more destructive factor in many cases is a dogged insistence on sexual exclusivity at all costs. Maybe some of these couples would still be together had they been willing to address their different sexual needs and what these might mean for the structure of their marriage. This conversation involves taking on the romantic ideal: monogamy.

Don't get me wrong: nonmonogamy is hardly a salve to all wounds or a buffer against betrayal. But when I see people hurting and feeling forced into decisions that are excruciating to all sides, I at least want to be able to offer another possibility. I grew up as the daughter of a seamstress and have long seen my work being similar to a tailor's fittings. I don't try to put the same suit on every couple.

For most people, the mention of sexually open relationships sets red lights flashing. Few subjects within the realm of committed love evoke such a visceral response. What if she never comes back? Can't he appreciate the good we have and accept that he can't have it all? What if she falls in love? Marriage is compromise! The idea that one can love one person and have sex with another makes some of us shudder. We fear that transgressing one limit leads to the potential breach of all limits. That may be so. But as too many people discover, closed marriage is hardly a bulwark against disaster.

Furthermore, I resist colluding with false premises. Too many people pretend they are working on rekindling their desire. They like the idea, but they actually don't want the reality. They want the family, the companionship, or the life they've built together; they don't really want to get down and dirty with each other. When that writing is on the wall, might nonmonogamy be a more propitious outcome than divorce? The unwillingness to even entertain the possibility ends up demolishing too many caring partnerships and happy, stable families.

Couples like Matt and Mercedes may decide to separate—maybe now, maybe later, maybe never. But I would hope whatever they choose will be the result of a thoughtful reflection on their respective needs and whether they can draw a circle that is big enough to encompass both of them with integrity. I'm sure that for all involved, this would be preferable to adulterous recidivism. When a second infidelity occurs, people are quick to say, "once a cheater, always a cheater," as if it were confirmation of a character flaw. But sometimes a more accurate explanation is that the core issue was never worked through.

Wholesale condemnation of an affair too easily distracts us from the real matters behind it. It also creates a fixed hierarchy of relational offenses. To this day, emotional and sexual rejection don't get the same press as lascivious wanderings. When we treat infidelity as the mother of all betrayals, we collectively resist a necessary reckoning, as couples and as a culture, with the complexity of marriage.

CHAPTER 13

THE LOVER'S DILEMMA

Conversations with the Other Woman

She is his selection, part time.
You know the story too! Look,
When it is over he places her,
Like a phone, back on the hook.
—Anne Sexton, "You All Know the Story of the Other Woman"

Vera checks her hair in the mirror and glances out the window. The table is elegantly set, the champagne is on ice, and the tomato salad, fresh from the garden, glistens invitingly. He said he'd be here an hour ago, but she won't let herself call. She paces the small but elegantly appointed one-bedroom, returning to the pane to watch for his car. Even after three decades, she still anticipates the rush when she first sees him step out onto the street below. Glowing, excited, and a little nervous, she looks like any other woman in love.

But she's not any other woman. She's *the* other woman. Also known as home wrecker. Man snatcher. Mistress. Secretary. Whore. These are the cultural labels that have been bestowed upon women like her since Lilith. Vera hates those labels, which is why she and

Ivan, the love of her life, go to elaborate lengths to conceal their thirty-year relationship. Ultimately she will take their secret to the grave. The only one who knows is her daughter, Beth. And at the age of fifty-five, having buried the two protagonists and packed away the evidence, Beth will reach out to me to tell her mother's story.

"My mother's long-standing lover, Ivan, was a rich and powerful married man. They had an apartment in a working-class part of town where they would meet three times a week, with a little garden they liked to work in. When she died unexpectedly at seventy-seven, I had the responsibility of closing up their love nest and helping Ivan, then eighty-five, reconcile his grief. There was no one else to dry his tears, because no one else even knew. Several years later, I attended his memorial service, though none of his family had any idea who I was."

Beth describes her mother as a great beauty—dynamic and adventurous. Abandoned by her first husband when she was pregnant, she had married again, but left when he became abusive. "She was tough and independent, buying houses when they weren't giving women loans. She got us out of that bad marriage."

"A big and beautiful love" is the way Beth describes her mother's relationship with Ivan. "I was happy she had that after all her bad luck with men. Ivan had already been married for decades when they met, and he knew he wasn't going to leave. He had just lost his eldest daughter and could not imagine inflicting another loss on his wife." Vera believed Ivan's wife knew about the relationship, but it was never acknowledged. A responsible and generous man, Ivan ensured her financial security.

"In many ways, their arrangement worked for her, because she had a lot of freedom," Beth concludes. "She could go to the love nest, be all sexy, have him think she was wonderful, make a delicious lunch and drink a bottle of wine, and then go home alone."

But her only daughter and confidante sometimes wishes she hadn't been so intimate with their setup. "I've absorbed all the details of how an affair of this nature evolves and is maintained: the lies told to the wife; the excuses made to steal time together; the sexual dysfunction claimed in the marriage; the sexual exploration enjoyed with the lover. How my mother could never wear perfume in case it would leave a trace on him. How they paid the rent in cash and signed the lease under a false name.

"I had way too much information. Like the story of how Ivan went for his annual physical with his wife and the doctor asked them about sex. When Ivan said they didn't have sex, the doctor offered a prescription for Viagra, and his wife turned to him and said, 'Oh dear, you don't want to start that up again, do you?' When the appointment was over, Ivan pulled the doctor aside to tell him that actually he was having plenty of sex and he would like that prescription. I didn't really need all these details, but they are now mine to keep."

As Vera got older, Beth says, it became much more difficult for her "to be on the outside of his life, looking in." She was ethically conflicted—not about her relationship with Ivan, but about being complicit in his deception of his wife. Sometimes she felt she had sacrificed her best years for him. She had to show up at every family Christmas alone, take vacations alone, and present herself in the world as a woman alone.

I venture a few questions. "And where has this left you? Did it make you believe in the power of love? Did it make you realize the power of deception? Did it make you aware of the astuteness of lies?"

She smiles wryly. "Check. Check. Check. On one hand, I was very aware of my mother's pain, but also of her sense that the grass was greener on her side. Ivan's wife had all the trappings of success, but she was living with a husband who was emotionally absent and didn't want to touch her. He brought his best self to my mother, who reciprocated in kind. So yes, it has made me believe in the power of love. What I hadn't realized, until recently, was how this history has leached into my own twenty-six-year marriage." I'm reminded once again that infidelity casts its shadows far beyond the triangle of lovers.

"During periods of marital stress, I'm quick to suspect and distrust to an extent that's not necessarily fair or justified. I can hear the lies Ivan fed his wife, my mother's whispers of a sudden change in plans, the stories they would tell in order to be together. I have my mother's sensuality and I want the kind of love she had, but I fear ending up in the position of Ivan's wife."

"How do you feel about Ivan?" I ask her.

"It was very hard for me, sitting at his funeral with five hundred people and hearing him being praised as a great family man. The worst moment was when someone got up and shared a memory of how he used to point to his wife and say, 'Isn't she gorgeous? Isn't she wonderful?' He used to say exactly the same thing to my mother. She gave him her love for thirty years, and she paid a high price. He never had to pay, beyond the money he gave her. I want her story told. She deserves that!"

Coming Out of the Shadows

Beth's mother did not tell me her story directly, but many others have. When word got out that I was writing a book on infidelity, I started receiving messages that began, "I am the lover of a married man . . ." "I am the proverbial other woman . . ." "I am the third person in the triangle . . ." They shared their stories, their hopes, their fears and their guilt pangs. They invited me into their dilemmas.

"How long should I wait?"

"Should I force him to choose?"

"How do I deal with the jealousy? The loneliness? The frustrations?"

"Will his marriage always dictate the schedule of our love?"

"Will I ever be able to have his child?"

"I wonder if all he wants is sex. Will he ever actually choose me?"

"I feel like I'm breaking the sisterhood—betraying another woman."

"He's lying to her. How can I be sure he's not lying to me?"

"I am a good person with morals and principles, but seem to be breaking all my personal rules. Can you help?"

"How can I keep pretending to my family that I'm single?"

"How can I maintain my dignity?"

"How can I end it? How can I not?"

All of these questions came with a request: Don't leave us out of the story. In message after message, the lovers have asserted their relevance to this inquiry—after all, it is a topic that would not exist without them.

Most of the clinical literature on affairs is dyadic, even though affairs are de facto triangular. The lover is barely mentioned, and in therapy, is either ignored or disparaged. Most therapists aim to close the loop around the couple as quickly as possible, and the mistress is treated more as pathogen than person. Her feelings are irrelevant to the recovery. Because it's rare for couples therapists to meet the unfaithful partner alone, there is also no place to talk about matters like how to end the affair with care or how much the lover is missed or grieved. "Cut her out" is the common refrain. "Break off all contact immediately."

As for the general public, we tend to judge the "other woman" far more harshly than the cheating husband. When Beyoncé dropped her infidelity-themed album *Lemonade*, the volume of online outrage directed toward identifying and shaming the mysterious "Becky with the good hair" far exceeded that toward her errant husband, Jay Z.

I use the pronoun "her" because it is almost exclusively women in this position who reach out to me. These are not the short-term flings, the one-night stands, or the casual extramarital friends with benefits. They are long-term lovers who have spent years, sometimes decades, single and involved with married men. Lest your immediate association be the stereotypical femme fatale, the young seductress barely older than his daughter, let me introduce the "other" other woman—often divorced or widowed, in her fifties, sixties, or seventies, smart, accomplished, and realistic. These are not simply naive, lonely, desperate women who'll take love in whatever form they can get it. In fact, they are pragmatic about their reasons for choosing to not only live with a secret but *be* a secret. This seems to be more typically a female variety of suffering, and it's no accident that the epithets applied to them do not have masculine equivalents. We do not refer to "woman snatchers" or "the other man." And besides, until recently, very few women had enough money of their own to be able to pay the rent on a *nid d'amour* (love nest) as well as the family home!

I have met plenty of men who were the lovers of married women (or married men, for that matter). But I have yet to meet a man who was single and gave his love to another man's wife for thirty years, hoping that she would leave and come and make a family with him. If a single man enters a triangle, it's more likely because he doesn't want a more involved commitment. I'm thinking of Greg, who had been happily seeing his married lover once a week for two years, but was horrified when one day she showed up at his door with a suitcase. "I never wanted her to get a divorce. Sure, we talked about it, but I thought that was just pillow talk." It suited him just fine to have a part-time relationship.

This business of the long-term lover intrigues me—why she makes the choices she makes, what she gets out of these, what price she pays, how she rationalizes her position. Whatever we may think about the ethics of her actions, she plays a central role in the drama and she too deserves compassion.

The narrative of the affair is worthy of attention, for it isn't always clear which of the two relationships, if any, will have a future. Was the affair meant to be just that—an affair? Or is it a love story waiting to live in broad daylight? What are the multiple entanglements? Are there children involved? What promises have been made, time invested, hopes deferred? In therapy, some questions are asked in front of the couple, like "How do you refer to him or her? Do you use a name? An epithet? Or is it simply 'that woman' or 'that guy'?" But others are reserved for discussion with the involved partner, alone.

"Do you meet with the lover?" people often ask. If the couple is intent on reconciliation, then no. But many lovers have come to me alone to share their woes. Some were strung along by false promises—led to believe the marriage was sexless, emotionless, or headed for divorce. Others were made unwitting adulterers by men who claimed not to be married at all. Still others found out they were not the only one. On occasion, the couple having the affair will come to me. Their questions include: "What if we were always meant to be together? What if both of our marriages were mistakes? Can we turn our backs on a chance to be with the loves of our lives? Can we ever be at peace knowing that our coming together will hurt so many people?" I have no simple answers to their questions. What I can do is hold space for their aching dilemmas and acknowledge that their marriages are not the only relationships that deserve empathic therapy.

"Is Our Connection Worth the Compromises?" A Lover's Ponderings

"I've never been loved so deeply, with such affection, in such an emotionally and sexually honest relationship. Nor have I ever been treated so well."

This is how Andrea, a fifty-nine-year-old divorced architect from Vancouver, describes her seven-year romance with Michael, a real estate developer. And, she adds, he's married, and has been for thirty years. "I'm looking for guidance," she writes, "but the literature seems trite and simplistic. I'm being used, it tells me, men can't be trusted, and I should leave him. Some friends say the same thing—as if I'm some naive woman who can't stand up for herself. It's an insult to my intelligence and self-awareness."

So begins a long and interesting conversation by email. This is a woman who conducts much of her relationship online—she and Michael exchange as many as fifty messages a night, she tells me. She welcomes an opportunity for written introspection.

Andrea is pragmatic about her lover's marriage, perhaps because she herself spent twenty-five years in an unhappy union with a man who withheld from her, both sexually and emotionally. "Do I wish he wasn't married? Absolutely. So does he. But he loves and respects his wife, and doesn't want to cause her pain, even if their connection is now flatlined. Thirty years makes even a listless relationship feel like home. I can relate. The comfort of an old shoe, the fear of making huge life changes. I had similar rationalizations."

"Surely it must be difficult for you to bear?" I respond. "What about your feelings?"

Andrea knows her insecurities. The sense of being inconsequential, subordinate to the wife. The judgment of others. The isolation of being a secret. But she says that she finds comfort in being able to talk to Michael about it all, as well as in his daily declarations of love. "How can I squander all that good love because he also respects and loves the mother of his children?"

For many women in her situation, even mentioning the marriage is tantamount to pressure, which could upset the delicate balance of the triangle. Then they reach the point where they are so damned tired of having to tiptoe around the topic. Finally they deliver the ultimatums, the deadlines, the threats: "If you don't make up your mind, I'll make it up for you."

Andrea knows that neither coercion nor manipulation nor anger will get her very far. "The fact is, I don't want him if he feels obliged or pressured; I only want him if it was his choice. So I don't ask him to leave her; I assume he won't, because he told me so from the beginning. And I don't ask him if he has sex with her—I just assume that he does, at least occasionally. I can choose to stay or leave, but I have to accept what is. There is strength in making a choice, with eyes wide open." When she thinks of it like that, she feels less helpless.

I wonder if she always manages to be so philosophical. Deep inside, does she think that if he truly loved her, he would overcome any obstacles to be with her? An hour later, another email is waiting.

"Of course, I do have fantasies about him ending his marriage and coming to join me," she writes. "I often wonder if I am undervaluing my own needs, and my answer is yes. Almost every day I go through an inner dialogue of what am I getting, what am I not getting?" Her answers wax and wane depending on how insecure she is feeling, but ultimately she concludes that it's worth it.

She also asks herself, would she even want to be with him full-time? She feels no need to be married. Furthermore, she confesses, "I wonder if I could maintain his interest or if I'd get bored with him or if he'd be faithful. I think we both worry that we could suffer the sad fate of many marriages. So seen from this angle, I may not be minimizing my own needs after all."

I ask her what helps her cope. She keeps herself busy with work and friends, and she particularly enjoys spending time with her male friends, especially if they have expressed romantic interest. The fact that Michael has introduced her to some of his close buddies helps her feel more legitimate.

Andrea's triangle is one type of configuration—she is a single woman, while her lover is married. It's different when both partners have their respective "official" relationships. I ask her if she would ever consider getting involved with another man. She admits that she's often thought it would be easier if she were married or had a boyfriend: "It would level the playing field. One way I have coped and boosted my self-esteem is to stay open to other possibilities. I have an online dating profile." Ultimately, though, her heart is with Michael. "Compromising our wonderful connection in order to feel a balance of power doesn't feel worth it somehow."

"Would anything change if you were an acknowledged mistress in his life, rather than a secret?" is my next query. She replies that she's never pondered that question because she didn't think it was possible. "Early in our relationship, after the first admissions of love, he said he was considering telling her, and I said, 'Don't do that! She'll make you choose.' I know he feels strong loyalty to her, even if important needs are unmet. And he's pretty sure that she would not be willing to share him. I've decided that as long as I'm confident that I alone have his romantic and sexual feelings, I can share his time and attention with her, albeit with a struggle."

Every woman in this situation ends up doing a mental allocation of resources—negotiating what the wife and family get versus what she gets. Many lovers go so far as to demand sexual exclusivity from their married partners: "He lives with her, eats breakfast with her, shares a bank account with her, and goes out in public with her. Since sex is basically the main thing he does with me, at least *this* should be ours only." Others delineate certain places or times when he is theirs alone. "Every summer his wife goes to Canada for a month to see her family. That's our time."

Andrea's balance sheet looks like this: "She gets his loyalty, family, financial support, daily companionship, holidays, shared friends. I get everything that was denied to me in my own marriage—a deep emotional, sexual, and intellectual connection, romance, mutual respect, trust, and joy. I value these things more than all the stuff he gives his wife, so I believe I get the best of him. She may well feel she has the best of him." Of course Michael's wife hasn't been offered the opportunity to weigh in on these economics. "But nor do I have any control over the distribution of resources," Andrea is quick to retort.

Every lover tallies up justifications—it's an unhappy marriage, they don't have sex, they're going to divorce soon anyway, there's one more year till the kids all leave home.

Of course, there's the wife's side of the story, too. She has negotiated her own deal, and it didn't include a mistress. Maybe her sex drive has tanked in response to her husband's emotional absence. She was willing to tolerate the void of intimacy in return for his loyalty. To then find out that even his loyalty was divided makes her apoplectic. It's painful enough to learn that he'd had other romantic partners, but when it's a long-term parallel relationship, with its own commitments, rituals, and routines, it stings all the more.

Andrea thinks about Michael's wife occasionally. "I never feel hostility toward her. I have compassion for her situation. I almost bumped into her one time at the grocery store, and I felt a crisis of conscience. But I don't generally feel guilt." As for the question, Does she know? "She's never said anything to him. But how could she not sense it after all this time? So I believe it must be a deliberate blind spot. If I thought she knew and was suffering, I would feel terrible, and I would probably end it." Andrea has just voiced one of the most common—and convenient—justifications.

When she compares herself to her friends, it confirms her conclusion that she has the better half of the deal. Many of them live behind a "mask of marital satisfaction"—seemingly contented in public, but sleeping in separate beds. "I don't think they are any better off than I am," she says. "We're all just stumbling around in search of happiness. We all compromise, and we all rely, to some extent, on rationalizations for staying in our relationships."

The Trade-Offs of the Hidden Woman

Clearly Andrea prefers to be the adored other woman than the avoided wife. Yes, there are trade-offs, but there are also benefits. In this, she reminds me of my patient Rose, whose mother suffered a sexless marriage and made her daughter vow never to be with a man who did not desire her. A married lover fit the bill perfectly—Rose and Tad have been meeting once or twice a week for three years, and his desire has never flagged. Being a mistress suited Rose—in the words of novelist Susan Cheever, "I had my freedom and I was someone else's fantasy." The lack of security and public commitment has been a price worth paying in her mind—until now.

Rose has tried to untangle herself from Tad several times, but he's always roped her back. She wants me to help her cut loose, but first she must understand what she has been getting out of the arrangement. To avoid being the rejected wife, she became the pursued mistress. "There are better ways to avoid your mother's sad fate," I tell her.

Despite the benefits, I've seen over and over the heavy toll these covert liaisons take on the one who is the secret. Yes, the lover gets the lust without the laundry, but she lives without legitimacy—a position that inevitably erodes self-esteem and confidence. She feels special because he goes to such lengths to see her, but devalued by remaining unseen by others. She vacillates between feeling adored and feeling ignored. Oftentimes, psychological issues of self-worth, childhood abandonment, and insecure attachment keep her entangled. Her sense of herself as "not enough" is matched by her willingness to accept crumbs as more than enough.

In Sweden, I meet Ingrid, who captures these dichotomies perfectly. For years, she has struggled to end a long-standing on-and-off affair. Last year she thought she'd walked away for good, but then he won her back. For the past six months, they have been seeing each other daily, before and after he goes to work. She describes their love as "an almost religious communion," but she also covets the mundane bond of chopping veggies for dinner. Lately he has been whispering sweet nothings about them getting married and living together, which has cranked up her hopes but also her anxieties. "When it was clear that we were lovers, and only that, I still had my own life, free of false hope and free to date other people. But now, I have become addicted to his dream and made it mine as well."

Ingrid feels ashamed and angry at herself for getting sucked in, but is afraid that if she breaks it off, she'll never experience this type of love or erotic bliss again. "I simply do not understand why he does not leave his wife!" she declares, listing the many unflattering ways her lover has characterized his marriage. "In our country, we are experts in 'friendly divorce,' and money and custody are not an issue. So why does he stay with her? But he does. And I'm sure he'll still be with her at seventy-five, and still be saying he does not love her and he loves me."

"What is it you need?" I ask her.

"Some type of revenge for my pain and the pain that my pain has inflicted on people that depend on me," she answers honestly. "Irrationally, I want to shout out to the world that he has betrayed his family for ten years. But I also long for some restoration of my dignity in the eyes of all the people in my life who have questioned his love for me, his intentions, his sincerity. I long to feel chosen by him and for the world to know it."

The illegitimacy of her relationship is unbearable for Ingrid. "I have this image of being at his funeral and not having the right to mourn or receive other people's affection for my loss. What will happen when he dies and nobody is a witness to our intense love? Our story will just dissolve to nothingness the moment he is gone and I will be left alone."

It's a poignant and all-too-accurate image. I think of Beth, quietly attending the funeral of her mother's thirty-year secret partner. I think of Andrea, who is grateful that just a few of Michael's friends know her name. I think of Roxana, who disguised herself as a nurse so that she could visit her lover in the ER after he had a heart attack. And I think of Kathy, who wrote to me that she found out that her long-term married boyfriend had died only when she read it in the local paper. Each of these women lives with the pain of being disenfranchised. However we judge their actions, we can also acknowledge their suffering.

In Ingrid's case, I hope to help her extricate herself. I sense the direct resonance between the plot of her illicit relationship and the lack of recognition she experienced as a child. She has told me that she was very close to her father as a young girl, but that as she grew older he grew distant, physically and emotionally, which made her feel ashamed. "The only time I hugged him as an adult was when he was in a coma on his deathbed," she says. "I longed for his expression of love but his only language was money." Ingrid was left not believing that she was worthy of love.

"Did that ever change?" I ask.

"Just before he died my father completed an autobiography, in which he made it clear to the entire world how important I was to him." Ingrid stops, tears filling her eyes. She too sees the connection: Now she would like her lover to do the same—to tell the world he loves her, but without dying.

"In many ways, my lover heals the wounds of the past by giving me the love I have always longed for," she reflects. "But he also reignites my need for acknowledgment. I guess this relationship is both repair and replay." Ingrid is shaken and thankful. Maybe now she can finally break this destructive pattern.

The End of the Affair

Ingrid had the maturity to sever her compromised relationship. But many others find themselves caught in a holding pattern for decades, watching their hopes (and often their fertility) fade. A term used by Terry Real is quite apt for such affairs: stable ambiguity. These are relationships of undefined status but well-established patterns, hard to break out of but just as hard to depend on. By remaining in a diffuse state, people avoid both loneliness and commitment. This strange mix of comforting consistency and uncertainty is increasingly common to relationships in the age of Tinder, but it's long been characteristic of extramarital liaisons.

Lia, a single mother of two young children, twice divorced, recently moved to New York from Tennessee and struck up a romance with the young married man who does occupational therapy for her youngest son. She doesn't beat herself up too much for their involvement—"I was lonely, I had no friends, and he wore me down with his attentions"—but she feels bad about her inability to end it. For a year she's been caught in a loop: "He's so sweet to me, and the kids love him. I'm afraid to end up alone. But I deserve better—a full relationship, not scraps. But how do I know I'll meet somebody else? Maybe I won't. Maybe he's the one. And yet I'm not just going to sit and wait for him to leave his wife." Her chronic ruminations accompany her as she halfheartedly peruses profiles on Match.com.

There is no easy answer to Lia's conundrum. Although her current situation feels fraught with uncertainty, one thing is certain: Her lover will never give her what she longs for. Ending the relationship will propel her into a real uncertainty, but also into choice and potential. She needs to break out of the sense of helplessness and reclaim her personal power and agency. There will be pain, but there will also be pride and the possibility of a better future.

Sometimes I am working with the married partner, but all the while I am thinking of the trapped woman and hoping that through him, I can liberate her. Jim, fifty-three, married with three kids, has been seeing Lauren, twenty-eight, for almost seven years. When their affair began, she was a college intern at his firm; now she's a young artist struggling to build a reputation. She longs for her future to include a family, and Jim. Meeting him, however, I see clearly that he has no incentive to make big changes. He has it all: a functional marriage and a comfortable life, with a lover and a steamy sex life on the side. More important, he's had his turn at fatherhood and is not eager for a replay. He has exactly the equilibrium he wants, and he's learned how to keep it that way.

Whenever she voices her unhappiness, he lures her back with extravagant romantic gestures. Time goes by. She starts to feel used and puts pressure on him to leave his wife. He makes promises to placate her, but she knows they are hollow, so she pulls back and starts seeing other men. Scared he'll lose her, he casts his hook once again. He knows exactly how to reel her in—renting her a new studio, paying for her next exhibition. Selfishly, he's buying time— time that her fertility clock will never get back.

"You have to set her free," I tell him. He insists that he's not stopping her and never made any promises to leave his family. I'm sure technically that's true—he's said he won't leave. But does he also tell her he loves her?

"Of course," he says. "I do love her!" I believe him. But that's why he needs to end it. Those sweet words that he whispers to her in the postcoital glow translate into hope in her mind. The lover's dreams and longings almost never exist in a vacuum—they are fueled by declarations of love and complaints of marital unhappiness. It's up to Jim to loosen the triangle so that she can remove herself. I will help him do so with care and mourn her loss. It's easy to write off men like Jim as selfish and entitled, but often, they too are deeply in love, and they too need a witness to their grief.

Whether the ending is done in person or in writing, it must be responsible, mature, caring, and clear. I coach Jim in great detail on what to say, working through several iterations. He needs to acknowledge the reciprocity of their feelings, appreciate the depth of what they shared, apologize for the false promises, set clear boundaries, and give her closure. These are the essential elements of a goodbye. It is not that he doesn't love her, but rather, that because he loves her he is leaving her. And once it is done, it needs to be definitive; he can't leave her any threads of hope to grab on to. There is no way for this not to be painful, but it makes a world of difference if Lauren knows that she's not the only one feeling heartbroken.

This approach is different from that of many therapists, who counsel a more abrupt ending. Typically, the advice is to cease all communication, delete her contact details, unfriend her on Facebook, and not mention her name. But seeing the fallout of this practice has made me seek more humane interventions. I've comforted many women who were "ghosted," to use the contemporary term, by men whose therapists (or wives) insisted that they walk away from long-standing love stories with not so much as a goodbye.

"He never said anything except how he adored me and how amazing I was, and then suddenly—silence," Jill recalls. "I searched online to see if he or his family had been in an accident or something. It was much more damaging than if he had just come out and said: It's over."

Casey's affair with Reid suffered a slower death—the variety of breakup known as "simmering." "He began to feel guilty, then started to withdraw. He didn't text as often. He was late for our assignations. He talked about his wife in more admiring tones." In the end, Casey called it quits when she heard his wife was pregnant. "I knew that eventually he'd just disappear."

Kat is furious that Joel thinks he can just walk away and go back to life as normal. "What a coward! If only he'd had the decency to tell me himself." She knew her lover's routines all too well, so she made a point of showing up at his favorite restaurant when he was having dinner with his wife, at his kid's baseball game, at the coffee shop before work. "Did he think I was just going to quietly disappear?" she fumes.

Darby at least got one text from her married lover of ten years, but it wasn't much comfort. "I have to go dark for a bit," he said, and so he did. Two years later, the darkness inside her is still heavy. "I've been depressed, even suicidal," she says. "My friends tell me I have to move on, but it's hard when he gave me no closure. My mama tells me, 'What do you expect from a man who cheated on his wife?' Maybe she's right, but I at least expected to be treated like a human being."

If the painful disclosure of a parallel love is to lead to a more honest future—for either one of the relationships involved—the other woman needs to be treated as a human being. She needs a voice and a place to dignify her experience. If the affair needs to be ended so the marriage can survive, it should be done with care and respect. If the lover needs to break it off to regain her own self-esteem and integrity, she needs support, not judgment. If the marriage is to end and the hidden love is to come out of the shadows, it will need help to go through the awkward transition to legitimacy. Without the perspective of the third, we can never have more than a partial understanding of the way that love carves its twisting course through the landscape of our lives.

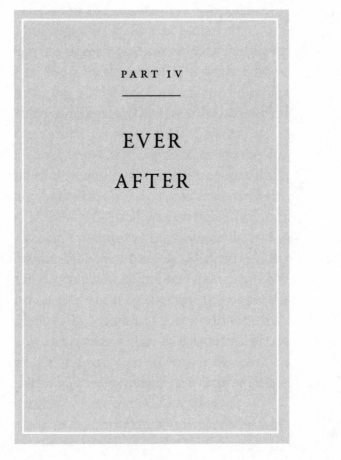

PART IV

EVER

AFTER

CHAPTER 14

MONOGAMY AND ITS DISCONTENTS

Rethinking Marriage

[T]hey'll say you are bad
or perhaps you are mad
or at least you should stay undercover.
Your mind must be bare
if you would dare
to think you can love more than one lover.
—David Rovics, "The Polyamory Song"

"Isn't the extent of infidelity proof that monogamy is simply not human nature?"

That question comes up over and over. Today it comes from a young woman who has stepped up to the mic during a workshop. "Wouldn't we avoid a lot of the pain, suffering, and deceit of infidelity if we just did away with the unnatural tyranny of monogamy?" she asks. "Why can't we have marriages built around consensual nonmonogamy and solve the problem of cheating?" I see several heads nodding in agreement.

A man in his forties stands up to respond. "Look, I think it's fine if people want to sleep around. But let's not pretend that's marriage! Why not just stay free and single? Real marriage means true commitment."

"Why does commitment have to be reserved for one person?" another man counters. "We can be committed to many friends or many children. Why not many lovers?"

"It's not the same thing," argues the defender of monogamy. "The Bible says love and sex are sacred. You can't just spread them around."

"But that's what everyone's doing anyway!" exclaims the woman who initiated the now-heated debate. "They just lie about it. The difference is that some of us have accepted that monogamy goes against our nature, and we're being honest with ourselves and our partners."

I understand the logic behind her argument: If monogamy is not natural, then imposing it on people gives them no option but to cheat. If you don't want them to lie, set them free and no one will get hurt.

When it comes to the innate-versus-learned debate, I share the view of activist-academic Meg-John Barker, who emphasizes that our relationship styles are "not a matter of nature or nurture, hardwiring or social construct. Rather the way we form relationships is influenced by a complex web of biological, psychological, and social aspects which would be impossible to disentangle." Natural or not, what matters to us is that presently many men and women seem to find monogamy, translated as mandatory sexual and emotional exclusiveness, quite difficult to maintain. Hence it may be time to at least take a fresh look at the topic.

We should be careful, however, not to conflate the conversation about monogamy with the conversation about infidelity. They are not the same. Let's parse out a few important distinctions. Infidelity is but one type of nonmonogamy—the nonconsensual variety. There are many other forms of consensual nonmonogamy—where partners explicitly negotiate the sexual and emotional boundaries of their relationships. However, it does not follow that consensual nonmonogamy is a safeguard against betrayal, jealousy, or heartbreak. You may think that affairs don't happen in open relationships, but they do.

Wherever There Are Rules, There Will Be Trespassers

As with any illicit trade, when adultery becomes legalized, the black market suffers a slump. But it never ceases to intrigue me that even when we have the freedom to direct our gaze toward other sexual partners, we still seem to be lured by the power of the forbidden. Monogamy may or may not be natural to human beings, but transgression surely is.

Every relationship, from the most stringent to the most lenient, has boundaries, and boundaries invite trespassers. Breaking the rules is thrilling and erotic—whether those rules are "one person for life" or "sex is okay but no falling in love" or "always use a condom" or "he can't come inside you" or "you can fuck other people, but only when I'm watching." Hence there is plenty of infidelity in open relationships, with all of the ensuing turmoil. If the desire to transgress is the driving force, opening the gate will not prevent adventurers from climbing the fence.

"We've always had an open policy for flings," says Sophie, "but I told him, not with my students or friends. And what did he do? Not only did he choose one of my girls, but he fell seriously in love with her."

"We make a distinction between sex for love and sex for play," Dominic tells me. "Nick was free to cruise. I couldn't even relate to the word 'cheating' until I found out that he'd developed an emotional relationship with a guy from New Zealand. That was supposed to be just for us."

Ethical nonmonogamy rests on the principles of trust and transparency. But human mischief will have its way with this as well. Consider Marcel, a forty-one-year-old sports coach. His wife, Grace, a science teacher at the same high school, had often proposed a more limber marital structure during their decade of marriage, but until he found himself attracted to a woman midway through a rock climb, he was staunchly opposed. Now the idea went from repelling to appealing, so he asked Grace for her okay, which she gave. "I felt a huge debt of gratitude to her," he says. "I finally understood what she had been trying to tell me all along."

From that day on, Marcel and Grace agreed to an open marriage based on honesty and communication. When Grace asked his permission to sleep with someone else, it was challenging, but he let her go, finding himself "surprisingly aroused" to watch her getting dressed up for her date. "I felt immensely proud of the commitment that we had made to each other, of how far we had come," he recalls.

Marcel's pride was about to take a fall, however, when a friend let it slip that Grace had been carrying on a secret affair, after their new emancipation agreement. When he confronted her, his surprise turned to shock at the many trysts she confessed to—before and after their renegotiation. "And here I was thinking we were so 'evolved'! How naive! Why, after I agreed to openness, would she go behind my back?"

The answer is all too clear. As Katherine Frank and John De-Lamater point out, "The exhortation to 'always use protection' enhances the thrill of barebacking; the pledge against sex in the marital bed is tossed aside like the comforter, becoming part of the adventure. . . . the goal of 'responsible nonmonogamy' may eventually provide fodder for rebellion and eroticization." In the realm of the erotic, negotiated freedom is not nearly as enticing as stolen pleasures.

You may be thinking, "I told you so—open marriages don't work." As it stands, Marcel and Grace are still together, and still open. But his idealism has been tempered and he no longer sees their flexibility as a shield against betrayal.

Opening Up Monogamy Without Taking It Apart

Cheating and lying aside, I see the conversation about ethical nonmonogamy as a valiant attempt to tackle the core existential paradoxes that every couple wrestles with—security and adventure, togetherness and autonomy, stability and novelty. The debate over monogamy often appears to be about sex. To me, it asks a more fundamental question: Can a new configuration of commitment help us to achieve what French philosopher Pascal Bruckner calls "the improbable union of belonging and independence"?

Iris, the thirty-something product of a marriage that was as long as it was miserable, has no intention of ever getting stuck. She wants an "intentional relationship." "When we come home, I want to know that it's out of free choice rather than obligation." She sees her agreement with Ella as reinforcing their trust. "We are devoted, but we don't own each other. We respect each other's independence and individuality."

Barney, now in his fifties, has been married and divorced twice, and in more therapy sessions than he can count. "People tell me I have issues with intimacy and commitment, but that's not true. I'm as loyal as they come, but it's time for me to be honest: I'm not monogamous. I don't want to keep trying to please everyone. I'd rather be authentic and create a workable relationship that's aboveboard from the start."

"I've always wanted to be meaningfully connected with many people, and I'm bisexual," explains Diana, a feisty lawyer in her thirties. "It's not going to cut it for me to just have an occasional threesome for my boyfriend's birthday—I want a committed relationship that encompasses all my loves. Monogamy feels like offering someone else ownership of my sexuality, and that's anathema to my values as a feminist."

Her primary partner of thirteen years, Ed, a scientist who is also bi, feels similarly. "Neither of us feels that our bond with each other is threatened by our appreciation for newness and variety. We both love the fact that the other is a sexual being, and neither of us would dare to quash that desire in the other." However, these dedicated parents play differently. Diana has a few steady lovers who "feel like part of our extended family." Ed, on the other hand, is more likely to seek out new connections. With new partners comes risk. So when Ed has a date with a lover, health considerations top the agenda. To ensure safe picks, Diana has been known to conduct reconnaissance and do matchmaking. Such are the rules of engagement that make this innovative union work.

For these romantic reformists, convention leads to constriction and dishonesty. They want truthfulness, choice, and authenticity. And they want a connection with their partners that doesn't disconnect them from themselves or from other people. They want to weave a tapestry together without losing their own threads.

Today's nonmonogamists—at least the ones who sit on my couch—are very different from the free-love pioneers of the sixties and seventies. Some of them are the children of the divorced and the disillusioned. They are not rebelling against commitment per se; they are looking for more realistic ways to make their vows last, and have concluded that the quest includes other lovers. The form this takes can vary enormously—from married couples who allow each other occasional "hall passes," to swingers who play with others together, to established three- or foursomes, to complex polyamorous networks that are reconfiguring love and family life.

Trust, loyalty, and attachment come in many forms. As feminist theorist Shalanda Phillips notes, "Experiences such as these call into question the integrity of monogamy as a stable construct, not rejecting it intact, but pulling it apart from the inside out." Rather than simply dismissing monogamy, these nonconformists aim for a more holistic, malleable definition of the term, one that no longer rests solely on the pedestal of sexual exclusiveness. Hence some observers, including psychologist Tammy Nelson, have characterized this movement not as *non*monogamy but as a "new monogamy"—a shift in the way the architecture of commitment is designed and constructed.

Of course, this is not the first time that the marital rules of engagement are being called into question. Over the last couple of hundred years, various communities have experimented with new models. The gay community in particular has been at the forefront of this endeavor. Since the sanctioned heteronormative model was not available to them until recently, they took it upon themselves to be creative and have practiced nonexclusive forms of relating with much success. Now, in our era of egalitarianism and inclusion, more and more straight folks seek the same license. A recent study published in the *Journal of Sex & Marital Therapy* found that one in five currently single people have experimented with some form of open relationship.

I meet many people who are involved in this project of redrawing the silhouette of love. Couples often ask me for help in navigating the new terrain of plural connections. Few social scripts exist as yet. We are all improvising. When I was training to become a therapist, a relationship by definition was a party of two. I never encountered the words "triad," "quad," or "polyamorous pod," since alternative relational systems had no legitimacy. And yet all of this is part of my practice today.

Some pairs are interested in embracing a multiplicity of intimate partners from the start; others, after decades of exclusivity, become curious about how to draw fresh lines around their long-established coupledom. And then there are those who, in the aftermath of an affair, wonder if opening the doors of their relationship would be a more mature response to the crisis than closing the door on decades of companionate life.

All of them are trying to wrap their arms around the imponderables: Can love be plural? Is possessiveness intrinsic to love or is it merely a vestige of patriarchy? Can jealousy be transcended? Can commitment and freedom coexist?

It will never work! you may be thinking. *Marriage is complicated enough. It will destroy the family! It's bad for the kids!* But people used to make exactly the same predictions in the 1980s with couples pioneering religious, racial, and cultural intermarriage or blending families upon remarriage. And they have done so at every other milestone in the ongoing sexual revolution that has defined the past half-century. Maybe we should give the marital innovators some time to figure it out. After all, does the old monogamy work so well?

If relational originality just sounds too damn messy, I can assure you, after listening to thousands of infidelity stories, that the messiness of affairs makes many of these situations seem rather orderly.

Marital sufferings and family crises as a result of infidelity are so damaging that it behooves us to seek new strategies that fit the world in which we live. I'm not suggesting that dissolving monogamy is the answer for everyone. But it is obvious that the current model is hardly a universal fit. Hence I respect monogamy's dissidents and their contribution to creating new templates for relating.

Redefining Fidelity

In order to engage in a constructive critique of monogamy, we must look beyond the prosaic question of how many sexual partners one is allowed and embark on a deeper examination of fidelity. As sex columnist Dan Savage argues, it is reductionist to make sexual exclusivity the sole marker of devotion. He likes to illustrate this with the story of a five-times-married woman who accused him of not being committed because he and his husband of twenty years are nonexclusive. "Which of us is more committed?"

Sitting in my office, post-affair, with his wife, Amelia, Dawson echoes a similar frustration. "I have been faithful to you for twenty-five years. The first twenty-four were happily monogamous. The last one was happy, with the addition of another woman. That said, my loyalty has never wavered. I've been there for you. When your brother lived with us for a year while he was in alcohol recovery, when you had breast cancer, when your father died, I was always there. I am so sorry. I never meant to hurt you. But when you measure my allegiance only by where I stick my dick, it's as if the rest doesn't count for anything."

For many people, sexual exclusivity feels inextricable from trust, security, commitment, and loyalty. It seems unimaginable that we could retain those virtues in a more permeable relationship. However, as the psychiatrist Stephen B. Levine posits, changing values is an integral part of life experience. We do it with our political and our religious values, as well as with our professional ones. So why not with our sexual ones as well? He invites us to recognize that our values evolve as we mature and "move from an understanding of ethical and moral issues in black and white absolutist terms to comprehending the gray ambiguity of most matters."

What if we were to consider fidelity as a relational constancy that encompasses respect, loyalty, and emotional intimacy? It may or may not include sexual exclusiveness, depending on the agreements of those involved. As we consider a redefinition, let's acknowledge those who are already engaged in the project.

Today's romantic pluralists have done more thinking about the meaning of fidelity, sexuality, love, and commitment than many monogamous couples ever do, and are often closer to each other as a result. What strikes me about many of their alternative renderings of relatedness is that they are anything but frivolous. Contrary to the stereotypes of bored, immature, commitment-phobic people engaging in a licentious romp, these experiments in living are built on thoughtful communication and careful consideration. If there's anything they've taught me, it's that there is tremendous merit in having open discussions about the subject of monogamy and the nature of fidelity, whether they result in open marriage or not.

Navigating the Monogamy Continuum

In a culture that places such importance on monogamy and attaches such dire consequences to breaking it, one would think it would be a prime topic of deliberation. But for many, even raising the question seems too risky. If we need to talk about it, it is an admission that love has not irrevocably tamed our roving desires. "I've only been dating this guy for a few months and yesterday he casually asked me if I was really into monogamy. The message is pretty clear: he's not that into me."

Plus, if you thought infidelity was a polarizing topic, monogamy is even more so. It's another of those typically "for or against" standoffs. People go instantly to the notion of "closed" and "open," caught in a binary perspective. Either you're sleeping only with your spouse or you're sleeping with everyone else. There are no gradations—you can't be mostly monogamous, or 95 percent faithful. Dan Savage has attempted to soften the hard edges with his term "monogamish," which signifies remaining emotionally committed to each other but making space for the third, whether in fantasy, flirtation, flings, threesomes, sex parties, or Grindr pickups. My patient Tyrone likes the term because, as he puts it, "It speaks to how there is a fundamental fidelity to our fifteen-year partnership, but it also contains a bit of levity and flexibility, which is great."

Monogamy is anything but monochromatic, particularly in our digital age. Today we each negotiate our particular brand. We decide whether it allows for fantasizing about someone else while making love to our partner, for extracurricular orgasms, for enjoying memories of one's wild youth, for porn, for sexting, app browsing, or more. In other words, monogamy exists on a continuum. When you ask people if they are monogamous, I suggest you ask them first what their definition of monogamy is.

Tammy Nelson makes the pertinent observation that most couples live with two separate monogamy contracts. The explicit agreement is their official declaration, like the marriage vows, and it defines the partnership's overt rules. In contrast, the implicit agreement is unspoken and "may never be openly visited before the commitment ceremony, or even after." It is a reflection of cultural, religious, and personal values. Nelson affirms that, contrary to the unified public stance, couples tend to hold very different implicit views of monogamy, and that "often a sudden collision between each partner's implicit contract precipitates a marital crisis." In our business, that collision is usually called an affair. Hence, we would rather say what society sanctions and what our partner wants to hear, and keep our truths to ourselves. Not because we are inherently deceptive, but because the culture that we live in provides little space for such frankness.

Until now monogamy has been the default setting, and it sits on the premise (however unrealistic) that if you truly love, you should no longer be attracted to others. This is why it often takes a fling or a betrayal to launch the conversation. Once the fiction has been cracked and you are no longer protecting it, you can begin to craft a more truthful narrative together. But it would be nice if this were not always precipitated by crisis. Drawing on the experience of gay men, Savage suggests that monogamy should be an "opt-in." If people were given more opportunity to choose, he offers, maybe some of them wouldn't have opted in and then they wouldn't be in trouble for adultery. Rather than penalize those who fail monogamy's standardized test, we should recognize that the test is disproportionately difficult. Savage is a fine pragmatist, but he's also more philosophical than his flippant demeanor lets on. He highlights a point that is both obvious and profound. Having feelings and desires for others is natural, *and* we have a choice whether to act on them or not.

The Economics of Addition

Are love and sex finite resources, with only so much to go around? Or is sex with other people a risky investment with high returns, paying unexpected erotic dividends? In the past, the fear driving monogamy was that you'd end up feeding children who were not your own. Now, when contraception and paternity testing can take care of that, what are we afraid of? For many, it comes down to this: Today's intimate commitment is predicated on love. The austerity of duty has been replaced by fluctuating emotions. If we get too close to others, one of us might fall in love with someone else and leave. It's pure dread that loosening the grip on monogamy, even in the slightest, could unravel the strongest bond.

What the vanguardists are trying to tell me (and perhaps themselves) is that the opposite is true. They believe that if they subject themselves to the constraints of monogamy, they're more likely to bolt. The more freedom they have, the thinking goes, the more stable their relationships will be.

For Kyle and Lucy, this seems to be true. Their story began as an adventure of the mind. Kyle is an engineer in his late forties who lives in Minneapolis. He had always fantasized about inviting a third into his relationship—specifically, a man to have sex with his wife while he watched. One day he found the courage to whisper his preferred scenario in her ear while they were making love. Seeing her turned on by his words gave him the feeling he was "riding on the edge of marriage." Their sexual play went on for eight years. Then Kyle began to long for something less ephemeral. Besides finding the idea of a real third arousing, he saw it as a hedge against adultery. "I know that it's difficult to be faithful and stay interested in one person for a lifetime. But there has to be a better way than the typical 'betrayal.'"

One day, in year nine, Lucy, a vivacious interior designer and the mother of two, met a charming stranger on the train and struck up a conversation. He invited her to the opera. She texted Kyle to ask, "Should I go?" and he replied, "Yes, but buy an extra ticket for me." That night, he recalls, "I sat just behind them incognito. I was excited to see if he would touch her."

A few months later Lucy was propositioned by a younger man—sex with no strings attached. "I encouraged her to go for it," Kyle says. "Since then, our sex life, which had dwindled after the kids were born, has boomed." Lucy needed reassurance that he was really okay with it, so they would make love before she left. When she returned, Kyle needed to know every detail, and she was comfortable telling him only if they were again making love. They took it a step further last month when Lucy went to a hotel with her lover and Kyle booked the room next door so he could listen. "When he checked out, she came to join me."

Kyle and Lucy relish the buzz of transgression—not against each other, but together, against cultural norms. Ninety-five percent of the time, they are exclusive; occasionally, they open the door. Their scheme maintains the ideal of the dyadic relationship and of faithfulness, albeit in an unorthodox form. It is a limited excursion that feels safe and can be a guard against straying. Playing with others stokes their ardor for each other.

In my study of desire, there is a question I have taken with me around the globe: "When do you feel most drawn to your partner?" One of the most common answers I hear is "When others are attracted to him or to her." The triangular gaze is highly erotic, which is why stories like Kyle and Lucy's are much less unusual than you may expect. Opening up a relationship does not always deplete the intimacy of the couple; sometimes it serves to replenish it. The fantasy of inviting in a third comes in many variations—imagining, enacting, watching, joining in, waiting at home, listening behind a door, enjoying the detailed report.

"Monogamy and nonmonogamy feed off each other and are inextricably linked," writes therapist Dee McDonald. Her focus is swingers, but I would extend the observation to many inclusive couples: Sex with others isn't only about being with others. "It is perhaps more accurate to consider it a rather intricate, perhaps dangerous, method of teasing and arousing the primary partner." McDonald raises the pertinent question: When couples are physically interacting with another, while psychologically and emotionally interacting with each other, "Who is having sex with whom?"

Couples using others for a libidinal reboot is common enough, but it doesn't always last. After a decade of marriage that has included recreational sex in various configurations, Xavier and Phil are coming to terms with the somber realization that their entire sex life has been farmed out, leaving a void between them.

By many standards, these two young men have a good thing going. Included in each other's families, they've built a home and a large circle of friends. They are interested in each other's careers— Xavier, the quintessential bearded hipster, owns a vegan chocolate company, while Phil is the founder of a coworking facility for young entrepreneurs.

As part of a close group of young gay men, they have plenty of sex, often in each other's presence, but rarely with each other. "Even on our anniversary, when we invited someone to have a threesome, we barely touched each other," Xavier tells me. "How is that for you?" I inquire. Turning to Phil, he says, "I feel like you try hard not to make me feel excluded, but that's not the same as feeling included." For a time, the sexual energy of their collective encounters was masking the lack of energy between them, but it's become unavoidable. Phil protests that it's not so bad—he thinks it's just a phase, a natural ebb and flow. "I'm not looking to replace you," he insists. But Xavier is rattled. "It's not that we're choosing other people as well as each other—it's that we're choosing other people instead of each other." Sadly, for this couple outsourcing sex led to a recession at home.

Closing the borders is not an option that Xavier and Phil want to consider. But I suggest to them that limiting their crossings for a period may be helpful while they get their juice back. Consensual nonmonogamy requires both sexual diversity *and* intimacy, crossings and barriers. They have favored variety over closeness, and this is depleting their relationship.

Reserving sexual attentions for each other is not the only way to tighten a bond. But when we decide that sex will not be the boundary that secludes us from others, it behooves us to think about alternative markers of specialness. Philosopher Aaron Ben-Ze'ev makes a distinction between two relationship models, one defined by exclusiveness, the other by uniqueness. The first one focuses on what is forbidden with another, whereas the second one centers on what is special about the beloved. One emphasizes the negative consequences; the other, the positive possibilities. I ask Xavier and Phil to consider: "If sex is something you share with others, what is exceptional to the two of you?" Exploring this question together helps them reclaim their common ground without giving up their freedom.

The Nonmonogamy Playbook

In order for commitment to take on new meaning beyond sexual exclusivity, we need to talk about boundaries. Nonmonogamists don't just indulge in a sexual free-for-all. Rather, many create explicit relational agreements with as much precision as a legal document. Common features include stipulations around honesty and transparency; where and how often liaisons with other lovers can take place; who those lovers can be and which specific sex acts can and cannot be shared with them; degrees of emotional involvement; and of course, rules about protection. Ally, Tara, and Richie are a triad who live and sleep together, and each is also free to play with others. "Our one rule," Ally explains, "is the use of condoms with external partners. The three of us are fluid-bonded, so if one person takes chances it puts us all at risk."

"Fluid" is an important term in these discussions, and not just in reference to the bodily variety. The boundaries in these carnal contracts are more fluid than the rigid restrictions of traditional monogamy, designed to be inclusive and adaptable. This distinction is particularly well captured by scholar and activist Jamie Heckert, who highlights the difference between boundaries and borders:

> Whereas borders are constructed as unquestionably right . . . boundaries are what is right at the time, for particular people involved in a particular situation. . . . Whereas borders claim the unquestionable and rigid authority of law, boundaries have a fluidity, and openness to change; more a riverbank, less a stone canal. Borders demand respect, boundaries invite it. Borders divide desirables from undesirables, boundaries respect the diversity of desires.

Boundaries vary greatly from one relationship to another, and they may also vary between partners. Partner A may feel fine about Partner B having intercourse with someone else, but prefers no kissing, while Partner B may be comfortable with Partner A doing whatever she likes. Partner C doesn't want to know much at all—just a text so he's not caught unawares. Partner D wants to be told the granular details in person, while he is holding her. These differing preferences speak to what the popular contemporary author Tristan Taormino calls the "myth of equality"—the common assumption in conventional relationships that each partner has the same needs and desires. Equality, she explains, has become synonymous with symmetry, leading couples to override the differences that likely exist between their sexual needs and emotional sensitivities. In these new contracts, symmetry is not required; agreement is.

Some couples take this a step further, with the privilege of plurality applying only to one partner, while the other remains exclusive. Celine tells me, "I have always known that I can compartmentalize, but my husband, Jerome, cannot. I'm emotionally monogamous. I can have my escapades and it will not be a risk to our relationship, but he is a true romantic. He falls for '*le grand amour.*' I know; I was his last affair. That was three decades ago, but he hasn't changed. If he fell for another woman, he would want to start all over—marriage, kids, and so on. So that's too risky." Jerome knows himself too, so he's agreed to their asymmetric setup. "At first it was hard for him to accept," Celine says, "as he wanted my attention to be solely on him, but I think he has enjoyed the times when I came to him energized from within. I didn't need to spell out the details."

Jax, a thirty-four-year-old music producer, came out only in his late twenties. When he moved in with Emmett, his first serious boyfriend, he was not prepared to live with a new set of restrictions. "Emmett is older and he had his fun for years—he's ready to settle down. I love him, but I'm not. Plus, I'm a submissive and Emmett does not want to dominate me, so we've agreed that I can go elsewhere for my sub needs." Jax and Emmett, like Celine and Jerome, practice what Michael LaSala calls "a monogamy of the heart."

While uneven agreements may be a good fit for some, they work best when based on differing preferences rather than on power imbalances. Sexual license is a symbol of power in a relationship, as are money, age, experience, confidence, and social standing. Tyler, a successful basketball player in his late twenties, came to see me with his girlfriend of six months, Joanie, who had recently given up her life in New York and moved across the country to be with him. Just twenty-one, she'd graduated from art school and was "trying to figure out who I want to be." Tyler was the one with the control. It was his city, his money, his career. So when she found out he'd still been hooking up with an old girlfriend, Joanie was less than thrilled.

Tyler tried to put a good spin on his dalliance. "I wasn't choosing her over you," he declared. "I'd love for the three of us to have a great time together." Although Joanie is not opposed to plus ones in principle, she resents him sneaking around behind her back and then trying to make it okay.

To me, what stands out are the multiple power imbalances in this couple, which make his proposal far less equitable than Tyler wants to admit. Their negotiation about fluidity is compromised because she is too vulnerable. Nonmonogamy requires equal footing and trust. A couple needs shared agency when they are going to enter an open relationship. Both parties need to feel that they are choosing from a position of parity.

Successful nonmonogamy means that two people straddle commitment and freedom together. In Joanie and Tyler's relationship, I can see that too easily they will polarize, with her becoming the protector of the union and him becoming the freedom fighter. He, more afraid of losing himself; she, more afraid of losing him. Their new contract will not work unless it helps to bridge this human dilemma, not accentuate it.

My concerns are confirmed when I probe further and he admits that actually he was envisioning the openness being reserved for him, since his girlfriend isn't really wired for casual sex. "She gets much more emotionally attached," he explains, "so I don't think it would work for her." I have had so many men sit in my office and tell me a version of this story. More often than not, they justify these conclusions on the questionable grounds that sexual diversity is more "natural" for men than it is for women. How convenient! They are usually taken aback when I point out that the "progressive" arrangement they are seeking is ultimately quite regressive—polygamy. There is nothing radical in a man imposing his mistress on his wife.

My conversations with Joanie highlight that until she is more empowered, she will never feel that she can choose freely. As we talk, I can see her beginning to relax and trust her own instincts. Tyler takes my challenge well—especially when I tell him that we don't really know what women are "wired" for, since they've never been allowed to figure it out. I leave them both with plenty to think and talk about. Inequality, gender, power, and a solid foundation are all considerations that need to be addressed before broaching how to open up a relationship.

Beta Testing New Families

The cultural shift toward more inclusive relationships is not just about expanding sexual frontiers; it's part of a larger societal movement to reimagine what constitutes a family. The lines once defined by blood and kinship are now being pushed out in all directions as people divorce, remarry, divorce again, cohabit, adopt, use donors and surrogates, and blend families. Alice is walked down the aisle by her father and her stepfather. Inga and Jeanine invite the sperm donor to become their son's godfather. Sandy opts for an open adoption and stays in touch with her twins as they are raised by Jo and Lincoln. Madeleine is becoming a first-time parent at fifty-two, thanks to an egg donor—an experience that until recently was only possible for men. Drew has five siblings who span four marriages, three affairs, three religions, and three racial backgrounds. None of these examples raises an eyebrow anymore—so how shocking is it that Drew grows up with a skepticism about old-fashioned monogamy?

Perhaps it won't be long before we are quite comfortable with an arrangement like Nila's, in which her girlfriend, Hanna, stays with her husband and three kids to help out when she's away on business. Or Oliver, whose boyfriend, Andres, comes to stay for the weekend, while his wife, Cara, moves into the spare bedroom. Their college-age son's first reaction was "Oh, so Dad has a boyfriend? Mom, do you want a girlfriend as well?" Or Kelli and Bentley, who are moving in with another couple to become a quad and raise their children together. In each of these new relational arrangements, we see up close the shift from inherited social structures to original improvisations.

These new formations come with new dilemmas. In a session in London, I meet a long-married forty-something couple, Deborah and William, and their lover of two years, Abigail, in her late thirties with a loudly ticking biological clock. Their unconventional union has been a beautiful love story, but now they are at an impasse. Abigail wants a child; Deborah, a mother of three, is excited to add a new baby to the household, but does not want William to be the biological father. That is something they have reserved as theirs alone. The snag is that William doesn't want Abigail to sleep with other men. What is she to do? She's frozen her eggs and is considering donors, but is struggling with a deeper existential question: "Am I just fitting into their life, or are we building a life together? What is my place in this relationship?" Abigail is grasping for legitimacy, but is not even sure what it looks like.

Many people are looking for a safe place to examine feelings like jealousy without being told that the presence of those feelings is proof that these groupings don't work. Others seek guidance on the intricacies of scrupulous honesty that govern life on the relational edge.

If there is one person who has orbited this space, it's Diana Adams. A lawyer in her mid-thirties, Diana is a passionate advocate for alternative relationships and families. She aims to invest them with as much legal stability as possible, helping them create clear agreements and ironing out disputes that come up. In her personal life she and her partner Ed (whom we met earlier in the chapter) are active in the polyamorous community.

Polyamorists (a term that entered *The Oxford English Dictionary* in 2006) emphasize creating meaningful connections, in contrast with those who seek casual hookups or playful short-term encounters. It's not "just sex" that they share with many partners—it's also love, not to mention domestic life. Polyamorists tend to characterize their lifestyle as a serious endeavor, involving mindfulness, maturity, and a lot of talking—hence the common joke in poly circles, "Swingers have sex. Polys have conversations."

Joking aside, polyamory is a growing movement in the United States and around the world. Many who choose this lifestyle do so with an entrepreneurial mind-set that aspires to a greater freedom of choice, authenticity, and flexibility. It's no surprise, then, that there are particularly high concentrations of polyamorists in hotbeds of start-up culture like Silicon Valley.

It has often struck me that the polyamorous lifestyle is more than just sex and freedom. It is a new type of community-building. Its flexible network of attachments, including multiple parental figures, is an attempt to counterbalance the isolation felt by so many modern couples trapped in the nuclear model. These diversified lovers are seeking a new sense of collectivity, belonging, and identity—

aspects of life they would have received from the traditional social and religious institutions.

The modern ethos of individualism, as attractive as it may be, leaves many of us beleaguered with uncertainty. Polyamory seeks to honor these values while embedding them in a communal context.

Of course, this is not without its challenges. As Pascal Bruckner writes, "Freedom does not release us from responsibilities but instead increases them. It does not lighten our burden but weighs us down further. It resolves problems less than it multiplies paradoxes. If this world sometimes seems brutal, that is because it is 'emancipated' and each individual's autonomy collides with that of others and is injured by them: never have people had to bear on their shoulders so many constraints." The collision of autonomies threatens every modern romance, but in polyamory it can become a multi-vehicle pileup.

When the rules are broken, the fallout ripples through the relational network. Should the transgressor be ostracized from the entire community? If one of your lovers "cheats" on you, for example, by pursuing a secretive relationship when disclosure had been agreed upon, should your other lovers now break it off with him, too? And how do you keep track of the relative status of so many different relationships? A poly friend recounted a story in which she was happily sexting with a new boyfriend, with the understanding that they were both free to see other people. Then she found out from a mutual friend that he had a girlfriend, with whom he had agreed to monogamy. "This hit me like a ton of bricks. By sexting me, he was cheating. I had been made a party to infidelity without my consent, which gutted me."

Polyamorists tend to attach a great deal of moral weight to their commitment to transparency and individual liberty—in fact, many seem firmly convinced that it's a stance more virtuous than that of the lying and cheating monogamists. Their critics highlight the inherently privileged nature of their lifestyle, with its aura of being entitled to have it all. Furthermore, it is easy to underestimate the degree of self-knowledge that such inventive boundary breaking demands. Freedom saddles us with the burden of having to know what we want. Be that as it may, the polyamorous experiment is a natural offshoot of the societal trend toward greater personal license and self-expression.

Will we see a day when a group form of marriage becomes acceptable, with triads or quads saying "We do"? Perhaps. But in the meantime, Diana Adams is more interested in seeing increased social protections for alternative families. While same-sex marriage was an important victory for gay rights and opened up a cultural conversation about the definition of marriage and love, she says, we shouldn't forget that the movement was also "a queer critique of the nuclear family and traditional monogamous sexuality." The same is true of monogamy's insurgents. Rather than "cram people into the institution of marriage," she says, "we ultimately want to get the government out of the business of deciding whether you get tax benefits, health insurance, and immigration status based on whom you're having sex with."

Her thoughts remind me of the late psychologist and gay activist Michael Shernoff, who reflected critically on the shift "from gay men radically transforming American society" to gay men "assimilating into it in conservative and hetero-normative ways." He lauded consensual nonmonogamy as a "vibrant, normative, and healthy part" of the gay community, and expressed concern that the advent of gay marriage might consign this "venerable, multigenerational tradition" to the category of adultery. "Couples who successfully negotiate sexual nonexclusivity," he wrote, "are, whether or not they are conscious of it, being genuinely subversive, in one of

the most constructive ways possible . . . by challenging the patriarchal notion that there is only one 'proper' and 'legitimate' (hetero-
normative) way that loving relationships should and need to be
conducted."

Monogamy was once a subject that was never even discussed in
the therapist's office, but today as a matter of course I ask every couple, What is your monogamy agreement? Marriage without virginity was once inconceivable. So, too, sex without marriage. We are
touching the new frontier, where sex outside can live within a marriage. Is our culture ready for the heretic notion that a relationship
could be reinforced by fluid boundaries, rather than destroyed? Is it
the end of monogamy? Or is it just one more step in its long history
of redefinitions?

CHAPTER 15

AFTER THE STORM

The Legacy of an Affair

How can I begin anything new with all of yesterday in me?
—Leonard Cohen, *Beautiful Losers*

All suffering prepares one for vision.
—Martin Buber

Once the storm has passed and the crisis is over, what then? What can we learn from looking at the affair in retrospect? We know that a breach is a decisive moment in the history of a couple, with one of two expected outcomes: together or apart. But that doesn't tell us much about the quality of the future togetherness or separation. Did the insight gleaned from the ordeal carry the couple through the slings and arrows of continued married life? Was there a brief second honeymoon before the relationship reverted to its pre-affair condition? Did he do it again? Did she ever stop? Once out of the therapist's benevolent gaze, did they file for divorce?

Tracking the long-term legacy is key to developing a holistic understanding of infidelity. We look not just at the facts but at the stories we tell—to ourselves and others. Does time alter the narrative? Are we susceptible to revisionism? I reached out to people with these questions, one, three, five, or ten years after the fateful events. A handful doesn't make for statistical evidence, but their personal testimonies inform both my thinking and clinical practice.

The stories I heard ran the gamut. Marriages fell apart, the affair an irreparable breach. For some, a cataclysmic ending; for others, kinder closure and grace. Marriages limped along, at times locking horns and other times locked in silence. Marriages came out stronger, the crisis of infidelity serving as a springboard to greater intimacy, commitment, and sexuality. And sometimes a new marriage emerged, with the former affair partners becoming the new spouses. In effect, infidelity can destroy a relationship, sustain it, force it to change, or create a new one. Every affair redefines a relationship, and every relationship will determine what the legacy of the affair will be.

The Affair as Dealbreaker

Quite a number of affairs do finish off a marriage. Whether the breach itself was the fatal blow or it simply legitimized a long-desired exit, there is no question that infidelity is often a story that ends in divorce court.

I remember Kate and Rhys as a couple who were trying hard to rebuild. But after five years her pain is as raw as if it were yesterday. She left him, she tells me, because he was a repeat offender and "there was no way I could ever trust him again." But Rhys's infidelity accompanied Kate wherever she went, becoming a specter that haunted her future relationships. After driving away several boyfriends with her incessant jealousy, she married a man who had experienced the same pain when his previous wife left him for a mutual friend. "We met through SurvivingInfidelity.com. We understood each other's hurt all too well and knew how to make each other feel safe," she tells me.

In the case of Jaime and Flo, Jaime was the one who broke the commitment, but she too lives with the bitter taste of resentment. "I tried to do everything I could to win Flo back, to show her my love. But she was constantly pushing me away, intent on making me pay. She was more interested in punishing me than in reconnecting with me. Finally I gave up. And now she blames me for being a coward and for not trying. She gets to be twice the victim—of my affair and what she calls 'my bullshit,' even though she defeated every attempt to put things right. I accept that I broke her trust, but she destroyed whatever was left."

When I am working with infidelity, my role is not to be a public defender of marriage or an advocate for divorce. But sometimes the inevitable outcome is so clear to me that I feel it would be kinder to cut to the chase. Although it was a decade ago, I've never forgotten my first session with Luke and Anais, because very soon I found myself telling them, "Your marriage is over." Luke was shocked: he'd been determined to make it work, despite the fact that Anais had systematically rebuffed him in bed and then went on to have a two-year affair.

I can still see his face. He looked like a hit man with a loaded gun. I told him as much, and suggested that we might need to put the gun in a drawer for the duration of our sessions. When I reached out to him recently, I wanted to know how he saw my bold proclamation in hindsight. Luke remembered it all too well. When I brought up divorce so quickly, he says, he felt that I had given up on him and sided with his wife. "I felt she had conned me into seeing a therapist who wouldn't even try to keep us together. When I told my cousin, she was so alarmed she said I should fire you. In that moment, I wanted to throw the coffee table at you and throw Anais out the window. But you saw right away what took me months to recognize—that we were dead upon arrival and I deserved better."

I was glad to hear that he eventually understood that if any siding was taking place, it was with him. At the time I'd known from speaking with Anais alone that their sexual gridlock was unlikely ever to change. I knew he felt lonely, humiliated, and sometimes enraged by her withdrawal, but saw no way out. Infidelity had marked and marred his childhood, and now that he had a young daughter, keeping the family together was his number one priority. This was a man in the grip of triple betrayal—her rejection, her affair, and worst of all, her lack of contrition. Someone needed to open a door for him that he would not dare enter alone.

In retrospect, he tells me, "It was brutal, but you were right. I think you knew that in my case, the best thing was to rip off the Band-Aid. I was completely hung up on the fact that she wouldn't express the kind of guilt I wanted her to feel."

In some situations, partners will never get the remorse that they want. "You told me I needed to stop banging my head against the wall," he remembers. "That was key. Letting me know there might not be any closure from her was helpful, if maddening at first." In situations like this, it's critical that one's ability to move on is not contingent on the other person feeling the "appropriate" amount of guilt and regret. Luke understands that now. "All these years later, I know she could never come up with the right words, because it doesn't work that way. It would never be 'enough.'"

Luke also remembered that I assured him there'd be a future. "You said I'd be banging babes aplenty and that I'd feel that electricity because I'd be getting a 'chargeback' from someone who actually wanted me as much as I wanted them. You were right. I even found myself saying a silent and very sincere 'thank you' to Anais and her boyfriend. And you know what? I used to have this excruciating back pain. It stopped the day Anais moved out."

I asked Luke if anything had changed in his world view as a result of his experience. "When Anais and I split, at first people saw it as a failure. They were wrong. I came to see that staying together at any cost was the wrong goal. Being happy is what counts. We were done, and now I get to live again."

Anais may not have been the right romantic partner for Luke, but he makes a point of saying that she's been "a great partner to raise a kid with." They are friends. They go to their daughter's soccer games together, and often he buys her lunch afterward.

"What about trust?" I ask him.

"I'm still hurt, deep inside," he says, "but I have lived and loved again. People thought I would be fucked up forever and unable to truly trust. They are partially right, but it's more that I trust differently. Before, I trusted too much and was naive. Now I realize that even the best people can't always get it right and end up acting out. We are all human and anyone is capable of doing what Anais did, even me."

"Have you forgiven her?" I ask him. "Yes," he replies, "though at first it seemed impossible." He recalls how I told him that one day he would understand that forgiving doesn't mean giving the other a free pass. It's a gift one gives oneself. Sure enough, as time passed, he got it. As Lewis B. Smedes writes, "To forgive is to set a prisoner free and discover that the prisoner was you."

Ending a Marriage with Dignity and Grace

As Luke expressed all too clearly, our culture views divorce as a failure, and even more so when it is precipitated by an infidelity.

Longevity is seen as the ultimate indicator of marital achievement, but plenty of people who stayed "till death do us part" have been miserable. A successful marriage doesn't end only at the funeral parlor—especially in our era of increasing life expectancy. Sometimes a relationship has run its course, and in such cases, when I can, I try to help it end with dignity and integrity. I see no contradiction in asking a couple about the success of their breakup. Hence my check-in with Clive and Jade.

I first met them as newlyweds, twenty-two years ago, when I led a workshop for mixed-race couples. They were carefree, full of promise. Two decades, three kids, and one affair later, their marriage was on its last legs, and they came to me for help. Clive had recently come clean about his secret relationship with Kyra. He felt terribly guilty, but had resolved to move on and make a life with his new love. Jade was desperate, fighting to hold on to him. I remember her hanging on to every word, gesture, and smile from Clive, but all of it was in vain.

I felt it was my responsibility to decrypt the message that was right in front of us: "Jade, he's not coming back. Your sadness makes him feel guilty, and that guilt instantly morphs into anger at you for making him feel bad that he's making you feel bad. He may not be gone, but he's not here, either."

I told him, "You keep waiting till you can leave without guilt, and that's never going to happen. It's time to set her free." He vacillated between being paralyzed and wanting to run as fast as he could, for fear that if he didn't bolt, he'd get stuck again. Yet I thought they needed to take the time to say a proper goodbye. So I suggested a separation ceremony.

Just as we have marriage ceremonies to mark the beginning of a union, we also need rituals to mark the end. A marriage is the nexus of an entire life—history, memories, habits, experiences, children, friends, family, celebrations, losses, homes, trips, holidays, treasures, jokes, pictures. Why throw all of this out and treat the relationship, in the poetic words of Marguerite Yourcenar, like "an abandoned cemetery where lie, unsung and unhonored, the dead whom they have ceased to cherish."

Rituals facilitate transitions. They also honor what was. Clive and Jade once exchanged vows; now they are tearing them up. But just because he fell in love with another woman doesn't mean their entire past together was a fraud. Such a summation is cruel and shortsighted. The legacy of two decades of a shared life is larger than the legacy of the affair.

When a couple arrives at the finishing line, drained after two years of back and forth—his confusion, her false hopes, his guilt about leaving, her holding on—it's easy to undervalue what they're leaving behind. The purpose of the ceremony I suggested was to not let Clive's affair eclipse all the positive aspects of their otherwise good marriage.

Sometimes departing spouses are reluctant to shift their focus to the good things in their relationship because they are afraid it will take the wind out of their sails. It's as if they feel the need to trash what they had to justify leaving. What they don't realize is that by doing so, they simultaneously degrade their own past and all the people they shared it with—leaving a trail of angry children, parents, friends, and exes.

We need a concept of a terminated marriage that doesn't damn it—one that helps to create emotional coherence and narrative continuity. Ending a marriage goes beyond the signing of divorce papers. And divorce is not the end of a family; it's a reorganization. This kind of ritual has caught the public imagination in recent years, dubbed "conscious uncoupling" by author Katherine Woodward Thomas.

I invite couples to write goodbye letters to each other. Letters that capture what they'll miss, what they cherish, what they take responsibility for, and what they wish for each other. This allows them to honor the riches of their relationship, to mourn the pain of its loss, and to mark its legacy. Even if it is done with a cooled heart, it can nonetheless provide solace.

When Clive and Jade came in for the following session, they had their letters on their iPhones. One click and the reading began.

Entitled "What I'll Miss," Jade's letter was a ten-page list, divided into categories, wistfully evoking the multilayered tapestry of their history. Their personal sayings—*Hola, chickly . . . Dame un beso* . . . the baaaaaby. The early days—love notes, mixtapes, salsa and more salsa, dog parks, parking meters, the opera. The food they loved. Their friends. The places that held meaning for them—from Martha's Vineyard to Paris to the Cornelia Street Café to apartment 5C. Their "sexy spots." Their "firsts" . . .

No one else will ever share the particular meanings these everyday things hold for them. She listed the connections she'd miss: "feeling protected, safe, beautiful, loved." Her final category was simply "You": "Your scent. Your smile. Your enthusiasm. Your ideas. Your hugs. Your big strong hands. Your balding head. Your dreams. You, next to me."

When she finished reading, we were all in tears and there was no need to trample the tenderness with any extraneous verbiage. But it is important for the scribe to hear her own words read back to her, so I asked Clive to do so. Then he read his own pages.

Hers was a love letter; his, a diplomatic farewell, thanking her profusely for the life they had shared, expressing regret for having fallen short, and assuring her that he would always treasure their bond. He was kind and caring, but his tone was purely formal. His opening and closing sentences say as much: "Thank you for being an amazing person and a truly wonderful force in my life over the past twenty-two years" . . . "I want you to know that despite its outcome, I see the good in our marriage, and will always cherish it and hold it deeply within my heart."

A year later, when I follow up with Jade, she emphasizes how the ritual of uncoupling helped her to see the writing on the wall. "At first I thought it was a little new agey, but I was also proud to be doing it and even shared it with some friends. We were doing something right despite all the wrong that had come before. I often wondered, how is he going to leave? Is he just one day going to wake up, say, 'Okay, bye,' and walk out the door? The separation ceremony put an end to my ruminations. I desperately needed a way to help me accept that he loved another woman and it was really over."

Some affairs are temporary side stories; others are the beginnings of a new life. Clive's was the latter, and no amount of waiting on Jade's part would have changed that. The tone of his letter made that all too clear to her. "It wasn't a 'what I'll miss' letter," she says. "It was a 'we are over' letter. He said some nice things, but this was definitely a man no longer in love. It struck me right then and there that while I was still suffering, still very much in love, he was gone. It hurt, more than you know, but it opened my eyes."

Next I caught up with Clive, who remembered the ceremony as "emotional and effective." Guilt was turned into gratitude, denial replaced by memory. Gradually he was able to simultaneously hold his attachment to Jade and his children and the calling of a new life with Kyra. "Until that moment, it hadn't felt real. The symbolism gave it a seal of finality."

This cathartic closure proved to be the right ritual for this couple. But sadly, many spew out a long list of curses rather than a list of sweet memories. Wherever I can, I try to help people create narratives that are empowering rather than victimizing. It doesn't always involve forgiveness, it makes room for anger, but hopefully it is an anger that mobilizes rather than keeps them trapped in bitterness. We need to go on with life—hope again, love again, and trust again.

The Marriage That Began as an Affair

Of course, the legacy of the affair does not end with the removal of the wedding rings. It can be the beginning of a new life for the lovers who were once hidden. The affair has finally been legitimized and becomes the primary relationship. What at one point may have seemed an impossible union is normalized—sometimes after years of waiting for the kids to leave home, the spouse to find a new job, the mother-in-law to die, the mortgage to be paid off, the divorce to finally come through. For better or for worse, a relationship that begins as a secret will always be influenced by its origins. When I meet couples who embark on a new odyssey together, I want to know to what extent their past affects and shapes their future.

Undoubtedly, there is great relief when a love story can finally emerge from the shadows. But it comes with a fresh set of concerns. Sometimes the affair was better off in its clandestine form, because when it became a marriage, the fantasy was lost. I remember Nicole and Ron as passionate and determined to be together no matter what the cost. "But once he said, 'I do,' it was 'I don't,'" Nicole tells me three years later. She is vexed that after five long years of waiting in the wings, Ron is finally hers—and now he won't touch her. Worse still, she suspects he's having a new affair. This is his third marriage. He seems to have a knack for turning every wife into his mother, with sex as the inevitable casualty. He loves his mamas; he just can't get it up for them. Desire is repeatedly reserved for the mistress. Nicole was that woman, but now she too has been relegated to the sexless status of wife.

For those affairs that do stay alive past the altar, there is the pressure to "make it seem worth the cost," as Eric puts it. To be together, he and Vickie both had to dismantle domestic bastions. Between the two of them, they left behind four children, three grandchildren, two cities, two beach cottages, a grand piano, ancient oaks, a dog, two cats, and dozens of friends. When so much destruction had to take place for them to exist, it's no wonder that the expectations are ratcheted up. When I got in touch with Eric recently, he confirmed that he is suffering stresses he never could have imagined while in the throes of fantasy. It's been three years since his divorce from Gabrielle, and while their eldest child has grudgingly come around, the younger has taken her mother's side. Does Eric have any regrets? I inquire.

"No," he says, "I love Vickie. But I do miss the life I left behind. I feel a lot of guilt and sorrow and loneliness. I particularly miss seeing my kids every day. I wish I could speak more freely with Vickie about my past life. But it's tricky. She immediately takes it as meaning I want to be back with Gabrielle."

"Do you ever fantasize about going back?"

"Sometimes," he admits.

Ironically, where the affair was once a secret in the marriage, nostalgia for the marriage becomes a secret in the now-legitimized affair. It's often hard for new partners to accept that missing the past relationship does not necessarily equate to wanting to return to it. The sadness isn't meant to be a threat. To break the pattern of internal lies, it's essential to make space for each person to talk about the past—including the loss, the regret, and the guilt. Every relationship incorporates multiple histories.

While the affair existed in a secluded world, cocooned from the practicalities of life, the new marriage finds itself swamped in logistics and complexities. How to introduce the children? How to relate to the ex? The implant needs time to "take."

In Brazil, I meet Paolo and Rafael. They met in college and fell in love, but in their Catholic community, love between men was an aberration. They parted ways, and both went on to do what was expected of them: wives, children, respectable lives. Two decades later, they met by chance in the Amsterdam airport. They claimed their baggage and reclaimed their hearts, beginning an affair that lasted two years before it was discovered, sending shock waves through their families and social circles. There were no bad guys to blame here—just the raw pain of taking apart two lives to build a new one. They've lost friends; some of their family members are refusing to speak to them; one divorce has been more amicable than the other. While being tarred as selfish, they risked everything for a truth that had been denied for too long. Time has vindicated their choice.

The Many Faces of Staying Together

While some couples who come to me choose to part ways, many more enter therapy with the intention of staying together, and they do just that. But togetherness has many faces. One of my patients told me, "A few years ago when I had a car accident, I remember thinking how much support I got from friends and family. With a broken leg, the pain is visible and everybody sympathizes. But when a couple decides to stay together after an affair, people think everything is fine and you're left living with an invisible pain."

Other patients have told me quite a different story. "We almost sank, but we didn't. Our relationship is more robust today. Too bad we had to go through all that to get here, but I wouldn't go back."

In my work I have identified three basic post-infidelity outcomes for couples who choose to stay together (with thanks to Helen Fisher for the typology): those who get stuck in the past (the sufferers); those who pull themselves up by the bootstraps and let it go (the builders); and those who rise above the ashes and create a better union (the explorers).

The Sufferers

In some marriages, the affair is not a transitional crisis, but a black hole ensnaring both parties in an endless round of bitterness, revenge, and self-pity. Even five or ten years after the events, the affair is still the epicenter of their relationships. These couples endlessly gnaw at the same bone, circle and recircle the same grievances, reiterate the same mutual recriminations, and blame each other for their agony. In fact, it is quite likely that they would have ended up in the same conflicts had there been no infidelity at all. Why they stay in the marriage is often as puzzling as why they cannot get beyond their mutual antagonism. They are sharing a cell in marital prison.

The affair is tagged onto every disagreement between them. Such couples keep score with moral superiority; no amount of remorse is ever enough. Debbie, who stayed with Marc after a string of extramarital exploits, ostensibly to preserve the family, constantly makes him feel that he is lucky she didn't kick him out, as if only he stands to lose everything they've built. Marc's quota of wrongdoing was filled years ago, and now he is no longer permitted any deviation. His pleas to let bygones be bygones only stoke her sarcasm. When asked if she misses their intimacy, she offers a response meant to protect herself, but ultimately self-defeating. "I want to make love," Debbie says, "but it'd be like saying everything is okay now." They haven't had sex since the affair three years ago. Sadly, Marc's dalliances take up more space in their bed today than when they were happening.

Marc asks Debbie why she has to bring up the affairs every time she is unhappy about anything. Often, he says, she ruins what might otherwise be perfect moments between them—their daughter's piano recital or a dinner with friends. "There are no perfect moments," she sneers. "You took those away." In these highly reactive couples, there is little room for neutrality, because the partners take the call for self-reflection as a personal attack.

Couples like these live in a permanent state of contraction. To the unfaithful, the betrayed spouse becomes the sum total of her vengeful fury. To the betrayed spouse, the unfaithful becomes the sum total of his transgressions, with few redeeming qualities. Marriages like these may survive, but the protagonists are emotionally dead. In any case, when past infidelity becomes the hallmark of a couple's life, whatever was broken can't be pieced back together. The relationship wears a permanent cast.

The Builders

A second pattern is found in couples who remain together because they value commitment and the life they've created. They care about each other and want to preserve the family and the community. These couples can move past the infidelity, but they don't necessarily transcend it. Their marriages revert to a more or less peaceful version of the status quo antebellum—the way things were, without their relationship undergoing any significant change.

An affair is revealed in a relationship, and an affair reveals a lot about a relationship. It sheds a stark light on its constructs—the cracks, the imbalances, the dry rot, the subsidence, but also the strong foundations, the solid walls, and the cozy corners. The builders focus on these structural strengths. They are not looking for massive renovations; they simply want to come back to the home they know and the pillow they can rest on. Along the way, they make amends, they renew their vows, and make sure to plug any leaks. Although a glimmer of passion can be intoxicating, they shudder at the prospect of losing everything. Ultimately, lying and deceiving are more agonizing than thrilling, and the end of the affair is simply a relief. When they look back, the whole episode is an anomaly best forgotten.

"Part of me was very disappointed in myself for not being able to leave my husband, and I wondered if I was letting go of the love of my life," Joanna recalled after ending her passionate affair with Jaron. "But another part of me felt relief that I was going to stay and not destroy my family."

She reflects that they almost divorced. She didn't think he would be able to forgive her. And she needed him to forgive her so that she could forgive herself. When forgiveness did come for them, it did so "not with the fanfare of epiphany but with pain gathering up its things, packing up, and slipping away unannounced in the middle of the night," to borrow the words of Khaled Hosseini.

Lyle feels more regret. Recalling his brief infatuation with a colleague, he says, "I never wanted an outside love affair. I appreciated all the great things about my marriage—I love and respect my wife—and I didn't want to leave my kids. I still harbor a lot of guilt. Eighteen months later I'd be in therapy with the next woman. But I'm also very sad because sex with my wife has been so lackluster throughout my marriage—she really has never been very interested in sex and has no idea how important this is to me. That part feels hopeless. Even so, I'd still rather look at porn and stay out of trouble than risk losing my family."

For builders, sexual disappointment and what they regards self-centered desires for more romantic "fulfillment" are not powerful enough incentives to turn them away from the more meaningful long-term rewards and vital obligations of family and community. Ultimately, these couples report favoring familiarity over the roller coaster of risky romantic love and sexual passion. Self-fulfillment without an ethical mooring feels hollow. They privilege deep, enduring love and loyalty. Doing what's right restores a sense of wholeness that is worth far more to them than any extramarital enticements. To the builders, commitment stands for something greater than themselves.

The Explorers

I've been particularly interested in a third category of couples, those for whom the affair becomes a catalyst for transformation. These explorers come to see the infidelity as an event that, though insanely painful, contained the seeds of something positive.

When faced with the collapse of the world they know, these couples home in on each other with a level of intensity they haven't experienced in years. It is not uncommon for them to experience a combustive rekindling of desire that is a potent mixture of anxiety and lust. Fear of loss is the spark plug that sets it off. They're deeply engaged—in pain, but alive.

The explorers have taught me much about what lies at the core of resilient relationships. Madison and Dennis always struck me as being this kind of couple. The uncovering of his affair threw them into turmoil, but I remember noting during our sessions that they had an uncanny ability to express and accept a wide range of feelings without demanding premature "closure." Their tolerance for ambiguity and uncertainty opened up a space for exploration, in which they could more deeply reconnect.

In contrast with the sufferers, who conceive of their ordeal in moral absolutes, the viewpoint of the explorers is more fluid. They more readily distinguish wrong from hurtful, paving a smoother road for clemency.

Several years later, when I touch base with Dennis and Madison, they affirm that they managed to sustain their wild swings without either one marching off to a divorce lawyer. Their grief revealed new facets of themselves and each other. Their first marriage was over, and they could never get it back, but they chose to have a second one. In the process, they were able to turn the experience of infidelity into an enlarging emotional journey.

When they speak about the affair, it is clear that they identify it as one event—not the definitive event—in their long history together. One sign that they have successfully metabolized the events appears in their language: Shifting from "you" and "me" to "our," Madison does not talk about "When you did this to *me*." Rather, they both talk about "When we had *our* crisis," recounting a shared experience. Now they are joint scriptwriters, sharing credit for what they produce. What started outside the relationship is now housed within. For Madison and Dennis, the affair has become a landmark integrated into the broader geography of their lives together. Above all, they know there are no clear-cut answers, so they're able to discuss the betrayal with a fundamental acceptance of their human flaws.

Madison and Dennis's relationship feels much richer and more interesting, but it also can feel less secure. They have added novelty to the enduring, mystery to the familiar, and risk to the predictable. "I'm not sure at all where this is going to take us, but dull it certainly is not," Dennis says. If before they were facing dead ends, now they don't know where they'll end up. But that very fact is more exciting than frightening, and they are in it together. To repair is to re-pair.

What Can Marriage Learn from Infidelity?

Some relationships die, some survive and revive. What are the lessons of infidelity, for all of us who love? I hope these pages have served to illustrate that affairs are many things, but at best they can be transformative for a couple. I began this book with the analogy that while many people have positive, life-changing experiences as a result of terminal illness, I would no more recommend having an affair than I would recommend getting cancer. What many people want to know, then, is what they can learn from affairs without necessarily having to go through one. It comes down to two questions: How can we better fortify our relationship against infidelity? And how can we bring some of the erotic vitality of illicit love into our authorized unions?

The answer is counterintuitive. The impulse to protect your marriage is natural, but if you take the common "affair-proofing" approach, you risk heading back down the narrow road of stifling constraints. Outlawing friendships with the opposite sex, censoring emotionally intimate confidences in others, nixing water-cooler conversations, curtailing online activity, banning porn, checking up on each other, doing everything together, cutting off exes—all of these homeland security measures can backfire. Katherine Frank argues persuasively that the "marital safety narrative" creates its own demise. When a couple tries to safeguard their relationship through various forms of surveillance and self-policing, they risk setting themselves up for the exact opposite: the "enhanced eroticization of transgressions." The more we try to suppress our primal longings, the more forcefully we may rebel.

The Irish poet-philosopher John O'Donohue reminds us, "It is always astonishing how love can strike. No context is love-proof, no convention or commitment impervious. Even a lifestyle which is perfectly insulated, where the personality is controlled, all the days ordered and all actions in sequence, can to its own dismay find that an unexpected spark has landed; it begins to smolder until it is finally unquenchable. The force of Eros always brings disturbance; in the concealed terrain of the human heart Eros remains a light sleeper."

Our romantic ideals are too entangled with the belief that a perfect marriage should deafen us against the rumblings of eros. We reject our unruly yearnings as immaturities we should have outgrown, and double down on our comfort and safety—which, as Stephen Mitchell points out, is no less of an illusion than our most passionate fantasies. We may long for constancy, labor for permanence, but it is never guaranteed.

Rather than insulate ourselves with the false notion that *it could never happen to me*, we must learn to live with the uncertainties, the allures, the attractions, the fantasies—both our own and our partners'. Couples who feel free to talk honestly about their desires, even when they are not directed at each other, paradoxically become closer.

The explorers model this. Their marriages may or may not be "open" in structure, but all of them are open in their communication. They are having conversations they never had before the breach: open-ended, vulnerable, emotionally risky conversations that elicit curiosity about someone who is at once familiar and also entirely new. When we validate each other's freedom within the relationship, we may be less inclined to go looking for it elsewhere.

Moreover, when we acknowledge the existence of the third, we affirm the erotic separateness of our partner. We admit that as much as we may want it to, their sexuality does not revolve solely around us. They may choose to share it only with us, but its roots are far-reaching. We are the recipients, not the sole sources, of their unfurling desires. This recognition of the other as an independent agent is part of the shock of infidelity, but it is also what can reignite the erotic spark at home. While it may be a scary proposition, it is also exquisitely intimate.

What about trust? Trust is at the center of the marital plot, and affairs are a violation of that trust. Many of us feel that in order to trust, we need to know. We conflate trust with safety, as a rational risk assessment to ensure we won't get hurt. We want a guarantee that our partner has our back and would never be so selfish as to put their needs ahead of our feelings. We demand certainty, or at least the illusion of it, before we are willing to make ourselves vulnerable to another.

But there's another way of looking at trust: as a force that enables us to cope with uncertainty and vulnerability. To quote Rachel Botsman, "Trust is a confident relationship to the unknown." If we accept that the certainty we long for is something we may never truly have, we can reframe the notion of trust. Yes, trust is built and strengthened by actions over time, but by the same token, trust is also a leap of faith—"a risk masquerading as a promise," as Adam Phillips writes. An affair throws a couple into a new reality, and those who are willing to venture forward together discover that for them, trust no longer solely hinges on the predictable, but rather, trust is an active engagement with the unpredictable.

We also learn from affairs that for most, the forbidden will always hold an allure. The ongoing challenge for steady couples is to find ways to collaborate in transgression, rather than transgressing against each other or their bond. These illicit acts do not have to be dramatic, reckless, or risqué, but they must be authentic. I can offer suggestions and examples, but what works for one couple may fall flat for another. Only you know when you are finally breaking your own rules and stepping outside your comfort zone. Only you can sense what activates the erotic energy—the élan vital—in your relationship.

For Viola and Ross, it meant creating secret email accounts through which they could conduct private, X-rated conversations during meetings, playdates, and parent-teacher conferences. For Allan and Joy, it was occasionally leaving the kids with her mom and going out with no curfew. Dancing all night with a sense of unboundedness is the opposite of the regimentation of family life. Bianca and Mags can't afford to go out, but they want to affirm that they're not just parents. So once a week they put the babies to bed, light candles, dress up, and have a date at home. They call it "meeting at the bar."

Alia took up singing again; Mahmoud, her husband of ten years, would come to watch her but make no contact—sitting in the back of the club like any other casual observer and seeing his wife through a stranger's eyes. Rita and Ben go to carefully chosen sex parties, where they speak only French. Nate and Bobby love to occasionally sneak back home after they've dropped the twins at preschool and have an uninterrupted adult breakfast. Amber and Liam enjoy searching online together for someone attractive they can invite home to play.

Rikki and Wes have given each other license to flirt, all the way to the edge but never over the line. When guys hit on her, "It's an ego boost," Rikki says. But it works both ways. Seeing girls lusting after Wes makes it all the more affirming when he goes home with her. Renouncing others reaffirms their choice of each other. They play with their roving desires, yet channel the energy back into their marriage. Commitment and freedom feed off each other. From the commitment springs a sense of security and openness, and the ability to feel liberated and alive with each other deepens their sense of commitment.

Each of these long-standing couples has chosen not to ignore the lure of the forbidden, but rather to subvert its power by inviting it in. Plainly, these tactics strengthen their connection, and when the connection is stronger, they are less likely to cheat. "It would be fun, but it's not worth it" becomes a voice of the inner boundary. That still does not mean their relationships are "affair proof." And it is precisely because they know this that they are continuously adding new pages to their love stories.

Our partners do not belong to us; they are only on loan, with an option to renew—or not. Knowing that we can lose them does not have to undermine commitment; rather, it mandates an active engagement that long-term couples often lose. The realization that our loved ones are forever elusive should jolt us out of complacency, in the most positive sense.

The current of aliveness, once awoken, is a force hard to resist. What must be resisted are the dwindling curiosity, the flaccid engagements, the grim resignation, the desiccating routines. Domestic deadness is often a crisis of imagination.

At their peak, affairs rarely lack imagination. Nor do they lack desire, abundance of attention, romance, and playfulness. Shared dreams, affection, passion, and endless curiosity—all these are natural ingredients found in the adulterous plot. They are also the ingredients of thriving relationships. It is no accident that many of the most erotic couples lift their marital strategies directly from the infidelity playbook.

NOTES

CHAPTER 2: DEFINING INFIDELITY

18 **Because there is no** Susan H. Eaves and Misty Robertson-Smith, "The Relationship Between Self-Worth and Marital Infidelity: A Pilot Study," *The Family Journal* 15(4): 382–386.

18 **research indicates a 40 percent jump** National Opinion Research Center General Social Survey, cited in Frank Bass, "Cheating Wives Narrowed the Infidelity Gap over Two Decades," July 2, 2013, *Bloomberg News*, https://www.bloomberg.com /news/articles/2013–07–02/cheating-wives-narrowed-infidelity-gap-over-two-decades.

19 **In fact, when the definition** Rebecca J. Brand, Charlotte M. Markey, Ana Mills, and Sara D. Hodges, "Sex Differences in Self-Reported Infidelity and Its Correlates," *Sex Roles* 57(1): 101–109.

21 **The possibilities for dalliance** Aziz Ansari and Eric Klinenberg, *Modern Romance* (New York: Penguin Books, 2015), 31.

21 **"accessible, affordable, and anonymous"** Al Cooper, *Sex and the Internet* (New York: Routledge, 2002), 140.

24 **three constitutive elements** I am indebted to Shirley Glass, whose "three red flags" inspired the line of thinking that led to my own triad.

24 **"Sex and subterfuge"** Julia Keller, "Your Cheatin' Art: The Literature of Infidelity," *Chicago Tribune*, August 17, 2008, http://articles.chicagotribune .com/2008–08–17/news/0808150473_1_scarlet-letter-anna-karenina-adultery.

26 **As Marcel Proust understood** Marcel Proust, *In Search of Lost Time*, Vol. VI (Modern Library, 2000).

27 **"dry dating"** Cheryl Strayed, *Tiny Beautiful Things* (New York: Vintage, 2012), 136.

27 **"It wasn't sex because"** Francesca Gentille, in private correspondence with the author.

28 **"The move from passive"** Aaron Ben-Ze'ev, *Love Online: Emotions on the Internet* (Cambridge, UK: Cambridge University Press, 2012), 2.

CHAPTER 3: AFFAIRS ARE NOT WHAT THEY USED TO BE

38 **"Most societies have"** Stephanie Coontz, personal correspondence with the author, March 2017.

39   The fact that she Statistic Brain Research Institute, 2016, http://www.statisticbrain .com/arranged-marriage-statistics/.

42   "property of the self" Anthony Giddens, *The Transformation of Intimacy: Sexuality, Love, and Eroticism in Modern Societies* (Palo Alto, CA: Stanford University Press, 1993), 14.

44   "unholy muddle of two" Robert A. Johnson, *We: Understanding the Psychology of Romantic Love* (San Francisco: HarperOne, 2009), xi.

46   "personal gain, low cost" William Doherty, *Take Back Your Marriage: Sticking Together in a World That Pulls Us Apart, 2nd ed.* (New York: Guilford Press, 2013), 34.

46   "from being an institution" Alain de Botton, "Marriage, Sex and Adultery," *The Independent*, May 23, 2012, http://www.independent.ie/style/sex-relationships /marriage-sex-and-adultery-26856694.html, accessed November 2016.

47   "Our high expectations" Pamela Druckerman, *Lust in Translation: Infidelity from Tokyo to Tennessee* (New York: Penguin Books, 2008), 273.

48   "Culturally, young adults" "Knot Yet: The Benefits and Costs of Delayed Marriage in America," In Brief, http://twentysomethingmarriage.org/in-brief/.

49   Hugo Schwyzer comments Hugo Schwyzer, "How Marital Infidelity Became America's Last Taboo," *The Atlantic*, May 2013, http://www.theatlantic .com/sexes/archive/2013/05/how-marital-infidelity-became-americas-last-sexual-taboo/276341/.

50   "Swept away" Janis Abrahms Spring, *After the Affair: Healing the Pain and Rebuilding Trust When a Partner Has Been Unfaithful, 2nd ed.* (New York: William Morrow, 2012), 14.

CHAPTER 4: WHY BETRAYAL HURTS SO MUCH

58   Couples therapist Michele Scheinkman Michele Scheinkman, "Beyond the Trauma of Betrayal: Reconsidering Affairs in Couples Therapy," *Family Process* 44(2): 227–244.

64   "rigidly stuck in the present" Peter Fraenkel, private correspondence with the author, January 2017.

64   "internal structure that helps" Anna Fels, "Great Betrayals," *New York Times*, October 5, 2013, http://www.nytimes.com/2013/10/06/opinion/sunday /great-betrayals.html.

68   "the only place" Jessa Crispin, "An Interview with Eva Illouz," *Bookslut*, July 2012, http://www.bookslut.com/features/2012_07_019157.php.

71   The shift from shame Julie Fitness, "Betrayal and Rejection, Revenge and Forgiveness: An Interpersonal Script Approach" in ed. M. Leary, *Interpersonal Rejection* (New York: Oxford University Press, 2006), 73–103.

73   "The dance of anger" Maria Popova, "Philosopher Martha Nussbaum on Anger, Forgiveness, the Emotional Machinery of Trust, and the Only Fruit-

ful Response to Betrayal in Intimate Relationships," *Brain Pickings*, https://www
.brainpickings.org/2016/05/03/martha-nussbaum-anger-and-forgiveness/.

73 **"transfer of vigilance"** Janis Abrahms Spring, *How Can I Forgive You?: The
Courage to Forgive, the Freedom Not To* (New York: William Morrow, 2005), 123.

74 **"if loss of power"** Steven Stosny, *Living and Loving After Betrayal: How
to Heal from Emotional Abuse, Deceit, Infidelity, and Chronic Resentment* (Oakland,
CA: New Harbinger Publications, 2013).

75 **"Everything can be taken"** Victor Frankl, *Man's Search for Meaning* (New
York: Touchstone, 1984), 74–75.

CHAPTER 5: LITTLE SHOP OF HORRORS
77 **Researcher Brené Brown** Brené Brown speaking at the Emerging Women
Live conference, San Francisco, October 2015.

CHAPTER 6: JEALOUSY
92 **"that sickening combination"** Helen Fisher, "Jealousy: The Monster," *O Magazine*, September 2009, http://www.oprah.com/relationships/Understanding-Jealousy
-Helen-Fisher-PhD-on-Relationships#ixzz3lwnRswS9.

93 **"The literature on infidelity"** M. Scheinkman and D. Werneck (2010),
"Disarming Jealousy in Couples Relationships: A Multidimensional Approach,"
Family Process 49(4): 486–502.

93 **"Recognized all over"** Ibid.

94 **"erotic rage"** Giulia Sissa, *La Jalousie: Une passion inavouable [Jealousy:
An Inadmissible Passion]* (Paris: Les Éditions Odile Jacob, 2015). Translated from the
French by the author.

94 **Sociologist Gordon Clanton** Ayala Malach Pines, *Romantic Jealousy:
Causes, Symptoms, Cures* (New York: Routledge, 2013) 123.

95 **As Sissa points out** Giulia Sissa, "Jaloux, deux souffrances pour le prix
d'une," *Liberation*, http://www.liberation.fr/livres/2015/03/11/jaloux-deux-
souffrances-pour-le-prix-d-une_1218772, translated from the French by the author.

95 **"Two's company"** Adam Phillips, *Monogamy*, (New York, Vintage, 1999) 95.

95 **"suffer[s] four times over"** Roland Barthes, *A Lover's Discourse: Frag-
ments* (New York: Macmillan, 1978), 146.

97 **"the demon that cannot be exorcised"** William C. Carter, *Proust In Love*
(Yale University Press, 2006), 56.

98 **"Jealousy is the shadow"** Pines, *Romantic Jealousy*, 200.

99 **"an honest feeling"** Sissa, *Liberation*.

100 **"Four Cornerstones of Eroticism"** Jack Morin, *The Erotic Mind: Unlocking
the Inner Sources of Passion and Fulfillment* (New York: HarperPerennial, 1996), 60.

101 **"Jealousy feeds on doubts"** François de La Rochefoucauld, *Maxims* (New York: Penguin classics, 1982) 41.

103 **"I was, in both senses"** Annie Ernaux, *L'occupation* [Occupation] (Paris: Éditions Gallimard, 2003). Translated from the French by the author.

104 **Weaning oneself off** Helen Fisher, TED Talk, "The Brain in Love." http://www.ted.com/talks/helen_fisher_studies_the_brain_in_love/transcript ?language=en.

107 **"an exquisitely tailored"** David Buss, *Evolutionary Psychology: The New Science of the Mind, 5th ed.* (Psychology Press, 2015), 51.

CHAPTER 7: SELF-BLAME OR VENGEANCE

120 **"it is difficult to unlearn"** Ayala Malach Pines, *Romantic Jealousy: Causes, Symptoms, Cures* (Taylor and Francis, 2013, kindle edition), loc. 2622–2625.

121 **"Bouts of anger"** Steven Stosny, *Living and Loving After Betrayal: How to Heal from Emotional Abuse, Deceit, Infidelity, and Chronic Resentment* (Oakland, CA: New Harbinger Publications, 2013), 10.

CHAPTER 8: TO TELL OR NOT TO TELL?

133 **"A no-secrets policy"** Michele Scheinkman, "Beyond the Trauma of Betrayal: Reconsidering Affairs in Couples Therapy," *Family Process* 44(2): 227–244.

133 **"We live in a culture"** Evan Imber-Black, *The Secret Life of Families* (New York: Bantam Books, 1999), xv.

134 **The same erotic longings** Stephen Levine, *Demystifying Love: Plain Talk for the Mental Health Professional* (New York: Routledge, 2006), 102.

135 **"favor the implicit"** Debra Ollivier, *What French Women Know: About Love, Sex, and Other Matters of the Heart and Mind* (New York: Berkley, 2010), 50.

135 **"Discretion seems to be"** Pamela Druckerman, *Lust in Translation: Infidelity from Tokyo to Tennessee* (New York: Penguin Books, 2008), 124.

135 **"French affairs can"** Ibid., 125.

137 **"puts a crack in the foundation"** Harriet Lerner, personal correspondence with the author, March 2017.

139 **"The tendency toward infidelity"** Dan Ariely, *The (Honest) Truth About Dishonesty: How We Lie to Everyone–Especially Ourselves* (New York: Harper, 2012), 244.

147 **"You can't 'prevent'"** Marty Klein, "After the Affair . . . What?" *Sexual Intelligence*, Issue 164, October 2013, http://www.sexualintelligence.org/newsletters/issue164.html.

CHAPTER 9: EVEN HAPPY PEOPLE CHEAT

156 **Mexican essayist Octavio Paz** Octavio Paz, *The Double Flame: Essays on Love and Eroticism* (New York: Houghton Mifflin Harcourt, 1996), 15.

159 **Hence, forbidden love stories** Lise VanderVoort and Steve Duck, "Sex, Lies, and . . . Transformation," in ed. Jean Duncombe, Kaeren Harrison, Graham Allan, and Dennis Marsden, *The State of Affairs: Explorations in Infidelity and Commitment* (Mahwah, NJ: Lawrence Erlbaum, 2004), 1–14.

159 **"lives that could"** Anna Pulley, "The Only Way to Love a Married Woman," Salon.com, July 21, 2015, http://www.salon.com/2015/07/21/the_only_way_to_love_a_married_woman/.

160 **"rearranges all our priorities"** Francesco Alberoni, *L'erotisme* (Pocket, 1994), 192. Translated from the French by the author.

161 **"Perhaps," he suggests** Jack Morin, *The Erotic Mind: Unlocking the Inner Sources of Passion and Fulfillment* (New York: Harper Perennial, 1996), 81–82.

161 **"erotic equation"** Ibid., 56.

161 **"poised on the perilous"** Ibid., 39.

165 **"there is always a suspicion"** Zygmunt Bauman, *Liquid Love: On the Frailty of Human Bonds* (Polity, 2003), 55.

CHAPTER 10: AN ANTIDOTE TO DEADNESS
175 **"Love and Eros"** Francesco Alberoni, *L'erotisme* (Pocket, 1994), 192.

178 **we crave security** Stephen Mitchell, *Can Love Last?* (New York: W. W. Norton, 2002).

179 **"expressions of exuberant defiance,"** Ibid., 51.

180 **"melancholy marriages"** Pamela Haag, *Marriage Confidential: Love in the Post-Romantic Age* (New York: HarperCollins, 2011), 15.

181 **"The adulterous wish"** Laura Kipnis, "Adultery," *Critical Inquiry* 24(2): 289–327.

182 **"The transformative allure"** Lise VanderVoort and Steve Duck, "Sex, Lies, and . . . Transformation," in ed. Jean Duncombe, Kaeren Harrison, Graham Allan, and Dennis Marsden, *The State of Affairs* (Mahwah, NJ: Lawrence Erlbaum, 2004), 6.

183 **"touchy-feely"** M. Meana, *"Putting the Fun Back in Female Sexual Function: Reclaiming Pleasure and Satisfaction."* Paper presented at the annual meeting of the Society for the Scientific Study of Sexuality, Las Vegas, Nevada (November 2006).

184 **"Erotic silence"** Dalma Heyn, *The Erotic Silence of the American Wife* (New York: Plume, 1997), xv.

185 **"Whereas before their affairs"** Heyn, *The Erotic Silence of the American Wife*, 188.

186 **Meana's research with** K. Sims and M. Meana, "Why Did Passion Wane? A Qualitative Study of Married Women's Attributions for Declines in Desire," *Journal of Sex & Marital Therapy* 36(4): 360–380.

186 **"Rather than being anchored"** Ibid., 97.

CHAPTER 11: IS SEX EVER JUST SEX?

193 "One of the key challenges" Jack Morin, *The Erotic Mind: Unlocking the Inner Sources of Passion and Fulfillment* (New York: Harper Perennial, 1996) 180.

195 "unholy triangle" Terry Real, in conversation with the author, February 2016.

200 "Men are finding" Irma Kurtz, *Mantalk: A Book for Women Only* (Sag Harbor, NY: Beech Tree Books, 1987), 56.

201 "This macho view" Ethel Person, "Male Sexuality and Power," *Psychoanalytic Inquiry* 6(1): 3–25.

208 "No bill of sexual rights" Daphne Merkin, "Behind Closed Doors: The Last Taboo," *New York Times Magazine*, December 3, 2000. http://www.nytimes.com/2000/12/03/magazine/behind-closed-doors-the-last-taboo.html.

210 "You may eventually discover" Janis Abrahms Spring, *After the Affair: Healing the Pain and Rebuilding Trust When a Partner Has Been Unfaithful, 2nd ed.* (New York: William Morrow, 2012), 6.

CHAPTER 12: THE MOTHER OF ALL BETRAYALS?

215 In a 2013 Gallup poll Eleanor Barkhorn, "Cheating on Your Spouse Is Bad; Divorcing Your Spouse Is Not," *The Atlantic*, May 23, 2013, http://www.theatlantic.com/sexes/archive/2013/05/cheating-on-your-spouse-is-bad-divorcing-your-spouse-is-not/276162/.

216 Sometimes we need David Schnarch, "Normal Marital Sadism," *Psychology Today* blog, May 2015, https://www.psychologytoday.com/blog/intimacy-and-desire/201205/normal-marital-sadism.

221 Big data analyst Seth Stephens-Davidowitz, "Searching for Sex," *New York Times*, January 25, 2015, http://www.nytimes.com/2015/01/25/opinion/sunday/seth-stephens-davidowitz-searching-for-sex.html?ref=topics&_r=0.

228 "infidelity sometimes provides" Irwin Hirsch, "Imperfect Love, Imperfect Lives: Making Love, Making Sex, Making Moral Judgments," *Studies in Gender and Sexuality* 8(4): 355–371.

228 Psychologists Janet Reibstein Martin Richards and Janet Reibstein, *Sexual Arrangements: Marriage and Affairs* (Portsmouth, NH: William Heinemann, 1992), 79.

230 As Pamela Haag observes Pamela Haag, *Marriage Confidential: Love in the Post-Romantic Age* (New York: HarperCollins, 2011), 23.

CHAPTER 13: THE LOVER'S DILEMMA

244 "I had my freedom" Susan Cheever, interviewed on Dear Sugar episode 52, WBUR, April 24, 2016, http://www.wbur.org/dearsugar/2016/04/24/dear-sugar-episode-fifty-two.

CHAPTER 14: MONOGAMY AND ITS DISCONTENTS

256 **"not a matter of nature"** Meg-John Barker, "Rewriting the Rules," http://rewriting-the-rules.com/love-commitment/monogamy/.

258 **"The exhortation"** Katherine Frank and John DeLamater, "Deconstructing Monogamy: Boundaries, Identities, and Fluidities Across Relationships," in ed. Meg Barker and Darren Langdridge, *Understanding Non-Monogamies* (New York: Routledge, 2009), 9.

259 **"the improbable union"** Pascal Bruckner, *The Paradox of Love* (Princeton, NJ: Princeton University Press, 2012), 3.

261 **"Experiences such as these"** Shalanda Phillips, "There Were Three in the Bed: Discursive Desire and the Sex Lives of Swingers," in ed. Barker and Langdridge, *Understanding Non-Monogamies*, 85.

261 **A recent study** M. L. Haupert et al., "Prevalence of Experiences with Consensual Nonmonogamous Relationships: Findings from Two National Samples of Single Americans," *Journal of Sex & Marital Therapy*, April 20, 2016, 1–17.

264 **our values evolve** Stephen Levine, *Demystifying Love: Plain Talk for the Mental Health Professional* (New York: Routledge, 2006), 116.

265 **"may never be openly"** Tammy Nelson, "The New Monogamy," *Psychotherapy Networker,* July/August 2012, https://www.psychotherapynetworker.org/magazine/article/428/the-new-monogamy.

268 **"Monogamy and nonmonogamy"** Dee McDonald, "Swinging: Pushing the Boundaries of Monogamy?" in ed. Barker and Langdridge, *Understanding Non-Monogamies*, 71–72.

269 **"Who is having sex"** Ibid., 71–78.

270 **Philosopher Aaron Ben-Ze'ev** Aaron Ben-Ze'ev, "Can Uniqueness Replace Exclusivity in Romantic Love?" *Psychology Today*, July 19. 2008, https://www.psychologytoday.com/blog/in-the-name-love/200807/can-uniqueness-replace-exclusivity-in-romantic-love.

271 **"Whereas borders are constructed"** Jamie Heckert, "Love Without Borders? Intimacy, Identity and the State of Compulsory Monogamy," in ed. Barker and Langdridge, *Understanding Non-Monogamies*, 255.

271 **the "myth of equality"** Tristan Taormino, *Opening Up: A Guide to Creating and Sustaining Open Relationships* (New York: Simon & Schuster, 2008), 147.

277 **"Freedom does not release"** Bruckner, *The Paradox of Love*, 5.

278 **Their critics highlight** Monica Hesse, "Pairs with Spares: For Polyamorists with a Whole Lotta Love, Three, or More, Is Never a Crowd." *Washington Post*, February 13, 2008.

278 **"a queer critique"** Diana Adams, in conversation with the author, September 2016.

278 **"from gay men"** Michael Shernoff, "Resisting Conservative Social and Sexual Trends: Sexual Nonexclusivity and Male Couples in the United States," unpublished paper shared by author.

CHAPTER 15: AFTER THE STORM

284 **"To forgive is to set a prisoner"** Lewis B. Smedes, *Forgive and Forget* (New York: HarperCollins), 133.

286 **"an abandoned cemetery"** Marguerite Yourcenar, *Memoirs of Hadrian* (New York: Macmillan, 2005), 209.

294 **"not with the fanfare"** Khaled Hosseini, *The Kite Runner* (New York: Riverhead Books, 2003), 313.

297 **"marital safety narrative"** Katherine Frank and John DeLamater, "Deconstructing Monogamy: Boundaries, Identities, and Fluidities Across Relationships," in ed. Meg Barker and Darren Langdridge, *Understanding Non-Monogamies* (New York: Routledge, 2009).

297 **"It is always"** John O'Donohue, *Divine Beauty: The Invisible Embrace* (New York: Harper Perennial, 2005), 155.

299 **"Trust is a confident relationship"** Rachel Botsman, TED Talk: "We've stopped trusting institutions and started trusting strangers," June 2016, https://www.ted.com/talks/rachel_botsman_we_ve_stopped_trusting_institutions_and_started_trusting_strangers.

299 **"a risk masquerading"** Adam Phillips, *Monogamy* (New York: Vintage, 1999), 58.

INDEX

INDEX

INDEX

ABOUT THE AUTHOR

Psychotherapist ESTHER PEREL is recognized as one of the most insightful and original voices on modern love. Fluent in nine languages, she has a therapy practice in New York City and serves as an organizational consultant for Fortune 500 companies around the world. Her celebrated TED Talks have garnered eighteen million viewers and her bestseller *Mating in Captivity* became a global phenomenon translated into twenty-four languages. Perel is also an executive producer and the host of the Audible original audio series *Where Should We Begin?*

www.estherperel.com